A Secret Madness

'I read it once and then I started over again. It is compelling and heartbreaking. At once an exposition of a married woman's life in the second half of the twentieth century; an account of obsessive compulsive disorder, a struggle for sanity within a destructive marriage and a must read for psychotherapists and counsellors who are allowed to enter the troubling state of mind of a man anguished by repetitive thoughts and the isolation it produced.' Susie Orbach

'Many touching moments … [a] remarkable book.' Hilary Spurling, *Daily Telegraph*

'She is a keenly observant writer who maintains a fine balance between the drama of her failing marriage and her awakening, independent self.' Julie Wheelwright, *Independent*

'It's a harrowing and thought-provoking book, and should cure any nostalgia for the way we lived in the fifties. The reader feels the author's lonely plight acutely. And one must admire a woman, isolated and unsupported, who uses her own intelligence to construct sense in the strange and frightening world into which her marriage took her. And one who has such emotional stamina.' Hilary Mantel

'Countless lessons can be learnt by reading A Secret Madness.' Dr Thomas Stuttaford, *The Times*

'This is a study in saintly forbearance, but also in the innocence of a time that knew little of OCD, was shocked by sexual deviance, and when the Freudian precepts we take for granted were not yet in place.' Lesley White, *Sunday Times*

'Bass has written a powerful and emotive book.' *Saga*

ELAINE BASS is eighty-four-years old. She has two children and lives with her second husband in Norfolk. This is her first book.

A Secret Madness

The Story of a Marriage

ELAINE BASS

P

PROFILE BOOKS

This paperback edition published in 2007

First published in Great
PROFILE BOOKS LTD
3A Exmouth House
Pine Street
Exmouth Market
London EC1R 0JH
www.profilebooks.com

Copyright © Elaine Bass

10 9 8 7 6 5 4 3 2 1

Typeset in Goudy Old Style by MacGuru Ltd
info@macguru.org.uk

Printed and bound in Great Britain by
Bookmarque Ltd, Croydon, Surrey

The moral right of the author has been asserted.

A CIP catalogue record for this book is available from the British Library.

ISBN-10 1 86197 964 9
ISBN-13 978 1 86197 964 3

For my daughter

One

'I know you'll think I'm mad,' Gerald says.

He pauses as I look up from my book, then he quickly turns his head away and stares at the fire, and I know then that we're back to last night's trouble. He had come home a worrying three hours late from one of his cinema matinees looking gaunt and ill, in a state of shock, hardly able to move or speak. 'Don't question me now,' he muttered, waving me away. He didn't even check the *Radio Times*, though there was usually something he had earmarked. Hunched in his chair he ate his shepherd's pie in complete silence while I choked my own food down along with my questions.

Tonight, after worrying about it all day at the office I came home to find him apparently recovered. He wanted to listen to a Shaw play on the radio, then we began to read, and I wondered if last night would ever be mentioned again.

He was still staring at the fire. I closed my book and leaned back in the chair, trying to ignore the rising fears and find the right expression to encourage a confidence. Impassive was probably the safest, or as near to it as I could get.

At last he looked up, and the fears edged their way back like insects crawling up my spine. He was strangely nervous and agitated, his eyes flitting about uncertainly, his fingers fluttering on his lap.

'I know we can't afford it,' he said, 'and it's a waste of money, but …'

'Yes, darling – what – what is it?'

He took a deep breath. 'Do you – do you think I could go to the cinema again tomorrow?'

1

Such a simple solution to a serious problem! I wanted to laugh aloud in relief, though it was odd that he should suddenly want to go again when he usually showed no interest for weeks on end. Very odd. And very puzzling.

When we had married we had given up our London jobs to go in search of country life and immediately fell under the spell of Devon, and wanted to stay here for good. I quickly found secretarial work, but after two years Gerald had still not been able to find any kind of clerical job, and to relieve the monotony of the long days at home he sometimes took the bus to a cinema matinee in Plymouth. Provincial salaries were low and any extra expense was a worry, but if he wanted to go again …

'Of course you can go,' I said in a cheerful voice.

He looked no less worried.

'Is that all, darling?'

'No, you don't understand, I –' With a despairing shake of the head he suddenly sprang from his chair and strode over to the window. He pulled the curtain aside and stood looking out into the dark, and I waited with growing impatience. But when at last he turned round he still couldn't bring himself to speak. I could hardly bear to watch as he fumbled in his jacket pocket for cigarettes and matches and then broke three matches before getting his cigarette alight. I looked down in embarrassment. This wasn't Gerald. It was nothing like him.

When I looked up again he was staring straight past me, exhaling cigarette smoke very slowly. How much longer? He let out another long trail of smoke and stood watching it slowly rise until it had completely disappeared. Then he lowered his eyes and met my gaze with a level stare.

Very quietly, with a hint of defiance, he said, 'I want to go to the same cinema.'

'The same cinema?'

'Yes.'

He would see the same programme. I tried to hide my amazement. He never wanted to see a film twice. Regardless of any inconvenience, we had to arrive in time for the beginning and leave at the end, though I myself – especially if it was a love story – would sometimes have liked to stay for a repeat. But my wishes were somehow never mentioned, and neither of us had ever seen anything wrong in that.

'Whatever for?' I said, careful to betray only mild curiosity; but he still turned away in pique.

'Oh, well, if you're going to cross-examine me …'

I rose and went over to the window and put my arms round his long, lean body. 'Of course I'm not, darling. If you want to go, just go, there's no need to worry about it.' (I was worrying enough for two.)

'You're sure you don't mind?'

'Of course not!'

'You're good to me; you're always so good to me.' He patted my head, a sign of his affection which I treasured. 'I can't explain, not now.'

I smiled tolerantly, remembering the ridiculously long time it had taken me to learn that his 'not now' was no guarantee that all would be revealed in due course. Then I became cheerful, since his present problem appeared, however oddly or expensively, to be resolved.

'Come on, darling, let's go to bed.'

There was always bed, though it wasn't the panacea I had once confidently expected. I went upstairs, looking away from the pale unvarnished centres of the stairs left behind by the former tenant. One day, when Gerald had a job, we'd have our own stair-carpet. I favoured a traditional red Axminster richly interwoven with royal blue. It was on my list, along with all the items of furniture we needed to replace the small battered occasional table and two worn wooden-armed easy chairs supplied by the village second-hand shop.

A lucky chance had recently ended the long hopeless search from our small furnished town flat for a permanent home in the country at a low controlled rent. No more tiresome waiting for buses out of the city for our weekend jaunts. Straight out of the house into the depths of our own quiet country lane, one of those narrow tracks that carve a meandering route between the numerous small farms of the undulating South Hams. Old Bob Bates had donated his farmhouse down the lane to his married son and retired to this new house, which upon his death was let, keeping it in the family. In the kitchen a worn-out old Rayburn emitted plenty of smoke but little heat for cooking, and I had to budget for an electric cooker on instalments. But the big boon was the commanding position on high ground, the large south-facing bay windows giving extensive views of the colourful curving valley of the Erme; not another house to be seen.

Gerald's present behaviour was a reminder of one or two of his habits that were equally incomprehensible. Like the procedure doubtless taking place downstairs at this moment, the routine collecting up of his small pile of books, carried up and down, morning and night, like a kind of personal baggage. After initial surprise I had come to accept the ever-present little pile as just another of his whims. It also served to impress me with his considerable erudition: comprising as it did the *Concise Oxford Dictionary*, Webster's *Dictionary of Synonyms*, Partridge's *Usage and Abusage*, Fowler's *Modern English Usage*, and the indispensable black leather notebook and gold propelling pencil. (Grinning, he had said this was a present from a former girlfriend.) He was always perusing one or another of these fonts of knowledge with great concentration, sometimes for hours, frequently breaking off to make notes.

I sometimes wondered about all this. If the dictionary habit, the constant careful perusal and note-taking, were indeed due to mere pedantry, then the habit was carried somewhat to extremes in that the dictionaries were consulted with a meticulousness and regularity suggesting something more than mere scholarly curiosity. But who was I to judge? After school, a fairly solitary life largely confined to office and bedsitter had left me little chance to experience the niceties of adult behaviour. Gerald's intense interest in the dictionaries might well be nothing unusual.

From the sitting-room doorway he would be making his careful scrutiny of the room before closing the door to conserve the precious heat.

When he took his turn in the bathroom I sat up in bed, trying to think. Had he, in fact, already stayed to see the film twice through when he first went on Tuesday? Did that account for his late return? But what of his distressed state? What had caused that?

I looked round the room at the attractive modern suite made of Australian silky oak which had come our way cheaply from a young couple going abroad. For once I had asserted myself and insisted that Gerald find the money from his dwindling savings. There was no carpet as yet, but we could now put our clothes away, though, surprisingly, this seemed to be of no importance to Gerald.

Other matters, however, did seem to be important to him, like the nightly emptying of his pockets on top of the chest of drawers. The neat array left me slightly perplexed: keys, wallet (placed exactly parallel to the straight edge of the chest), unused handkerchief, coins in two neat piles, silver and copper, each arranged in graduated sizes, the largest at the bottom. I once playfully rearranged the piles as he put them down, and, frowning with displeasure, he fussily restored them. I said nothing and never interfered again.

The comparative serenity of Thursday vanished when I arrived home to find the house empty. Surely he couldn't be sitting through the film twice? Perhaps for some reason the bus had been cancelled. I hung up my coat and closed the curtains, trying to believe, again, that he'd be on the next bus; just enough time to prepare everything if I hurried.

At ten past seven all was ready, the bed made, the fire lit, the potatoes peeled, cabbage prepared and sausages in the pan ready to be grilled. I went to take a quick look in the mirror of the hall-stand, which together with an old bed and chest of drawers for the spare bedroom had been donated by Gerald's mother as a kind of wedding present. I grimaced at myself; no doubt the spare bed meant that she'd be visiting us in the summer.

I had changed into the new white sweater Gerald liked, one of my sale bargains. I scrutinised my bust-line. Was it too large? No, not when I remembered Gerald's approving glance. Too high? Not really; this bra was a very good fit. I thought of the luxury of buying another but that, of course, would have to wait. I went to sit by the fire, listening for his step.

Twenty past seven. He hadn't caught the six o'clock bus either. How could this be happening again? It was unreal, inexplicable.

The house lay cocooned in the dense silence reaching out from nearby Dartmoor like a great sheltering wing. A much-travelled friend of ours had remarked on an early visit that it was like the silence of the desert. He'd not come across it anywhere else. Usually we found it restful and relaxing, but now it was becoming oppressive, eerie. Gerald was a creature of habit; he always kept to the same times, arriving home before me. Renewed fears crept into my gut, hollowing out my belly. His chair shouted his absence into the empty air. If only he were here! Far better to find him bundled in his chair, problems and all, than this precarious blank. But I mustn't panic. Everything might still be all right; this second outing might have a quite innocuous explanation. He had seemed not exactly pleased but somehow at peace in his mind that he was going.

I picked up the *Radio Times*. A Brahms concert till nine o'clock, the Second Symphony, one of my favourites. I made a quick cup of tea and settled down by the fire to the unaccustomed treat. Despite some tentative efforts to convert him, Gerald didn't like orchestral music and it was a long time since I had listened to any.

I switched off the radio as the last long drawn-out chord sounded and almost at once heard footsteps outside. But in the hall I hesitated. Just as on Tuesday night, the footsteps were slow and uneven, an old person's footsteps. The pleasures of Brahms vanished; my legs felt weak; my heart turned into a mechanical hammer. Ridiculous! What was there to be afraid of?

Slowly, very slowly, the front door opened. Gerald at last. But I was right about those footsteps. Once again he stood wilting in the doorway, grey and exhausted as if he hadn't the strength to move.

I tried to smile. 'Hello, darling.'

No response.

I stepped forward and kissed his cold cheek.

No answering kiss.

I backed into the hall. Woodenly, like a winding down robot, he followed me inside.

'What's the matter, darling?'

No reply.

'Have you been to see the film?'

A long silence followed by a whispered 'Yes', as if he'd hardly the energy to speak, then he stood drooping in the middle of the hall. I moved forward and held him close, and his body sagged heavily against mine, like a leaden sack of potatoes. I drew back a little and kissed him on the lips. No response; like kissing a dead man.

Gerald had never departed from his strict arrival routine: the thorough brushing of his overcoat on its hanger on the hall-stand, the patting this way and that and the peering from side to side until he was satisfied that it hung centrally. Exactly the same performance with the jacket. Then into the conservatory to reverse his trouser turn-ups and brush the insides of the folds, restoring the turn-ups before returning to the hall to change into slippers, his shoes always replacing them at right angles to the wall beside the hall-stand.

Like a compliant child he now allowed me to unbutton and remove his overcoat and jacket. I turned to hang them up on the hall-stand, and when I turned back he still hadn't moved. I helped him into his old blue sports jacket, which in cold weather he always wore indoors.

'Come on, darling, go and sit down and I'll make some tea.'

In the kitchen I switched on the kettle and subsided on to the one chair, staring down at the bare deal floorboards. What was wrong now? Old fears which had been shelved for years were about to engulf me like an avalanche. But I must not give way. Gerald needed me.

He didn't look up when I brought in the tea, and I was upset at being ignored until I saw that he hadn't even lit a cigarette.

'Here you are, darling. You must be dying for some tea.'

When he took the cup mechanically without a word or a glance, this finally broke my nerve and I became tearful and quickly took my own tea into the kitchen in case he noticed. Why not simply tell me what was wrong? Why this stubborn ritual of secrecy and evasion, this wall of silence?

The hot tea was comforting; it helped to restore a sense of reality. I returned to find him slumped forward holding on to his empty cup. I took the cup away and he leaned back, eyes closed, and I stood there watching him until his shut face became unbearable. Kneeling down, I hugged him, kissed his dead face, his cheeks, his eyes, his forehead, his lips.

No response.

I turned his face to me.

'Darling, what's the matter? Kiss me.'

He pecked my lips and resumed his blank stare.

'Darling, what's wrong? Have you had bad news?' (Perhaps something had happened to his parents.)

'No.'

'Then what is it? Please tell me.'

No reply.

I took both his hands in mine and they lay there heavy and lifeless, elegant well-kept hands which had never done anything more strenuous than wield a school cricket bat. Not that I minded Gerald's helplessness and indolence. I worshipped; he accepted, graciously and gratefully. The gratitude was as important as the flashes of masculine approval; it made everything worthwhile. Kissing each of his hands, I replaced them in his lap and went to pour more tea.

He took the tea from me absently.

'You must be starving, darling.'

No reply. I was hungry, but I could wait. Gerald wouldn't eat before he was ready. I dug into his jacket pocket for the cigarettes and matches I had transferred from the jacket of his suit. When I handed him one he placed it between slack lips without an upward glance. I struck a match and lit it. When he took his first drag I removed his shoes and brought in his slippers, kneeling down to fit one on to each heavy foot in turn while he went on staring at the fire, sipping tea and smoking. I left him to it and went to get the dinner. Perhaps some hot food would revive him.

After the meal he sat with a book, I with a newspaper, but neither of us was reading. He continued to stare despondently at the fire; drained, defeated, no longer keeping up his former pretence that nothing in particular was wrong, that he was just tired. Best say nothing for the moment. I went to wash up and make more tea and we listened to a radio discussion about a new West End play (in London we had been keen theatregoers). But though outwardly attentive to the radio he looked no less strained and distant. Kneeling down by his chair again, I put my arms round him.

'Darling, can't you tell me what's wrong?'

'No. Not now, my dear.'

'Is it finding a job that's worrying you?'

Briefly rousing up, he snapped, 'No, no, it isn't that.' Slumping back again, he added in a more conciliatory tone, 'Don't question me now.'

My faith in the implied promise of future revelations was waning.

'Let's go to bed, darling.'

Without a word he gathered up his little pile of books and followed me up the stairs.

For once he didn't want to make love to me, and I was tired enough to be thankful for the respite but also slightly piqued not to be needed.

He was soon safely asleep, his demons held at bay while I lay awake contemplating them from afar. That five-year-old confession of his had been flitting round the edges of my mind all evening but had been disregarded. Now it came back stronger than ever, a ghost intent on haunting. Could Gerald's original disclosure have any relevance to today's problems? It seemed absurd and stupid even to begin to think about something so vague, so long ago. Yet there had to be some explanation, something that even I in my ignorance could understand. How could I ignore the fact that Gerald was creeping about like a condemned man? Like it or not – and I didn't like it, I hated it – I had to think about it, had to try to understand, find a way to help him. There was no one else. It was up to me.

So, think about it –

But there can't be any connection –

Think – think about Liverpool Street ...

Two

'What time is your train, darling?'

Gerald glanced at his watch. 'Ten-fifty. We still have twenty minutes.'

We were standing outside the glazed doors of the station refreshment room. After an evening at a West End cinema or theatre I always went with him on the tube the half-hour or so eastwards across London to Liverpool Street. It seemed the obvious thing to do, putting off the moment of parting. Returning westwards to Notting Hill Gate, I longed for an end to the partings. I couldn't really understand why we weren't married. It was true that we had only known each other for three months, but waiting for love till you're twenty-six seems an unbearably long time, and with my feelings apparently returned I had half expected to be married after just a few weeks. Gerald was thirty-one, the war was over, why delay? But there had been no proposal, no plans, no declaration of feelings or intentions, only meaningful looks, and urgent lovemaking in my bedsitter followed by endless pointless days between meetings.

The partings might have been more bearable if I'd known when we were to meet again. I'll phone you, he'd say, and eventually he did, after several uncertain days, a week, two desolate weeks of wondering if I'd ever see him again. In the adjoining bedsitter my best friend Helen seethed and fretted, but her advice and opinions were not what I wanted to hear as I put a stop to all outings and concert-going to listen through the open door for the ring of the telephone on the landing below. Helen instinctively mistrusted Gerald from the outset; no specific reason, she just sensed something wrong. Specific reasons might have helped. Without them I was lost, dizzied by a heady concoction of romantic Hollywood films and the words of popular songs: 'Love is all, Love is all.' Love, the big cure-all – an unshakeable belief, like a religion.

And now another parting. It occurred to me that Gerald had been especially quiet all evening and now he was silent, staring ahead at the long facing platforms.

'It was a marvellous film, wasn't it,' I said, a little distantly, trying to dispel the impression of something wrong.

'Yes, marvellous.'

'I do like that chap, what's his name?'

He half turned towards me. 'Jean-Louis Barrault.'

'I wish I'd learnt French at school instead of German.'

'Well, I learnt French for five years and I hardly understood a word.'

'Still, the subtitles are quite enough, aren't they.'

'Yes, it's surprising.' He was silent again for a moment. Then in the same conversational tone, he said, 'I've been mentally ill, you know.'

I stared at him, dumbfounded. His face was averted, and I watched the sleek side of his head, waiting for it to turn, waiting to be told it was all right, it wasn't as bad as I thought. But his head didn't move, didn't relent one bit. I gave up and gazed down at the grimy ground, trying to recover myself.

Unbelievable that Gerald, my charming, masterly lover, had just spoken those few unlikely, devastating words. Yet he had said them, no doubt about it, for they were resounding in my ears like hostile drums, repeating themselves but becoming no more intelligible. Gerald 'mentally ill'. Gerald, so knowledgeable about the many aspects of life of which I was ignorant, so apparently normal. What could it mean?

A strange fear gripped me, as if I had just found myself alone on an unknown planet which I was plainly not equipped to explore. Illogically I was afraid even to move, as if any action on my part – a small shift of feet – might plunge me into some perilous deep. To risk speaking seemed equally hazardous, as if anything that I might bring myself to say – even a preliminary cough – might in some indefinable way make the situation even worse.

But you have to respond to something like this even if it comes from a stranger, let alone from someone you love. I glanced up at Gerald. But he was still turned away, disconnected, as if there was nothing more to say.

I looked round the cavernous station. Dark scurrying figures. Black towering trains. Nothing seemed real any more; there were only murky shadows seen from a long way off. The only reality now was a mysterious new world conjured up by one short sentence, a few electrifying words. I turned away from the darkness to the window of the refreshment room, and the bright lights glinted off the green glass table tops with a curious hypnotic effect, pinning my gaze down on the shiny surfaces.

My trance was penetrated by a succession of metallic sounds issuing from the depths of the station. It so happened that I had never come across the changing of buffers and the clanking of chains as trains were being shunted, and this lack of identification lent a certain eeriness to my surroundings, adding to my sense of dislocation. What should I do? What exactly was mental illness, anyway? Unthinkable that this sinister phrase with its vague but powerful connotations of derangement and insanity could have any connection with gentle, lovable Gerald.

A few more interminable minutes dragged by before I could make myself turn back and seek an explanation, but his face was still unkindly averted, a red danger signal saying 'Keep Out'.

Never before had I been at such a loss. Early years of slum poverty; caring for the family during mother's miscarriages and illnesses; air-raids, job-hunting, money battles; in the past some course of action had always suggested itself, but now I could think of nothing I could say or do which might be in the least appropriate. In a world bristling

13

with knowledge and information I was stranded like a castaway on my little island of ignorance.

Our twofold silence had become intolerable. Precious minutes were slipping by. One of us had to say something.

I touched Gerald's sleeve, and found the contact with the rough tweed material – something real and tangible – oddly reassuring. I heard myself say, 'I – I don't know what you mean,' and there was tremendous relief in having spoken. Now he would explain himself, he would replace those resounding fears with some definite problem which, however dire, could in some way be tackled.

He half turned towards me, revealing a pale segment of cheek which, again, I found reassuring. But the reassurance was short-lived.

'It doesn't matter,' he said. 'There's nothing that can be done.'

His note of finality almost silenced me into submission. Then I rallied a little.

'But what's wrong with you?'

'Never mind.'

'But I do mind. How can I help you if you don't tell me what's wrong?'

'*You* can't help me.' He seemed first surprised, then amused at the idea. He shook his head decisively. 'Nobody can.'

'I could try.'

His face became stern. 'There's nothing you can do.'

'Then why did you say anything in the first place?' As well as piqued, I was puzzled.

Silence. Why place an unnecessary obstacle between us? Perhaps I was expected to disown him, turn and walk away without a qualm as if from an unwelcome street-beggar. I had to shed an uneasy feeling that that was indeed what he wanted, or thought he wanted, and I hesitated before my next question. It might give offence. But I could think of no other.

'Have you been to a doctor?' (He could not have been ill enough to need a doctor.)

14

'Oh yes, the doctors have done their worst. I'm incurable.'

'Now I don't believe that!'

My response had been automatic, then came reflection. He had seen a doctor. There really was an illness. No use entertaining the hope that nothing momentous was amiss, that those few dynamite words weren't so dreadful after all. Not that I'd really thought that. However odd, however hard to accept, I'd known right away that this must be serious.

He was entrenched once more behind his wall of silence. It was almost time for his train. Surely he couldn't mean to leave the matter there. I scrabbled for another opening.

'The illness you said you had after the war, was that connected with it?'

'Yes.'

'Was that when they said you were incurable?'

'No, not exactly.'

'What did they say?'

He didn't answer this. Then he turned to me as his train came in sight. 'Look, Elaine, I can't talk about it now. You – you won't mention this to anyone, will you? If you did, that would be the end of us.'

I hesitated only a moment before caving in. 'All right.'

A soft kiss on the lips, the kiss of a lover – a normal lover – then he was off along the platform, turning with a little wave of the hand before boarding the train.

I stumbled down the wide dusty passage to the underground, my mind in turmoil, his parting kiss a warning that his wishes had to be heeded. Forget about that desperate resolve to seek help. I dared not even mention his confession to Helen and risk having to lie to him about that.

The train burst out of the tunnel and hissed to a halt. I stepped inside and took an empty seat in the row of sealed faces, staring stupidly round at the familiar interior as the train tore through black holes: the same grubby, tickly upholstery; the same anonymous passengers; the same shiny black rectangular windows winking back mesmerically in the shifting light; and, curving up to the ceiling, the same little oblong advertisements for cigarettes, for drinks, magazines, cough cures, mints, chewing-gum; the same dreary succession of ill-lit stations. By some odd quirk, everything had been left unchanged whilst I had been catapulted on to this entirely new plane of existence where I did not belong.

For months after that evening, laborious attempts to find out more about Gerald's illness met with the deft resistance of a Hobbs defending his wicket. The term 'mental illness' haunted me. Night and day it gave me no peace. What could it mean? I must find out more. Someone must be able to help him. He couldn't be incurable.

But it wasn't easy to question him; in fact it turned out to be almost impossible. Extracting the merest snippet of information was like trying to find water in a desert. All was shrouded in mystery, enquiries were disposed of with a monosyllabic mutter, a change of subject or a defeating silence, and I could neither press for answers, nor ask too many questions.

By the way, are you mad? Imagine saying that; the big joke question, the one most needing an answer – and the only one that could never be asked. I would have to wait for the right moment, and then, rather than enjoying the evening, rather than remembering the way his face lit up when he saw me or how good and right it was to be with him, find leading questions to ask in the hope that he would talk about his mental illness, whatever that might be.

He disposed of one of my fears: his army service had comprised only administrative work in England, so he hadn't been exposed to horrific battlefield experiences.

Often, a whole evening would pass with no mention of the matter, then, shortly before we were to part, never earlier: 'Perhaps I ought to tell you …' A maddeningly long pause. 'No, I'll tell you about that some other time.' 'I remember once – no, I can't tell you about that.' 'Did I ever tell you about …? No, not now, my dear. Perhaps next time.'

Each opening raised me to a new pitch of expectancy from which to fall. I wished that he had never said a word, that I was not consumed by this obligation to pursue the truth, that I had never discovered the lines in his face. I wished that futile conjecture did not dog my every daytime moment, that it didn't keep me awake at night. I wished that I was not spurred on by his enigmatic remarks.

'Oh, you can't imagine, life is Hell –'

'No, I dare not tell you about that –'

'Oh, you little know; I suffer all the time.'

'You've no idea how awful it is.'

'Life is just Hell.'

'There's no respite; I can never escape –'

My guesses began to wear thin. For want of fresh stimulus the subject started to fade. The comforts of marriage would cure him of all his ills, if indeed he really had any …

Lying beside Gerald on this February night years later I realise that, apart from his insomnia, love and marriage have cured him of nothing. How could I have been so idiotically wrong about that?

After his bombshell at the railway station I'd lie awake at night besieged by images of madness: lunatics locked away in attics, murderers brandishing knives in pursuit of innocent girls, maniacs in padded cells struggling with straitjackets, white-coated figures poised menacingly with hypodermic needles …

The parade of madmen is starting up afresh, and I begin chanting to myself the old refrain:

Gerald isn't mad, Gerald isn't mad, Gerald isn't mad.

He can't be mad, he can't be mad, he can't be –

I go on chanting until fatigue finally does its work and I sleep.

Three

Should I speak or should I not?

If I do speak, what should I say?

What should I not say?

When should I speak?

In what tone?

When should I not speak?

The questions were not new. At times they mercifully receded, but not today. Gerald had woken up no less distressed, barely raising his head when I took up his tea and biscuits.

'See you later, darling.'

A grunted reply. I kissed two dead lips and left for the office, to be dogged all day by his tormented face.

I had always looked forward to Friday evenings, the important little brown wage-envelope safe in my handbag and the weekend ahead. It was also my favourite night for going out, but we weren't going out tonight; it hadn't even been mentioned.

Only three days since I'd hurried down the lane eager to get back to Gerald after the long day apart. A faint residue of light in the sky heralded our first summer in the country, and the February air was mild, almost spring-like. Charlie, our farmer landlord, liked to boast, as though it were a personal achievement of his, that down here you hardly ever needed an overcoat in winter, though we'd found that the damp could get at you.

Only three days since I'd thought that our one remaining problem was finding that elusive job. Now my legs no longer wanted to rush home. No glad thoughts of spring tonight, no smiling up at the wisp of grey sky skimming the tops of the hedges. I walked slowly, my head down, with every step the mysterious new worry closing in like one of those sudden thick Dartmoor mists.

You can't see the house above the high hedge until you arrive at the gap where the iron gate opens on to the flight of high stone steps. I reached the gate and saw that the light was on. He might have been out again; anything was possible now. But he was huddled as usual beside the lifeless grate clutching his notebook and pencil, and one glance at his funereal face was enough to demolish the last shreds of optimism about the weekend.

'Hello, darling.'

'Hello.'

The same dead lips brushed mine, the same old dirge accompanied me into the hall: Should I speak or should I not?

I hung up my coat, switched on the kettle and began cleaning out the grate. It upset me to find Gerald sitting in the cold, but if I sometimes managed to get the fire laid in the morning he still wouldn't light it. He didn't need it, he said, it would be a waste of money. If it occurred to me now and then that he might have laid the fire for me, the thought never lingered. Housework was woman's work; we all knew that.

The evening passed with hardly a word spoken, eye-contact avoided, Gerald's head bent over his notebook and dictionaries, mine over my book. The quiet flick of a page. The nine o'clock news.

By ten o'clock the strain had become unbearable. Abandoning poor Anna Karenina, I knelt down by Gerald's chair and began massaging his taut scalp, easing out the tensions, and quite unexpectedly he responded, leaning back, eyes closed. Up and down, up and down, little ripples of air drifted like autumn leaves across the aching silence. Gradually, his body slumped. Up and down, up and down …

He was dozing. I rested my aching hands.

After a few minutes his eyes opened. He looked rested; he was almost smiling. I waited for him to speak.

19

He said nothing.

'Darling, what's wrong?' Drawn perhaps by his placatory manner the words had slipped out against my better judgement.

No reply. But I thought I sensed a weakening of resistance, which I then dared not trust. Could this by some remote chance be capitulation? Was he going to speak after all this time, all these years? My heart was thudding as though I had just run all the way up the long escalator in Piccadilly Circus station. Several long minutes crawled by. My back went damp. I kept still as the silence dragged on painfully, like an exposed nerve.

'You may as well know,' he said at last, pausing uncertainly.

A delay at this point was only to be expected, I told myself. But had I detected an unprecedented note of submission? I waited, not daring to move my cramped legs.

'I – er – I –' Another torturous pause. If only I could move! I willed myself to stay still. And at last he spoke; quietly; resigned:

'I – er – I've – um – I've forgotten something –'

He lapsed into silence again, and I took a moment to try to digest this intelligence. Was it meant to be taken seriously?

It was probably safe to move now. I rose and stretched my legs, limping to my chair as pins and needles began stinging my left foot. I leaned back, eyes half closed. Was it I that was dreaming? Was it I that was mad? 'I've forgotten something' – Was this puny remark meant to have a bearing on the death-mask of the past few days?

I opened my eyes. 'What do you mean?' I spoke gently. Angrily demanding that he explain himself did not seem to be a good idea.

Another long pause. Then, half glancing up, he repeated impatiently, as if I should have understood him perfectly well the first time, 'I've forgotten something.'

'Forgotten what? What do you mean, darling?'

'I forgot something whilst I was in the cinema.'

'Do you mean yesterday?'

'No.'

'The first time?'

'Yes.'

'Do you mean something in the film?'

'I – er – I don't know. It – it may have been.'

I curbed my impatience.

'I don't understand you,' I said.

Looking up, he met my eyes with a new frankness.

'It – it isn't easy to explain.'

Nothing of Gerald's ever would be easy to explain, I thought in confusion, casting about for a likely lead.

'What kind of thing is it that you've forgotten?'

'That's just it, I don't know. It could be anything.'

'Darling, don't make a mystery out of it. You must know what sort of thing you've forgotten.'

'I don't.'

How was one supposed to reply to that? I didn't believe him, but there was his distraught face.

'Well, don't upset yourself about it, darling.' I tried to sound soothing without being patronising. 'It can't be very important, can it.'

'It IS important.'

'How can you know that? I mean, if you don't know what it is?'

He turned aside to gaze at the fire. Perhaps the matter would be left there. I half wished it would; it was too peculiar.

He looked up again with sudden determination.

'I suppose you may as well know –' He sounded portentous again, and my back grew clammy. He really was going to volunteer some vital information. Gerald never volunteered anything; he only allowed fragments of information to be extracted slowly and painfully, like wisdom teeth.

'You see, um –' Glancing down, he flicked ash into the glass ashtray beside his pile of books, keeping his eyes down as he went on.

'You see, whilst I was in the cinema something flitted across my mind. It could have been anything, but whatever it was, I wanted to

21

remember it –' Looking up, he added defiantly, 'I know that much.'
Lowering his eyes again, he added more amenably, 'I couldn't make a
note of it in the dark so I made a mental note to remember it.'

(So that was why he was always jotting down notes.)

'And then you found you'd forgotten it?'

'Yes.'

'So when you went again you thought –?'

'I thought it might come back to me.'

'But it might be nothing to do with the film.'

'No, but it might have been. Anyway, it might have been something triggered off during the film and then the same thing might
have happened again.'

'I see.' (I saw little, beyond a frightening mess at which one should
either laugh or cry – I didn't know which.)

'And you've still no idea what it is?'

'No.'

'Well, you don't have to worry about it, do you.' I made the effort
to avoid tartness. 'It'll come back to you when you least expect it.
Things like that always do.' (He must know this already.)

'Are you sure?' He looked as if his very life hung on the answer.

'Of course! Surely that happens to everyone?'

His tense face entreated reassurance. Uneasy in the role of adviser,
I deliberated.

'Surely you've often tried to think of a name or a tune or something like that that you've forgotten and you can't? Then when you
least expect it it comes back to you.'

'But does it always?'

'Yes, I suppose so.'

'But you can't be sure?'

'Well, I'm pretty sure.' I pondered carefully. 'Yes, I'm certain it
comes back if you really want it to; but it may take time.'

'Why should it take time? Why shouldn't it come back straight
away?'

A note of panic in his voice did nothing to boost my confidence. Lost in a maze which I had not consciously entered, I sought a way out.

'I suppose something has to remind you of it.'

'What if nothing happens to remind you?'

'I suppose something always does remind you.'

'How?'

'Well–' The subject was becoming tiresome. I glanced at Gerald's distraught face and dutifully sought an answer. 'I expect one sets a train of thought in motion when one first tries to remember and eventually the thing is traced back.'

'Back where?'

'Back into the unconscious where it has been all the time.' Was this right? And if it was right, how could I have come to know it?

'Has it?'

'Yes, of course. We don't ever really forget anything, do we?' My certainty on this surprised me. I must have heard or read it somewhere.

'But I want to remember it at the time.'

'Why is that so important? I mean to say, most of these things one forgets are trivialities, aren't they?'

'Ah! That's the point! Now you've got it!'

I didn't feel as though I had 'got' anything. But Gerald had spoken with vehemence, as if he thought I had. He went on, 'They usually are trivialities, and I always know it. That's the damnable part about it. I've got to remember straight away, whether I want to or not, all these damned trivialities which I know aren't in the least important, even to me. And I've got to keep trying to remember. I can't stop. I know very well it's stupid, but knowing that I'm being stupid – do you see? – only makes it worse. I've still got to keep trying.'

He was so distressed, so trapped, I felt obliged to come to the rescue. But how? Like a mother with a hurt child, I could only try to soothe away some of the pain.

'But you know,' I said, 'that even if you don't try, it'll probably come back anyway.'

'Ah! But it may not!' he snapped, pausing, and then adding rather sheepishly, 'Besides, there may be scores of other points before then, and I'll never know whether I've remembered that particular one or not.' He ended on a slightly plaintive note.

After five years of suspense and prevarication, Gerald was talking and I had very little idea of what he was talking about. Seeing my bewilderment, to my surprise he began to enlarge.

'You may as well know it all. This is the point. Things are flitting across my mind all the time and some of them – quite a lot of them – involve a point I have to remember. Usually I make a note of it.'

'What sort of things?'

'Oh, anything; absolutely anything; the merest trivialities.'

'Such as –?'

'Well, for example …' I tried to hide my discomfiture as he paused in confusion and then went on: 'It may be the name of a person, an acquaintance, an actor, anyone; it might be a time when something happened, the name of a place or a house or a tune, anything. Or there might be a word I want to look up, or something may remind me of something else which I can't place, and so on …' His voice tailed off.

'But everyone has this sort of thing going on, only –' he was regarding me defensively – 'only, well, one doesn't pay all that much attention to it.'

'Well, I have to.'

This I had been vaguely suspecting. But could one accept that somebody, anybody, driven by some freakish compulsion, had to pay attention to all these idiotic thoughts? Was this really possible?

'What do you mean by scores of other points?'

'Well, this activity is going on all the time and points are arising all the time. If I'm not careful I lose track of them. You see, while I'm trying to remember one, another may arise, and so on.' His voice faded, his head drooped for a moment and I tried in vain to make some kind of sense of this new conundrum. Looking up and meeting my eyes, he added earnestly, 'It gets very complicated.'

His strained face forbade dismissal of the whole story as some incomprehensible joke. But how far it was from a joke I now began to discover. It was already midnight but he wanted to recount the whole film to me in the hope of being reminded of his elusive 'point'. I listened to one commonplace detail after another, stoically enduring his prolonged pauses for reflection, stifling yawns and muttering, 'Yes', 'I see', 'Of course!'

Was I right, I was wondering at two in the morning, to be attempting this kind of help? Should I have insisted that this line was not worth pursuing? Perhaps I should have made a determined effort to change the subject. He still had not thought of his 'point' and he evidently wanted to continue. But for how long?

'Shall we go to bed, darling?'

'I can't. Not yet.'

'Yes you can. Come on, darling. It'll still be there tomorrow.' (By then, surely, his need would have evaporated.)

'Perhaps you're right.' He gathered up his books.

His prompt acquiescence came as a relief. Perhaps the problem was not as bad as I'd first thought. Perhaps he'd be better in the morning.

Long after Gerald was asleep I lay awake. What bearing, if any, did these revelations have on the mental illness of the past? Was it really past? Was it still going on? Was this unlikely explanation the answer to the mystery of five years ago? A mere habit of mind – could that be significant? Surely a habit of mind was no more important than any other habit, just nuisance value, something to be either largely ignored or dealt with positively.

I thought of Gerald's despairing face. Could so much misery be the result of a mere bad habit? I was used to practical everyday difficulties. Gerald's abstruse problems were new, different, far too

25

abstract and undefined for me to have any idea of their real nature, and therefore I could not entirely believe in their existence. In the morning, surely, they would all be forgotten.

Unforeseen problems seemed to have developed a nasty way of interfering with my idea of love. There had been a brief time when my future with Gerald had seemed assured. We had met at a farming camp in Suffolk, where I had taken a cheap healthy holiday between secretarial jobs and found Gerald an unlikely member of the staff. 'I'll be returning to London soon,' he promised at the end of my fortnight. And the agony of waiting six weeks without a word from him was immediately forgotten when I heard his voice on the phone, and then I felt a little foolish when he spoke as if there had been no doubts, as if we had seen each other only yesterday. And of course we were going to meet again soon, the very next day, in fact, for dinner in a Leicester Square restaurant. I wore my new light blue silky dress with the heart-shaped neckline which drew Gerald's eyes like a magnet.

We sat on at the table for hours while he listened to my chatter, smiling, saying little himself. The tube trains were about to finish for the night and he insisted on putting me into a taxi, ignoring my protests when he pressed a pound note for the fare into my hand. 'I'll ring you,' he said, and kissed me, there, in the street, in public.

I bounded up three flights of stairs and unlocked the door of my room to find it lit up with bright starlight, an ethereal white light like no other light I had ever seen. I went over to the window and gazed out, entranced, at the brilliant sky, the portent of a wonderful future. I was no longer alone. The slow years of suspense, of waiting for something to happen, were over, gone for good.

Four

'Come on, darling, nine o'clock.'

Saturday. No work. The tea tray waiting on the dressing-table. I nudged Gerald's shoulder, then raised his pillows as he dragged himself up. I pulled back the curtains to admit a blast of sunlight and settled down on the edge of the bed to chatter over tea and Gerald's favourite Nice biscuits. Yesterday's revelations were far too queer to be taken seriously. I'd have to get a move on, get dressed, do the dusting and shopping, make an early lunch and then we could get out for some fresh air. Gerald liked hoovering. I loved hearing him sing at the top of his voice above the racket made on the bare floorboards by the heavy old machine (a five-pound bargain from the village shop). Life was simple and easy, of course it was. I'd always been right about that.

Gerald put down his cup. He looked up. 'Do you mind if we go over it again?' he said.

The morning joy was washed clean off my face. How could this be happening? Looking away in confusion, I slowly drained my cup, and slowly, in a dream, replaced it on the saucer. I should have known, of course I should. Life wasn't simple. It wasn't easy. I glanced out of the window at the glinting greens of the garden and the coloured hinterland. The real world was out there waiting for us, but we weren't going out there. We were staying in here, incarcerated in the punishment cell on a sunny Saturday in spring.

Half hoping to be told he didn't mean it, it's just an idle thought, a joke, let's forget it and talk about where to go this weekend, I turned back. But his head was already bent over his notebook. Didn't he know that he was probably acting against his own best interests? Or, for that matter, against mine? Didn't he care about me, about my needs? I pulled myself up. Gerald's needs were what mattered.

'Why, er, of course, if you want to,' I said. And for the next three hours I sat trapped on the edge of the bed in my dressing-gown, getting chilly and more and more mystified and downcast as the film was again meticulously deconstructed: dialogue, costumes, settings, names of cast, hundreds, thousands of details recalled and examined; related matters, however remote, methodically explored, including anything that might have served as a reminder of something else such as other films the actors had appeared in. We drew a complete blank; the morning was frittered away; the precious weekend was disappearing.

I dressed hurriedly. Ignoring Gerald's protests that he didn't need food I prepared a hasty lunch of grilled cheese on toast before dashing to the village for groceries, returning to find him dressed, hunched in his chair, ready for the afternoon performance, a very peculiar kind of private matinee, one with no laughs. Once or twice during the inquisition I escaped to the kitchen to make tea, thinking at three o'clock that we must be nearing the end of this futile post-mortem. But at four o'clock I was again ferrying in tea in the blue-flowered china cups and saucers bought with such pleasure in a sale. The sunny afternoon was disappearing in the wake of the morning, swept away, swallowed up.

'Is it worth it, darling? Wouldn't it be best to leave it?'

The face looking from the notebook was so gripped, so fixed, I hadn't the heart to refuse him. A quick meal of eggs and chips, more tea, a cigarette … the evening, too, was being squandered.

At ten o'clock Gerald finally closed his notebook. He sank his head in his hands. Finished.

What was any sane person supposed to do in such a situation?

He looked up at last. 'It's no use,' he groaned. 'It must have been something that occurred to me while I was in the cinema, nothing to do with the film – I've lost it now!'

He was so crushed, so desolate, so grief-stricken, like a man who has lost his best friend, I was wrung with pity for him; and ashamed of a spasm of relief that the day's inquisition was over. If only there was something I could do! Something very serious was happening, something destructive, out of my control; and far worse, far more worrying, out of Gerald's control, too.

'Tell me, darling, how long has all this been going on?' I was sitting on his lap, rhythmically running my fingers through his hair, willing his troubles away.

'Oh, a long time.'

He sounded utterly weary and defeated. And, suddenly, I felt weary and defeated, too, and wanted to give in, relinquish all further effort and involvement and just weep and weep. But I had to keep my head.

My hands stopped moving.

'And does it really go on all the time, not just in cinemas?'

He met my gaze with unaccustomed frankness.

'Yes.'

'When you're talking to someone?'

He nodded his head and went on nodding dully, a victim resigned to his fate, as I said, with growing disbelief: 'Listening to the radio? Reading? Working? Walking? Even' – I hesitated – 'Even when you're making love to me?'

He smiled ironically. 'Yes.'

'Oh!' I drew a deep breath. Resting my face against his, I created a long silence of my own, trying and trying to digest the bizarre notion that anyone could spend all his waking hours compulsively pursuing unwanted trains of thought – but it was like grasping handfuls of air. I drew back a little, stroked his hair, kissed his face. The fire tried to cast a comforting glow as I ransacked my brain, not for answers but for questions, the right questions, the right line to take.

'Darling.' I tilted his head back to meet his eyes. 'You know you said you'd been ill soon after the war and you had treatment at some rehabilitation centre or nursing home or whatever it was.' This had once been mentioned, briefly, in passing.

'Yes.'

'Well, was all this activity going on then?'

'Yes.'

'Well, what did they say about it?'

'I didn't tell them.'

'You – you didn't tell them?'

'No.'

'But why ever not?' I didn't try to hide my amazement.

'There was nothing they could do about it.'

I contrived to keep my voice even. 'How do you know that?'

'I know.'

'But you can't be sure.'

'I am sure. Nothing could be done, I tell you.'

Again that note of quiet conviction, positive and dismissive, Gerald as usual knowing everything while I knew nothing. But I must fight this, contest it, discredit it, find a way through it, or round it. But how? The blank wall of his face offered up no answers. I stared at the fire, straining to unravel knots as the thick silence gathered about us like a choking fog, hemming us in.

I spied an opening, a little chink of light.

'Tell me this, darling. Was that the worst thing that was going on at the time? I mean, when you had your breakdown. Was that the main thing that was wrong?'

Sighing, he took his time about answering.

'Yes,' he admitted at last. 'I suppose so.'

'And you didn't tell them about it?' I was silent for a moment, trying to take this in.

Carefully avoiding any hint of reproach, I said, 'How could you expect them to help you if you didn't tell them?'

'It was up to them to find out.'

'Oh, now you're not being fair. Surely it was up to you to tell them all you could?' I spoke mildly, curbing the need to shriek at him, for what good would that do?

'Well, I didn't tell them.'

Considering this, I was guided by his defensive manner towards a rare flash of intuition.

'Was it because you were ashamed of it that you didn't tell them?'

Pitifully uncomfortable, he didn't at once reply. Then with a look of abject surrender, he whispered, 'Yes, I suppose so.'

I hugged him, kissed his weary face. 'But darling, it's nothing to be ashamed of. I'm sure of that.'

'How could YOU know?'

I ignored the scorn in his voice. 'But I do know. It's obvious.'

He was unconvinced.

'Look, darling, what you're doing – trying to remember things – we all do it. It's perfectly normal but it's got a bit out of control, that's all.'

His voice rose in agitation. 'But I should be able to control it.'

'Darling, I suppose that's what you need help for.'

'And how do you think anyone can help me to do that if I can't do it for myself?'

'I don't know, but there must be a way.' Of this I was convinced. Did we not live in a post-Freudian world of psychological expertise? I rose from his lap. 'I'm going to make some tea.' I paused at the door. 'Darling, tomorrow, do you think we can go out?'

He looked doubtful.

'Please –'

'We'll see.'

Hounding the myriad thoughts slumbering peacefully in the background, dragging them relentlessly, one by one, into the foreground. The prompters forever usurping the principal players, upstaging them. The whole of life subjugated to inner compulsions. Hard to comprehend, hard to accept. But explaining so well Gerald's habitual detachment, his lack of commitment to daily life, to work, to possessions, to other people, to me. Clearly this was no fanciful invention, no hallucination, no triviality. Not only was it happening, it had virtually made a successful takeover bid for the whole of our lives. I'd never be able to think of anything else again. Walking up the lane on Monday morning I couldn't even smile at the sight of fresh little clusters of primroses dotting the hedges, a treat for London eyes.

Gerald needed a doctor. He must know that, but of course he would never mention it himself. That would be left to me, and I trembled at the thought. The obstacles in the way of the merest hint at a doctor would be formidable. Of that, if of nothing else, I could be absolutely sure.

There was little choice but to rely on chance remarks made at just the right moment. And over several days, gentle prodding did produce a limited response. But not an encouraging one. He refused to see a doctor without a guarantee of foolproof treatment, and I could only protest (not vociferously) that there was no question of a guarantee. We could only put our trust in the doctors. The doctors would know how he could be helped.

To press the point would only ensure his opposition. Days passed: walking the lanes, watching out for birds, returning to the drone of the radio; pretending that it didn't matter if he went or not – an inept attempt at acting that was bound to fail.

To refer to it or not? And when, and how, to do so?

In desperation one day, I blurted out, 'I don't see why doctors shouldn't be able to cure your condition. After all, don't they sometimes even cure people who've been certified?' I seemed to have heard or read this somewhere.

The foolhardiness of making such a remark frightened me even as I spoke. A secret volcano might erupt, spewing forth buried deposits of anger. Something might so easily be said that would send Gerald into a mad frenzy. There was a film in which a man became murderous whenever he saw anything white – any everyday object – clothing, linen, furniture, a washbasin, a wall, a door …

Luckily, the remark seemed to appeal to his reason. 'Yes, that's true,' he muttered thoughtfully. And a point was scored, but the game far from won, his face saying that he wanted to go while his voice stayed silent. He didn't refer to it again, and he knew so well how to ward off my approaches with a forbidding look, a change of subject, an air of haste, or an intense preoccupation with other, weightier matters.

Now that he need no longer hide his thoughts from me, I was enlisted as an ally, I was privileged to descend into the pit with him.

'Did I ask you to do something for me the other day?' He had looked up with furrowed face from his notes.

'Which day, darling?'

'I'm not sure.'

'What sort of thing?'

'I don't know. It could be anything.'

'Haven't you any idea which day?'

'Well, it was probably yesterday, or the day before – or it might have been the day before that.' He was frowning over his notes, oblivious of the enormity of the task he had set me, which I naturally felt obliged to carry out to the letter. My book was relinquished. 'I'll try and think, darling.'

I leaned back in the chair, eyes half closed. Let's see, what happened yesterday? Nothing. Went to work, of course. Did Gerald ask me to get him anything? Cigarettes? No. Did I buy anything from the shops at lunchtime? No. What about the evening? What did we have for dinner? Sausages and mash. Did he say anything to me before dinner? No, I was talking about Mrs Cooper at the office and he wasn't listening. Did we have the radio on? What was on? I sat up and scanned the *Radio Times*.

'No, darling, I'm sure there was nothing yesterday. I'll think about

Tuesday.' My eyes half closed again. I can't remember anything about Tuesday. What did I have for breakfast? What did I wear? Was Mr West in? One answer followed another until the day's minutiae were spread out before me like a page out of Hansard – immensely intriguing, though, in the end, yielding no help to Gerald.

'I'm sorry, darling, I can't think of anything for Tuesday either. Do you want me to go over Monday?'

No reply. He was staring despondently at the fire.

I got up and went and put my arms round him. 'Darling, won't you go and see a doctor?'

He stiffened. 'No – I can't.'

'Do you want me to think about Monday?'

'Monday?'

'Yes, if you asked me to do anything.'

'Oh! Yes, please.' He gave an appreciative half-grin. 'If you don't mind.'

I chafed at the waste of time, but Gerald's needs came first.

Cautious mention of a doctor when he was at his lowest ebb met only with more refusals. Night after night 'points' were pursued into the small hours. Until one evening, my tentative mention of a doctor was met with a cautious, 'We'll see,' which sent me to bed hopeful for the first time. But the next day brought more opposition. I insisted that there must be a way out.

'There's no way out. It's incurable!'

'It isn't!'

'It must be!'

My conviction must have carried weight because a few days later, looking up from his notebook, he said unexpectedly, 'If we wanted to see a doctor, where should we go? We don't know anyone down here.'

I smothered the useless retort that we could see the local doctor even though we'd not yet registered with him. Gerald wasn't going to bare himself to a stranger.

'When you were ill after the war, did you go to your own doctor at Beston?'

'Yes, Doctor Mitchell. He knows all about me.'

'Do you like him?'

'Mitchell? Oh, yes, I've known him all my life.'

'And do you trust him?'

'As much as I trust anyone. He's well-intentioned, anyway.'

A great concession, this, coming from Gerald, who frequently warned me to 'trust no one', advice entirely wasted on one whose trust was given automatically, without question.

'Well ...' (Don't let him see you're excited.) 'Couldn't we go and see him and get his advice?'

'Oh, perhaps. I'll see.' He waved me away. 'I'll have to think about it.' He returned to his notebook.

A further week of suspense and I could wait no longer.

'Darling, have you decided yet?' Having washed up the evening dishes, I found him staring intently at some minute spiky writing on a scrap of newspaper. Sitting on his lap, I began to massage his scalp.

'Yes, go on doing that.' He leaned back with a sigh, and a few moments later had dozed off. Reluctantly moving away, I rejoined my neglected Anna Karenina.

A week later there was still no decision. Either he was overwrought and unapproachable, or he was tired and I hadn't the heart to bother him, or he urgently wanted to make love to me there on the battered old hearthrug in front of the fire, or we were listening to the radio, or going out. It was he who spoke about it at last, unexpectedly following me into the kitchen, where he was seldom seen.

'If we did go and see Mitchell, what should we tell him?'

'Why, what's been happening, of course.' (Stay calm!)

'You mean about the activity and so on?'

'Yes.'

'What would he do then?'

'I don't really know. Send you to a specialist, I suppose.'

'Where?'

'I don't know.'

'Suppose he questions me about it?'

'Well, just tell him what he wants to know.'

'What if he wants to see my notes? I shan't show him those.' He was in a panic.

I poured hot water from the kettle into the washing-up bowl. (Calm!)

'Darling, I'm sure you won't have to show him anything you don't want to, or tell him anything you don't want to.'

'Perhaps. I'm not sure.'

I swished the dishmop idly in the bowl. After a moment he observed thoughtfully, 'Mitchell's a man of the world, at any rate. Sensible. Not one of those pompous asses.'

I looked up. 'Shall we go and see him next Saturday, then?'

'Oh, perhaps. I don't know. We – we'll discuss it tomorrow. There's a programme I want to listen to now.'

The next evening he didn't mention it. When we were undressing I said lightly, 'Darling, shall we go on Saturday?'

'No, no; not yet. I'll have to think about it.' He was undoing his shirt buttons and staring blankly at the wall behind the chest of drawers, like all the walls in the house painted in flat cream distemper. I hungered for the texture and colour of wallpaper but hadn't bothered to mention this particular craving for unattainable luxury.

I got into bed, pretending to read. I can't bear it, I thought. I can't bear to wait another minute for him to make up his mind.

Returning from the washing up a few evenings later, I found him slumped in his chair, head in hands. Tilting his head back, I kissed soft passive lips.

'Oh, I don't know what I'm going to do,' he groaned.

A declaration of defeat. I was winning.

'Darling, let's go and see Mitchell.'

A long pause. I looked down, suppressing the urge to scream.

'If we did go ...'

I looked up.

'There's just one thing.' He paused, turning away again, and my patience fluctuated wildly. How much longer would this take?

He turned to face me at last, and very hesitantly he began to speak. And what he had to say was once again totally unexpected: 'There's a – there's a brain operation they do, you know. It's called leucotomy. They cut out a chunk of the memory. It cures people like me, yes, but by God, we pay for it! It destroys some memories of the past and can change the personality drastically.' He shuddered. 'I won't have that!'

Thank God he had spoken out! I had a particular horror of brain operations. Gerald, of all people, must be spared such an outrage. Still, for one wild moment I couldn't help wondering if he, and, indirectly (I was ashamed to admit it) I myself, could not gain by some kind of beneficent personality change. In great agitation, he continued, 'No one even knows if it's a permanent cure. The whole thing's experimental. No one knows very much about it –'

The uncertainty of the outcome was a decisive argument against surgical interference. 'Darling, no one can force you to have an operation if you don't want to. Besides, I wouldn't exactly be keen on it either.'

He looked grave. 'Are you sure?'

I was learning to dissemble. 'Yes, of course, darling. You do worry for nothing, don't you. I'll write to your mother, shall I? She'll be pleased to see you.'

'All right, then.'

I wondered for a moment if I might swoon with relief. But he was still uncertain.

'What about the appointment with Mitchell? He may not be free.'

'Don't worry. I'll ring him from the office and fix it.'

'You won't tell him anything on the phone, will you?'

'No, of course not.'

'All right, if you're sure. What shall we say when we –'

I gently touched his lips. 'Not now, darling; let's go to bed.'

Five

I should long ago have made it my business to look into one or two of Gerald's odd habits. Much as I hated to pry, if we were going to see a doctor I really should know as much as possible about him.

I thought of his strict rule that newspapers and periodicals must not, without his express permission, be thrown away or used to light the fire or wrap up the rubbish. I'd humoured him in this as just another of his fads, nothing very important, though sometimes idly, in passing, I'd wondered about it.

Now it began to tease me. I ought to know the reason behind it. It suddenly occurred to me one day why he might want them, and I waited for the right moment after dinner that evening when I was handing over last week's *Listener*.

'Is it in case there's anything in them you want to remember?' I had been hoping for a denial or perhaps some practical explanation, and was a little taken aback when he nodded, slightly shamefaced.

'Where are they all, then?' I kept to a neutral tone.

'In there.' He pointed to the adjoining empty room, earmarked by me as a future dining-room.

In the middle of the bare pine floor, well away from damp walls, stood several packing cases and large brown paper parcels which months ago, when we first moved in, had been sent on, under Gerald's detailed orders, by his mother. 'You won't touch them, will you,' he'd cautioned, and, obediently, and not given to curiosity, I'd scarcely glanced at them.

Also on the floor in several cardboard grocer's cartons was my small collection of books patiently awaiting their bookcase. I knew the kind I wanted, light oak with sliding glass doors. It would fit perfectly into the alcove on one side of the fireplace, nicely balanced on the other side by Gerald's bureau bookcase, his most treasured possession, which he hadn't asked to be sent on yet – a nagging source of insecurity for me.

What was in those packing cases? With Gerald safely in the bath one evening I decided that the time had come to investigate. I crept into the bare room, quietly closing the door and switching on the light, hating the need for secrecy. Or should I think of it as treachery? I seldom went into that room. It was probably the first time I'd entered it after dark, and the reflection of the naked light bulb in the shiny black window struck a lurid theatrical note, heightening the sense of unease. With a shudder I advanced the few feet to the huddled packages.

Flimsy plywood lids lay unfastened on top of Gerald's three packing cases, denoting a degree of trust on his part which contrasted uncomfortably with my own disloyalty. Being a spy is not a pleasant sensation. But this had to be tried. In some roundabout way it might help. I removed the lids, carefully propping them against the wall.

Inside each case, a large bulging hessian sack lay wide open at the top, hiding nothing. The first two were evidently filled with neatly stacked newspapers and copies of the *Radio Times* in strict date order. Hundreds of them. Irrefutable evidence. But evidence of what? Feeling slightly sick, I fingered through a few of the top copies before letting them drop back into place. No *Listeners*. Gerald seemed to be able to discard those.

I turned to the third sack, heaped to the top with what appeared to be scraps of newspaper, notepaper, envelopes, broken pieces of cigarette packs, each bearing one or two scribbled notes in Gerald's small, angular, almost indecipherable handwriting. Gerald's secrets, not meant for prying eyes. But it was too late for scruples. I picked up a handful and tried to read them. They referred mainly to points of English – odd words, grammar, punctuation – much of the writing amounting to little more than a spiky line. I remembered Gerald once very hesitantly passing me a similar slip and asking if I could read it. I hadn't been able to, and, after frowning over it all evening, neither had he. I had thought no more of it and it had duly vanished, superseded no doubt by numerous other 'problems'.

Gingerly – avoiding contamination – I replaced the pieces, and stood contemplating the plentiful hoard of notes; there were thousands of them, each probably representing hours of deliberation. All that wasted effort and concentration, the grinding misery, the hours of sleep for ever lost. I saw Gerald perched on the edge of his narrow bed, worrying away the small hours over his teasing personal hieroglyphics like a dog with a well-gnawed bone. This, then, had been the cause of his post-war insomnia. No wonder he'd refused to explain. But since he was always tired I had made ridiculous allowances for him, waiting for an hour or more outside a restaurant or cinema, accosted by leering men.

In a wave of revulsion I hastily restored the lids and left the room.

'Darling, all those newspapers in the dining-room, you'd never find anything in all that lot.' I was dutifully handing over the previous day's newspaper.

'Ah! But I know they're all there! I can't lose them!'

It was the first spontaneous remark ever to escape him which betrayed the existence of an obsession. Not that Gerald was given to spontaneous remarks, but I'd caught him unawares.

How had he got into this state? And even more importantly, how could he be got out of it? I had to know. How else discover a way of helping him, of curing him? A mere habit of mind, was that all it was? What were my own habits of mind? I wondered. What did I think about – that is, when I wasn't thinking about Gerald?

As an experiment I decided to keep track of all my thoughts in the course of the twenty-minute walk to the village. But after only five minutes I had to give up. Already dozens of apparently unconnected topics had arisen, until careful probing showed them to be linked into a continuous intricately woven strand.

Halfway to the village, I halted.

'We all of us think all the time!' I said aloud.

So obvious now that I'd thought of it. But nevertheless astounding, bringing a new vision of the human race. Millions of assorted men, women and children converted into innumerable private worlds, unique collections of words, impressions, feelings, memories, interactions, knowledge, prejudices! And until now I had thought of people as individuals acting under their own volition, their own free will. But what if unconscious inner compulsions, to some extent or other, denied the expression of free will?

I stood on the grass verge lost in thought, ignoring several passing motorists who slowed down, keen to offer a lift.

Stunning! Overwhelming! New concepts cascaded about me like a shower of meteors, a mesmerising mind dance. I'd felt something like this – like Columbus landing on the shores of a new continent – only once before, on leaving the Queen's Hall after my first orchestral concert.

So that's what people were like, what people were! All at the mercy of their own little powerhouse silently ticking away, twenty-four hours a day, every day – storing, sorting, hiding, converting, distorting innumerable complex filing systems. People, all of them, all of us, not quite masters of our own brains, our own minds.

Six

I sank back in my seat as the train began to move. A slight pressure from behind confirmed that we really were moving, and relief came stealing through my veins like strong drink. Safely on our way at last. At any moment in the past week Gerald might have changed his mind about this trip. There would be no warning. 'I'm not going,' he'd say, and that would be the end of it. Right up to the last minute, the last second, I was on tenterhooks: waiting for the bus to town; queuing for the train tickets; hanging about the platform. Even when we were finally in our seats we weren't safe; he could still have leapt up and bolted through the door, leaving me to grab his travel bag off the rack and tumble out after him. Certainly he'd never played quite such a trick, but I kept to the edge of my seat, staring down at the dusty grey platform, praying for the guard's whistle.

Agreeing to see the doctor had brought no relief to Gerald, no comforting sense of imminent salvation. Nothing like that. He immediately regretted his decision and sought an excuse, any excuse, to escape from the trap he'd sprung on himself, watching me for the flimsiest sign of being humoured, patronised, despised, ridiculed. One wrong word, one wrong look or gesture, would have been enough. Choose your words, I constantly told myself, control your facial expressions, the train is all that matters, getting him on to that train.

As we gathered speed I relaxed and looked around the crowded carriage. Intent, well-dressed people, smoking, rustling national newspapers, leafing through shiny magazines. In place of the attractive Devonian geniality we'd grown used to, alert, guarded faces trained warily down, an advance guard of London, a half-forgotten existence.

I slipped my arm through Gerald's as he half turned towards me and then found myself holding his hand for the first time in public without blushing. And it felt good to be out with my husband, belonging somewhere and to someone, an established person content with that rare sweet smile that made up for everything.

Five years it had taken since the night at Liverpool Street to get him to this point, and now there was nothing more to be done; it was out of my hands. The dull back gardens slid by, oblongs of grass bisected by narrow paved paths under washing lines. The waving washing reminded me of Gerald's mother collecting up his discarded clothes from the bedroom floor at six o'clock on Saturday morning, to be washed and blowing out on the line, then ironed dry ready for him to wear again after his weekend lie-in. Another of those early surprises.

Soon after returning to London from Suffolk, through an ex-army friend, Gerald had landed a temporary post as liaison officer in the planning stages of the Festival of Britain. No more listening for the telephone to ring: our offices were close enough to meet daily for lunch. We settled for the economical Lyons tea-shop in the Strand, and I scanned the *Evening News* for interesting films and plays, but we seldom met in the evenings. Gerald still never fell asleep before four or five in the morning, and now the early start and the long day at the office were leaving him more tired than ever.

It was over lunchtime coffee on a mild November day that he invited me to a Sunday film in his home town. 'It's that Marlene Dietrich film I was telling you about.' His face was shining as if Len Hutton had scored another century in the Test Match.

Marlene Dietrich held no more attraction for me than Len Hutton.

'Lovely!' I exclaimed.

'I'm afraid they're all slow trains on Sundays.'

'Never mind, darling. What time shall we meet?'

'I'm not sure of the Sunday train times.'

'Don't worry, I'll find out.' In my high heels and straight knee-length black skirt, breasts bouncing under tailored jacket and clinging white jumper, holding down my wide-brimmed black felt hat, I raced along the busy Strand, turning bowler-hatted heads.

The train, as Gerald had said, was slow, taking an hour for the thirty-minute weekday trip. Not that I minded. From my window-seat I beamed out at my lover's territory – sanctified ground. Why worry about the poor Sunday service or the reek of grime and stale cigarette smoke? Not only was I entering Gerald's domain, I was going to see him on a Sunday, usually a dead day to be filled in some-how by a concert at the Albert Hall with Helen or a visit to my mother in Clapham – anything to pass the time till we met again for Monday lunch.

I'm going to see him today, I'm going to see him today, I'd chanted all morning, soaking in the big old cast-iron enamelled bath, brushing my hair, drawing on the precious nylons, twisting before the mirror to admire the fluffy pink jumper bought impetuously at M&S out of Friday's salary. A light dusting of Yardley's face powder over a thin film of Pond's Vanishing Cream, a touch of pink lipstick …

The view from the window was disappointing: no resemblance here to the wooded South Downs seen on the familiar day-trip to Brighton. This was another country – mile upon mile of featureless flat fields shaved brown and green like army camouflage, breaking out here and there in a rash of red-tiled rooftops – the new housing estates, laid out in straight lines of identical brick pairs like drawings in a children's book. More drab fields and then suddenly, incongru-ously, a long squat new factory, flat-roofed, more glass than brick: post-war business springing up in out-of-the-way places.

The Beston in which Gerald grew up was a small market town with a railway station at one end of a short main street and a dozen or so modest shops, a small Woolworths, one or two pubs and a cinema. The more fortunate local housewives had progressed from outside lavatories, black-leaded stoves and linoleum floors to half-tiled bathrooms, carpets and vacuum-cleaners, and were now being lured by the gleaming banks of refrigerators and washing-machines stacked behind the new plate-glass shop windows. Very impressive, those shop windows, especially after wartime deprivations, like so many stands in the Ideal Home Exhibition, the face of the seductive future.

My heart raced like a revved-up engine when I saw Gerald's lanky figure on the station platform. In the friendly dark of the cinema we held hands and then turned to kiss, oblivious of the incriminating silhouette against the lighted screen.

Outside, the high-street lights woke us abruptly to the real world, and I clung to Gerald's arm, confidently expecting the long-awaited introduction to his home and some sustaining tea.

'Shall we walk?' he said.

Another little shock. Why did I never know what to expect from him? He led the way to a large park where we kissed hungrily against the broad trunk of an ancient oak tree. But the weather had turned and it was far too cold to linger. All the way from Siberia the pitiless easterly wind came blasting across the North Sea and the flat Essex farmlands to drive us on. But not to home and tea, nothing as normal as that.

On Sundays, the town centre forgot its modern facade and became sanctimoniously dead. Only one decent tea-shop was open. Gerald knew about it, hidden away in a little side street, fresh white net curtains on small-paned white-painted window-frames proclaiming a respectable place where a young man could safely take his young lady. A tinkling doorbell announced us to a dozen or so blameless white-draped tables. The sole occupants, a middle-aged couple in the far corner, gave the interlopers a brief appraising glance before returning to their toasted teacakes, resuming their conversation in the hushed reverential tones exacted by superior surroundings. Tucked discreetly away in the opposite corner, Gerald and I kept to the safe topics of the afternoon's film and the weather. His hand lay on the table and I longed to take it in mine. Out of the question, of course. Just speaking normally in this mortuary would be tantamount to dancing naked on one of those spotless tables. Lowering my eyes, I kept the improper thought to myself.

It was only six-thirty when a cold, almost empty train jolted me, like a lost parcel, back to town. I slowly mounted the wide stairs of the tall Victorian house and knocked on Helen's door, but there was no reply. Confronted in my own room by the dilapidated bargains resurrected from second-hand furniture shops, I wanted to turn and run away. But to where?

I grew to dread the moment when the white circle of Gerald's face dissolved into the dark, spirited away out of my life. Closing the carriage window, I sat down to the acrid smell of soiled upholstery and grimy floors. I don't want to go. Please don't make me go.

The guard's whistle blew. There was an urgent temptation to jump from the moving train and beg to be allowed to stay.

'Would you like to come home to tea?'

We were leaving a Sunday matinee the following spring.

I freed myself from the clutches of the film love story.

'Yes, of course, darling, I'd love to.' I took Gerald's arm. We were going to his home. I was going to meet his parents. D-Day had arrived.

We had walked some way down a long residential road before it occurred to me, for the first time, that all I knew about him was that he was thirty-one, he worked in London and lived with his parents, and had served in the army throughout the war. Yet glancing up at the longish, slightly haughty contained face, I knew that without a moment's hesitation I would gladly have followed him to the nearest registry office.

I had imagined him living in a large comfortable house set back from the road, his parents rising with gracious smiles from chintzy chairs.

'My father's a remarkable old boy, you know.'

I clicked to attention. Gerald was volunteering information.

'He retired more than twenty years ago and he's still going strong. He's seventy-three.'

'Retired from what?' Probably one of the professions, I thought. The law, perhaps.

'From his public house.'

I absorbed this message in surprised, almost stunned, silence.

'He sold it. Do you know' – Gerald's face was lit with an enthusiasm normally reserved for cricket and H. W. Fowler and Marlene Dietrich – 'for about twenty years before he retired, my father drank at least a bottle of whisky a day, more often two bottles. It would have killed an ordinary man. Of course, he was exceptionally strong!'

I was incapable of understanding the boyish boasting and misplaced admiration. 'What made him stop?' I asked.

Unusually relaxed and cheerful on his home ground, Gerald grinned. 'Well, one or two of his old drinking pals died suddenly and that scared the old man. It made him realise he was getting on and he was lucky to have got away with it for so long. He'd no intention of dying – he's far too fond of himself for that – so he gave up drinking, just like that! Sold up and retired.'

The large comfortable house gained credence, but public houses evoked a long forgotten picture of small ragged children crouched, winter and summer, on the steps of beery backstreet premises, waiting for parents to emerge at closing time.

'And does he drink now?'

'Not whisky any more. He can't afford it, anyway. He just toddles round to the local twice a day for a pint of beer. You'll see.'

What I would see, however unpredictable, mattered far less than the extra time with Gerald. And being officially accepted, belonging.

48

We turned into a side road. 'This is where I live,' Gerald said. 'On the next corner.'

There were no large houses with driveways, only identical pairs of small two-storey houses which turned out to be maisonettes with tiny front gardens and low wooden gates all painted the same grass-green shade. No sign anywhere of a smudged window, a crumpled net curtain, a chip of paint, a straggling blade of grass, an untrimmed hedge. No sign, in fact, that anyone actually lived in these dolls' houses. A chair on one of those mini-lawns would have suggested loose living. A toytown, lacking the familiar squalor of London slums or the once imposing tall houses of the Bayswater bedsitter area, run down by degrees during the war.

But there was no further time for reflection.

'Here we are!' Gerald was holding open a gate. He went ahead and unlocked the front door. Calling out 'Mother!' he ushered me along a dark narrow passageway and into the living-room, and a moment later his mother entered and I was shaking a strong bony hand. Wispy grey hair framed a lined even-featured face, the face of a woman who had always worked hard. In marked contrast to Gerald's easy manner, Mrs Gardner was as tense as a runner at the starting line, her body rigid, her steely grey-blue eyes darting nervously from him to me.

'Pleased ter meet yer.' The strong cockney accent was unexpected, and the edge to the voice was hardly reassuring. A marked facial resemblance between mother and son struck yet another discordant note.

'Can I take your coat?' The offer sounded as if it had cost Mrs Gardner five hard-earned pounds. Clutching my coat, she began tentatively jerking her lean body back past us towards the door. Halfway there, she halted, her eyes again flitting from Gerald to me. 'I'll get the tea,' she said hesitantly.

'Can I help?'

'No, no, that's all right. You sit down.' A hint of reproach suggested that I had perhaps said the wrong thing, had given offence. Turning round, Mrs Gardner scuttled away, leaving the door wide open.

Gerald carelessly pushed the door to, then his arms were round me, and the soft touch of his lips in these strange surroundings came as a delicious surprise, like the taste of the season's first strawberries. A seal was set on our relationship, and I felt no resentment when his mother's sudden re-entry forced us apart. As long as we were together, as long as I was spared the choice between Helen's commiserating stare and the cold cerebral company of the Third Programme.

With the door once again wide open to cold draughts of air from the passageway, Mrs Gardner was dashing to and fro. With much patting this way and that she managed to spread a starched white tablecloth on the table to her satisfaction, returning to the kitchen for cutlery and then for plates and yet again for bread and butter. Rather irritably, I wondered why a tray was not used to reduce the travel time.

We were sunk in the two large old brown leather armchairs on either side of the small brown tiled fireplace, and with the coal fire barely alight I felt cold. Gerald, obviously acclimatised, was occupied in admiring my legs and I was glad they were at their best in my sheer new American nylons. No female leg had ever appeared to better advantage than in the diaphanous stockings emerging amid sensational glamour from wartime austerity. The glowing reports about them had sounded grossly exaggerated, scarcely believable, but then Helen had overheard at the nearby bus stop that a local draper's had a supply. An unlikely story, a fairy tale, but we rushed to the shop and were astonished to find the rumour true. We were rationed to one pair each. Held ecstatically up to the light, the unfurled nylons were a wonder to behold, gossamer creations from another world. The post-war age had truly dawned.

I looked round the crowded room. The central floor space was covered by a large brown patterned carpet square dominated by a square oak table and four straight-backed matching chairs. I noticed that the stuffing under the shiny Rexine seats was worn into smooth little bumps and was immediately re-united with the identical chairs in my mother's parlour, reserved for entertaining and family Sundays, Christmas and birthdays. Most of our time was spent in the small kitchen cum living-room off the little scullery at the back – eating at the small deal table covered in the oilcloth worn through at the corners, ironing, sewing, reading, talking, listening to the 'wireless'. There was a great sense of occasion entering our 'front room': the festive white damask tablecloth setting off the pretty rose patterned best china; on the sideboard the framed sepia photographs, and the satin-lined box housing the bone-handled cutlery, a wedding present; in winter a coal fire; the food always something special, our usual vegetable stew ousted by chicken and roast potatoes followed by tinned fruit with evaporated milk, and mixed cakes from the baker's (seven for sixpence), or Peak Frean's cream biscuits for tea.

Displayed on Mrs Gardner's gleaming oak sideboard were four glass-bottomed pewter tankards in a range of sizes, a green glass bowl of apples and oranges, and two silver-framed sepia wedding photographs. I noticed three large wooden brass-handled trays propped up at the back and wondered if they were ever used. On the settee, two large plumped-up brown velvet cushions signalled another unexpected link with my past. I smiled to myself, remembering how the nicely rounded feather stuffing was rapidly reduced to a pancake when performing its role as a seat.

Gerald was not as acclimatised as I had thought. No doubt in search of absent heat he was now standing in front of the fireplace, mercifully hiding from view one or two of the hideous ornaments on the mantelpiece. He looked strangely at home in his Austin Reed suit when he clearly didn't belong here. He had seemed far more in his element in the expensive Leicester Square restaurant, studying the menu and casually ordering dinner.

Two platefuls of ham and eggs, luxuries bought with hoarded food coupons, landed on the table along with two cups of tea. 'Come on,' Mrs Gardner chirped, 'You sit here, Gerald. Here's yours, Elaine.'

Extricating myself from the clinging brown velvet, I glanced at my watch, wondering how long I would be exiled in Siberia away from the fire. Not that it deserved to be called a fire. But it was, marginally, I thought, warmer than Siberia. Having busily fetched a third plateful of ham and eggs and her own cup of tea, Mrs Gardner noticed that Gerald's cup was empty. Her spare body was arrested halfway down to her chair.

'More tea, Gerald?'

Nodding absently, Gerald reached for more bread and butter. Trained to wait on myself, I looked away to hide my surprise as his cup was scooped up, shortly to alight in front of him replenished.

Mrs Gardner's slate eyes immediately flashed to my empty cup. Useless to protest that I could wait. My cup, too, was whisked away.

With the meal finally under way, Mrs Gardner appeared to be more at ease. 'Frank's gawn for 'is little walk,' she said, grinning meaningfully at Gerald, who smiled back. ''E'll be 'ere presently,' she promised. The conspiratorial smiles, the unlikely rapport between the two, left me uneasy. Then a discussion about murders revealed an encyclopaedic knowledge of a subject which Gerald had never mentioned to me. I found it abhorrent. I was amazed at their shared interest.

'You a secretary, then?' Mrs Gardner had switched from murders to me.

'Yes, I'm a secretary.'

'Gerald says you like music, an' all that.' An unmistakable note of disapproval put me on the defensive.

'Yes, I like music.'

'What do you do, then, go to concerts an' all that?' A final thrust, this. No hope for me now. Denounced, shown up for what I was, a pretentious fraud. Because, of course, no one actually enjoyed listening to that funny music, everyone knew that. Just pretending, trying to be posh an' all that.

'Yes, I go to concerts.'

'Miss Hodges next door – she's a schoolteacher – she goes to concerts.' The derisory tone finally angered me, but, at the sound of a key in the front door, in one swift movement Mrs Gardner had sprung up and propelled herself from the room. I marvelled at her agility. Some whispering and bustling outside gave Gerald time to snatch some healing kisses, and then the bulk of an old man filled the doorway. I stood up as he shuffled forward, panting heavily.

There was no resemblance to Gerald in the massive head of thick short iron-grey hair, black beetle brows or large flabby face, the bulbous cheeks purple with the exertion of the long walk from the town centre. A pronounced stoop did not disguise a pair of powerful shoulders suggestive of an elderly prize fighter, one who could be respected for former prowess. We shook hands.

'Pleased ter meet yer.' The voice was low and guttural, the babbled words difficult to follow.

'Good to meet you.' Flashing my friendly smile, I returned to the cold embrace of the brown velvet. The old man was helped off with his coat, and with difficulty, still panting, he deposited his great bulk in the second armchair, allowing Gerald to resume his stance in front of the fireplace. In a great flurry of movement, Mrs Gardner placed a small sturdy table by the old man's side, and with the door once more wide open began darting to and from the kitchen in pursuit of her husband's high tea.

'Cold out, very cold,' Mr Gardner mumbled, rubbing his hands together. I noted, sourly, that he didn't bother to hold his hands out to the fire. It would hardly have been worth his while.

'Yes, it is.' Wrenching my gaze away from the gaping doorway, I abandoned all hope of the fire being replenished, if only for the sake of the old man, whose attention was now diverted by a plateful of jam sandwiches. In deference to his toothlessness these were cut very thin with the crusts removed, and his tea came in a very large old V-shaped china cup perched on a small saucer, producing an absurdly top-heavy effect, like a dainty woman burdened with a disproportionately large bust.

A brisk clatter of crockery from the kitchen indicated a virtuous attack on the washing-up, and I glanced at Gerald, wondering about offering help, but he went on blindly praising the afternoon's romantic film – 'They don't seem to be able to make films like that any more,' he concluded with a wistful smile.

The old man quickened to his favourite – in fact his only – topic of conversation. 'Well, I ask you, what is there that's any good these days?' The low sonorous mumble resembled the unintelligible gabble of a foreign tongue. 'I mean ter say, things ain't like what they was when I were a boy; look at the price of everythink! An' it's all a lotta rubbish! Rubbish!' The post-war increase in the cost of living had considerably upset the old man's retirement plans, but his indignation was mild, poor health after two attacks of apoplexy having drained his energy and left him lapsing into dignified senility. He stared vacantly in front of him as if he had already forgotten the discussion, as indeed he had, before returning ponderously to his jam sandwiches.

'Come and see my books.' Taking my hand, Gerald led the way down a dark icy-cold passage, and I glimpsed Mrs Gardner's head jerking round as we passed the open kitchen door.

A small oblong room, meticulously neat and clean. A narrow bed alongside one wall. An old oak dressing-table with triple-framed mirror. A small oak bureau-bookcase full of books. No wardrobe. My eyebrows rose at the sight of several sports jackets, a shirt and a raincoat hanging from the picture-rail, then the gaudy flower pattern on the lino caught my eye and I was eleven years old, scrubbing the identical pattern on our kitchen lino on Friday after school. Beside the bed a worn brownish rug gave a touch of comparative luxury. In my own childhood, rugs had been seen only in other people's homes.

Behind the glazed doors of the bookcase I noticed books of plays by Wilde, Shaw and Sartre, several thick volumes of Poe and a number of thrillers and books of light fiction unfamiliar to me; also several impressive-looking dictionaries and reference books, mainly on English, a mixed bag which was not discussed because we were clinging together behind the strategically open door. But we dared not linger. Our absence was probably being timed, at any moment Mrs Gardner would appear on some pretext. I suppressed a disrespectful giggle at a sudden image of her lean figure, washing-up abandoned, crouched over a stop-watch like a zealous sports official.

'We'd better go,' I whispered.

On the whole, despite surprises, the visit appeared to have been a success. A certain landmark had been reached.

The train was now nearing London, and I wondered if I would merit a welcoming smile from Gerald's mother on this first visit as his wife. And would I discover how she had reacted to Gerald's hurtful prohibition of parents and friends from our wedding three years ago? At the time my tearful pleas had met with a curt, 'If you don't agree, then I shan't get married.' I was cravenly stunned into agreement, and a long time was to pass before I could begin to understand my cowardice. For two years I had been obliged to keep quiet about Gerald's illness, which made him a special case, outside the established rules of romantic behaviour and procedure. Knowing what was right was one thing, understanding Gerald's viewpoint quite another. Only when, after the short practical ceremony, a humiliating search of the premises had to be made for a porter and cleaner to act as witnesses did I begin to realise how wrong this was, though it still never occurred to me that I should have taken a stand and insisted on parents and close friends being present. I was too sunk in the quagmire of Gerald's problems for that.

Helen, now married to Alan, was naturally angry and hurt, and I found myself minus my only friend. Later on it was not possible to leave London without attempting a reconciliation, and I waited in suspense for Helen to answer the phone.

'I'm glad you've rung,' she said softly.

I sighed with relief. 'It's so good to hear you. I couldn't help it, you know.'

'Yes, I know.' Never had I heard Helen's voice so affected. But mention of the impulsive migration to Devon brought a doubtful pause.

'Don't worry about me,' I said. 'I'm so looking forward to it. You will – you will visit us, won't you, when we get settled?'

'Yes, of course I will.' Helen's voice was warm. The friendship was intact.

My own mother had received Gerald's wedding decree with an apparent indifference which did not deceive me.

'I'm sorry, Mum, it's not my doing.'

Hurt or no, my mother's relief that her eldest daughter, at the end-of-shelf-life age of twenty-eight, was at last to be safely married outweighed both her aversion to the unholy steps of a registry office and her indignation at the outrageous banning of relatives. My kiss was accepted, and twenty clean pound notes were produced as a wedding present, a sum carefully garnered by her over the years for each of her three daughters.

I had never discovered whether Gerald's mother knew that the wedding arrangements had been solely his decision. 'You're not to talk about it,' he had instructed, 'not a word,' and, unsure of my ground, I was easily cowed into obedience.

The married couple were welcomed by a cordial handshake. No hugs or kisses, but I never expected those. Happily, no sign of any lingering resentment but an amusing hint of deference, and I congratulated myself on no longer being a nobody, a mere unmarried girl. Upgraded to the status of wife, I merited respect.

'You'll manage in Gerald's bedroom,' Mrs Gardner said in her new conciliatory tone. 'Go and take your things in and I'll make the tea.'

It seemed very odd to be allowed officially into the monk-like sanctity of Gerald's bedroom. I eyed the thirty-inch-wide bed doubtfully. Was it possible for two adults to lie side by side in that confined space, let alone sleep? The answer was that Gerald could sleep while I lay awake for most of the night balancing on the edge of the bed, trying not to disturb him by falling off. Never mind. The interview with the doctor tomorrow was all that mattered.

Promptly at eight o'clock by pre-arrangement Mrs Gardner brought in a huge wooden tray laden with a large old silver teapot, a silver milk jug and sugar bowl, two large platefuls of bacon and eggs, toast, butter and marmalade. We roused Gerald. Could we contrive not only to sit up side by side in that confined space but also to eat? It appeared that it was just possible. I was mildly astonished at the informality of breakfast in bed in this formal household. Arrayed in a fresh sleeveless cotton print overall, Mrs Gardner waited attentively, almost obsequiously, while elbows were arranged and the bacon and eggs were pronounced perfect and, yes, we should both like more tea. Second cups were carefully poured, the heavy teapot was borne militantly away for more hot water. Strangest of all was the casual acceptance of all the arrangements as the most normal thing in the world; no comment, not even a little joke or smile. Never mind, the doctor was forthcoming.

Upon Gerald's strict instructions, Mrs Gardner was not to be told the real reason for our visit, ostensibly purely social. 'We shall spend the morning in the town,' Gerald informed her regally. 'We'll be back for lunch at one.'

Dr Mitchell was a young fifty-five, bearded, brisk and kindly, inspiring confidence. Having known Gerald since birth, he had apparently been consulted about some kind of breakdown (not yet elaborated upon) after the war, and the two had become casual friends, meeting occasionally for a drink and a chat.

Warm Christian-name greetings were exchanged and then we all sat down to a big silence. I flushed with annoyance at being left to take the initiative, along with the responsibility for saying exactly the right thing. Only slightly mollified by Gerald's grateful glance I began to explain, trying, in consideration of the doctor's time, to be brief and unconsciously tending to under-emphasise our difficulties. Despite this, several times Gerald protested, 'It's not as bad as all that.'

'Now then, darling, don't try to make too light of it.'

The account was barely half over before Dr Mitchell, while deftly keeping up the flow of understanding nods and sympathetic grunts, began writing on note-paper. He handed Gerald a sealed envelope. 'I've written a letter to Mr Pritchard at your local hospital. He's a good man.'

A mere fifteen minutes and the interview was over, impressing us both – whether favourably or not we didn't know – with its brevity and efficiency. Not that we'd known what to expect beyond, perhaps, a more detailed interest in Gerald's problems.

Accepting the superior wisdom of the doctor, I took Gerald's arm. Our troubles were over. Help was on the way. Expert help. It was out of my hands. Free! Reprieved!

Seven

'The 19th September at ten-thirty, Mrs Gardner.'

Four months to wait. Four months!

'Mrs Gardner …?

I found my voice. 'Haven't you – haven't you anything sooner?'

'No, we haven't.' The receptionist was aggrieved. 'You're lucky, you know. The waiting period is usually six months, but we've had a cancellation.'

'I see – thank you.' Very slowly I replaced the telephone receiver and sat staring down at my typewriter. All was quiet in the office at this hour, Mr West not yet in, letters still being sorted in the post room.

The new fear wormed its way in like a virus. Waiting spelt disaster. Gerald was ready to see someone, he needed to see someone now. Four whole months, a slow walk on a tightrope when any number of things, all of them bad, might happen. I had somehow imagined Gerald to be a unique case but there was no consolation now in knowing that others, too, were waiting, trapped in their own anonymous hells. That didn't bear thinking about. Four more months, seventeen weeks, more than a hundred days of playing guardian angel, of seeing him suffer.

I pushed my typewriter away, sank my face in my hands.

I can't bear it, I can't –

I summoned up a smile as Maddox brought in the post. A decent man, touchingly anxious to please, a former grocer's assistant now enjoying the benefits of a higher income and higher status; middle-aged, ever effusive to the boss's secretary – Thank you, Mrs Gardner – Nice day, Mrs Gardner – The door closed behind him.

Slitting envelopes, reading, sorting ... Hearing Mr West go into his office next door, I matched up the last of the letters with previous correspondence and took in the sheaf of papers. Little smiles along with the good mornings. A warm day, the first summer-dress day, frank blue eyes darting towards my pale blue bust-line and then quickly away, but today the usual glint of pride at this veiled compliment was missing.

The day passed somehow: dictation, typing, bright telephone talk, insipid roast lamb awash in watery canteen gravy. Inner whispers: don't be silly; don't worry; it'll probably be all right.

By evening, the first panicky fears were beginning to subside. Stay calm and wait patiently. What alternative was there? In one way or another the time would pass, it would have to. And, however far away, definite relief was at least in sight.

Gerald took the news of the delay with remarkable unconcern, almost, I noticed with amazement, as though it was nothing to do with him. And was I right, had I detected in his face a flickering suggestion that he might even be secretly pleased? A mad idea! How could I have thought such a thing?

Life was resumed as though no doctor had ever been mentioned, and I was once more recruited to help trace missing 'points'. But is it right? I asked myself. Is it even good for him to get this kind of help, especially as he never seems to find the answer? Is all this co-operation of mine misguided? Does it just reinforce his obsession, give it the guise of a normal everyday activity? Might it not be better, help him to resist it, if I kept aloof?

I could find no answers. At least I was showing him that he wasn't alone, that I'd do anything to help.

The continuing late-night sittings had become exhausting, damping down the joy of going home. But I'll survive, I told myself as I left the office weeks later; I'll have to put up with it.

The view from the top of the bus was a special treat on these light summer evenings, but by now I was so tired I knew that as soon as my ticket had been clipped I would probably doze off. The conductor came along with his genial smile: Devon was conducive to genial smiles. The bus swayed.

Half smiling at the curving colours, I felt my eyes close and I thought of all the sleep lost in the Blitz: the rush home from work to breathe in the foul air of the brewery cellar, the rows of sleepers on the large stone floor, with just enough room to pick your way through to the smelly loos – we couldn't hear the bombs and guns down there so we felt safe. Until the night when the roof threatened to cave in under the weight of the water used on the fire bombs and we had to roll up our fat bundles and brave the punishing din of the moonlit street: the menacing throb and drone of powerful bombers, the resounding crump-crump of anti-aircraft fire, the whine and crash of a high-explosive bomb. Then finding that we hadn't been killed after all but had reached the comparative safety of the garden Anderson (you could only be killed there by a direct hit). Through the small opening you could watch the reddening sky and listen to the clang of fire engines and the shouted directions of firemen against the sustained hiss of the fire hoses.

Gerald hadn't wanted to hear about my air-raid experiences, he hadn't wanted to know anything about my life before we met any more than he had wanted to talk about himself, as if nothing else had ever happened to either of us.

By some inner telepathy I roused myself in time to alight at my stop, wondering as I turned into the lane whether tonight I would be spared the lengthy evening inquisition, which usually began at bedtime when Gerald's problems of the day were being resolved:

'What did we do last Sunday?'

'What were we talking about at supper last night?'

'Were we discussing an actor, or possibly a singer, the other day?'

'Did you say there was something you wanted to do tomorrow?'

'Did I ask you to remind me of something yesterday?'

Any humdrum action such as posting a letter, any ordinary remark – 'the bus was very late this morning' – could be the starting point for one of his problems, since any one of them might have triggered off, or might have occurred at the moment at which was triggered off independently, a query to which he did not know the answer. The remark, or action, then needed to be exhumed and, together with all related events, subjected to rigorous examination in the hope of reactivating the forgotten point. But tonight I was spared; and got to bed in reasonable time; and was glad that the lovemaking was of the usual brief duration; and woke to the old nagging question: are all Gerald's troubles purely imaginary on my part, just an exaggeration of trivialities; in fact, much ado about nothing?

A mild spring had turned into a warm sleepy summer. Along with bird-watching, we could explore the miles of local lanes and the picturesque rivers and villages, and at the weekends we could take the bus or train to the coasts of Devon and Cornwall. At home there was the radio and reading and friendly discussion. His secret revealed, Gerald was slightly less tense, there was less to hide, his compulsive needs could become openly integrated into the daily pattern, an accepted part of life.

It is striking how real life runs along in parallel with the inner tensions of mental illness ready to assume priority at any time. The charming lover with the approving smile maintained a presence, ensuring that I attended to my appearance, hunting for clothes in the sales, examining my bust-line anxiously in the mirror: is it too high? too low? too small? too big? Certainly not too big, not according to Gerald. Was this one good bra ever to be supplemented by another? Like other necessities, that would have to wait.

But sometimes charm and grateful smiles were not enough. Something more was needed. Gerald had never actually said that he loved me. 'Please say it,' I begged. 'It,' he'd say, laughing and then adding placatingly, 'You know I'm very fond of you, my dear,' – never 'darling' – but with his eyes appearing to say far more.

'But are you happy?'

'Happiness?' His face clouded. 'That's not for me. I know nothing about happiness.'

Aided by a deep-seated childish illusion that no one was incapable of happiness, I tried not to be too upset by this repeated denial. It was up to me to make him happy. Of course he had great problems, but there was all of our life together besides.

If he wouldn't say he loved me, I craved tactile reassurance. It might be unreasonable, even childish of me, but I longed to feel his arm round me when we were about to go to sleep. The longing was acute, it wouldn't go away. Telling myself not to be stupid didn't help. Like an aching tooth, the need persisted. Without the comforting arm I was adrift in an uncertain world, as insecure as an unloved baby. And incapable of sleep. Until I gave in and put my arm round him.

Ridiculous to be so dependent. I'll do without him. Turning on my back I'd lie awake, hoping with every slight shift that he was about to draw near. No such luck. He was soon asleep. Cold and tired, I'd hold out for a whole wretched hour or more before giving in and turning over.

One winter night I lay stretched out in misery along the edge of the bed between wastes of icy sheet, determined not to weaken. If it took all night I'd make him come to me.

Not a move. He was asleep, and eventually I could bear it no longer. I eased myself gently out of bed so as not to wake him, for that would not be right, and a temptation to make a disturbance by kicking off the bedclothes was easily resisted, for what should I do then? Huddled into my warm dressing-gown and slippers, I crept downstairs. It was one o'clock in the morning, the sitting-room cold and damp, in the grate the dead coals and ashes. There was no option but to curl up in the armchair under my thick red winter coat. Soon Gerald would stir and find me missing and then all would be healed.

Two desolate hours crawled by. I was tired, cramped and cold. At last, unbelievably, a sound from above. I waited. I heard the cistern flush. Would he come downstairs?

Please let him come down.

I heard his step on the stairs. The door opened and his face peered round it looking slightly mystified but very affable.

'What are you doing here?' It was the polite kind of enquiry you'd expect of a stranger, and the unforeseen combination of friendliness and unconcern, as though nothing was wrong, completely disarmed me.

'I couldn't sleep,' I said, very matter-of-fact.

'Oh!' A slow nod of polite comprehension stamped my answer as the only normal and rational one for such a situation. A quick look of friendly complicity as if we'd just arrived at the answer to a crossword clue, then his head vanished; the door closed; footsteps ascended.

Impossible! Incredible! Why had he said nothing more? Didn't he care about me at all? The tears came. It wasn't fair, wasn't right, that I should be made miserable like this; there was no reason for it; we loved each other; it shouldn't be happening. The tears soaked through my handkerchief on to the rough collar of my coat, and when they finally slowed I realised that I was horribly cold. My feet were numb. Might as well go to bed, if only to get warm.

I stole upstairs. Placing my dressing-gown across the end of the bed for extra warmth, I eased myself under the clammy bedclothes. Gerald's breath came soft and even. How could he sleep when I was so upset? For a while I kept to my side of the bed but I couldn't get in the least warm, and at last I gave in and turned over, drawing close to the enticing heat. He was lying on his back, the pale circle of his face lit by moonlight filtering through the thin blue curtains. No use having scruples, I had to sleep. My arm edged round him. The penetrating warmth was blissful, like getting into a hot bath.

Just the same, I shouldn't have given in.

I slept.

The next day I realised that he wasn't going to mention last night. Then neither would I. There was my dignity to consider.

I was left with my dignity, and the suspicion that I had perhaps made rather a fool of myself.

Eight

At nine-thirty on a warm June Saturday morning we walked the mile down to the village. I had been troubled by a persistent sore throat, and on the strict understanding that no mention was to be made of his 'problems' Gerald had agreed to register with the local doctor.

The surgery lay at the end of the long narrow curving main street of Stowbury, part of the old Plymouth to Exeter road. Boosted by ex-servicemen, babies, migrating businessmen and professionals attracted to country life, Stowbury was growing fast. A new estate of council houses had appeared in the latest 'System building' – prefabricated outside walls of hung horizontal concrete slabs over Cornish stone – a little strange to eyes brought up on bricks but with pleasing slate roofs, and attractively laid out in pairs on curved rising roads at the end of the village. There were generous front and back gardens and extensive views, but no garages. Cars were not yet a serious proposition for working people; the new small post-war cars, the Minis and Austin Sevens and Volkswagens were still some years away.

There was a handy string of shops: several grocers, two butchers, a baker, ironmonger, newsagent/sweet-shop, chemist, post office and a garage-filling-station. The last shop on the left was my favourite, a century-old dairy, low-roofed, dim and cool, with a special calm of its own. Stepping down from street level you came upon farm produce which had barely changed for decades: unpasteurised ('raw') milk dispensed directly into customers' jugs from a large floor-standing churn; and fresh farm butter from the half-barrel on the end of the pale grey marble counter. I loved watching the wetted wooden spatulas deftly removing the satin ivory wad. I breathed in the fragrant aroma and waited for the delightful plap-plopping as it was expertly shaped into a rectangle on its own small marble slab.

The greatest attraction of all was the delicious nutty Devonshire cream spooned into waxed containers direct from the large enamel bowl in which it was made. The eye was drawn to the rich thick crust, the cream of the cream, so to speak, glinting across the top of the bowl like a slab of gold inlaid with tiny diamonds.

We'd first encountered Devonshire cream at a small roadside café on an early walk in Devon. The plump friendly proprietress was astonished to learn that we'd never tasted the delicacy and insisted on giving us a generous free sample, together with her home-made strawberry jam and fragrant, freshly baked rolls. Standing over us, proudly smiling as we approved the feast, she explained how the crust was formed when the cream of the rich Jersey milk gradually rose to the top as it was warmed over a very low heat. 'It can take twelve hours or more, you know; the longer the time, the thicker the crust.'

On our country walks we later found that on many a smallholding a few cows were kept for family milk, butter and cream, any excess cream being sold to passers-by from the large enamel bowl placed between parted lace curtains on the cottage window-ledge.

An occasional spare shilling bought the smallest quantity of cream sold, four ounces, just enough to whet healthy appetites. Once Gerald had a job I planned to place a weekly order for a splendid eight ounces, enough to be heaped lavishly with jam on to fresh pulpy home-made scones, or, the ultimate luxury, a bowl of steaming porridge.

The doctor's surgery was in the small white-painted timber annexe of a large detached Georgian house at the end of the village street where the fields began. Sturdy wooden chairs were ranged round the walls of an empty waiting-room; we were evidently the last patients of the morning. I picked out a *National Geographic* magazine from the heap on the small central table while Gerald consulted his notebook, and presently a heftily built ruddy-cheeked young man emerged from the inner door and the ping of a little bell summoned us inside.

Seated at an open roll-top desk, Dr Harris's burly frame dominated the surgery, into which were crammed two wooden chairs and a bulky old wooden filing cabinet, with a tiny washbasin tucked away in one corner. The floor was covered with the same green polished linoleum as in the waiting-room, softened here by an Axminster rug.

The doctor's head of thick brown wavy hair was large and authoritative, the pleasant face looking up with a smile from note-writing gave an impression of solid reliability which I found oddly disturbing.

'Do sit down.' We were welcomed on to a crowded list: 'Nearly at the maximum of three thousand five hundred,' the doctor said amiably. Lolling back in his capacious swivel chair, he enquired about our presence in the county, our work and interests.

Acutely aware of the scrutiny of direct, lively blue eyes, I concentrated on not blushing. The face was not a handsome one, squarish with smooth skin and well-marked features. But whereas Gerald's appeal, his air of helplessness, drew heavily on the maternal instinct, Dr Harris gave off an aura of calm strength. When he drew near to examine my throat it constricted uncomfortably. I grew hot and told myself not to be silly.

Dr Harris drew a pack of antibiotic tablets from a wall cupboard. 'This should ease your throat for you,' he said, waving aside the prescription fee.

Gerald's mention of bird-watching and, in passing, the lack of a car to explore areas unserved by bus or train, brought a surprising offer: 'I'll take you both somewhere tomorrow morning if you like. My wife' – Dr Harris twinkled indulgently – 'is never ready to go out till the afternoon.' We accepted gratefully, mildly amazed at this unexpected hand of friendship.

Walking away, I admitted to being excited by something more

than Gerald's eagerness to visit a remote estuary.

'We shall have to find out when the tide is out at Mothecombe,' Gerald said.

'Yes, darling.'

I didn't care about the tide. I was trying hard to remember that Dr Harris had a wife.

At ten o'clock on Sunday morning a large green Rover car glided up to the gate where we were waiting, equipped with binoculars and Gerald's prized portable telescope. Seated beside the doctor, aware of his nearness, my normal shyness was redoubled and I was virtually incapable of speech. The conversation was left to run lightly between the doctor and Gerald, who this morning was at his best, talkative, relaxed and charming.

Dr Harris knew very little about birds but wanted to learn, he said with a friendly smile. He questioned me about my job and my fondness for Devon; he and his wife also came from London but she preferred town life. I smiled back but my answers were brief. My voice sounded choked and I was afraid Gerald would notice.

Scarcely wider than the car, the approach to the estuary was down a steep narrow lane bordered by the usual thick high green hedges, laced now with soft ferns and fairy-like pinks and whites and purples. We had the place to ourselves when we parked close to the hedge near the end of the lane. The tide was out. A small area of short damp grass separated us from a large expanse of glistening light brown mud.

It was one of those smiling summer days that spirit away the buzz and sting of the world, the air balmy, the sea glimmering complacently in the warm sunshine. Binoculars were directed down to the twinkling activity on the soft mud, and then up to hundreds of dunlin, oystercatchers and little plovers flashing and manoeuvring like small shooting stars against the limpid blue sky. From somewhere upriver came the long imploring call of the curlew, then the silence

69

was stirred by the gentle splash of a wave or the sweet piping of an oystercatcher.

A loud whirring sound drew the eye upwards again to a scintillating show of white and black and bright red as a flock of oystercatchers took to the air, wheeling about and then settling further on to forage anew. Raised arms began to ache. It was my favourite bird-watching arena, but today other claims prevailed. The docile bird-watching companion had undergone a drastic change of identity.

'Shall we explore upriver a bit?' Gerald was enjoying himself. And as he spoke it struck me suddenly, like a thunderbolt, that his voice sounded incredibly unfamiliar, almost as if I had never heard it before. A weird notion which showed no sign of abating as we walked on. I wasn't walking, I was coasting like the surfers in Newquay.

Followed by Dr Harris, Gerald eagerly led the way along a narrow path, while in the rear I fought an irrational desire, more than a desire an urgent need, an imperative which took a conscious effort to dispel, to close with the burly doctor and stay near to him. Not to gravitate naturally towards Gerald, indeed almost to wish to shun him after years of being drawn to him as to a magnet, was overwhelmingly odd and disturbing. I didn't know what to make of it. It was ridiculous, insane.

Returning along the path, we admired a pair of nesting swans, a kingfisher and a dipper, and on the low clifftop we watched a buzzard being mobbed by a pair of crows. Trailing along, I tried to ignore the pull towards Dr Harris's broad back and the curious feeling of estrangement from Gerald, but neither would go away.

Back in the car, Dr Harris offered large rosy apples. 'They're very good,' he said, 'from my garden. My name is Roger, by the way.'

Gerald accepted the apple, but my usual healthy appetite had deserted me. As the two men munched, I was keenly aware of Roger's approving eye on my flushed cheeks. I used little make-up, just a touch of lipstick. 'You don't need it,' Helen said enviously, she herself seldom seen without the pancake mask which suited her sallow skin.

Before parting came another delightful surprise. We were invited to Dr Harris's house the following Wednesday evening. He shared my love of music and boasted a record player and membership of a record club.

'I've got some Mozart this month,' he said, his blue eyes burning into mine, 'and some Beethoven. Would you like that?' I nodded dumbly, hoping I wasn't blushing too much, too overcome to enquire which works were on offer. It would be a rare treat to listen to music. In the circumstances, almost any music.

What, I wondered, should I wear on Wednesday?

Nine

My one effort to probe into Gerald's odd habits, his retention of newspapers, had not been carried forward into other areas. I'd never liked to prod and pry into his affairs. But with Helen intending to visit us soon, in August, I realised that questions were bound to arise and I didn't want to appear too much of a fool. I could at least make an effort to enquire into his background. Now that I had earned his trust he might be ready to talk.

Gerald had never talked freely about himself. Even unimportant factual questions were usually fended off. You could learn more about a stranger on a bus or a train than I had ever learnt about him.

There had been an attempt, on our first seaside holiday, to draw him out. The summer after returning from Suffolk I had persuaded him to take a week's holiday with me at Brighton, where I booked a furnished flat.

'We were bombed out during the war,' I began after breakfast one morning.

'Really!' He barely glanced up from his newspaper.

'Yes, my mother and I weren't there at the time, fortunately; the girls had been evacuated with their school and my father was away in the army. I packed my mother off to join the children in the country – their foster mother took her in for a basic pound a week – but she came back when the raids died down.'

'Really!' He went on reading. When he was turning a page I snatched the opportunity to ask, 'Have you any brothers and sisters?'

'I've one sister.'

'Older or younger than you?'

'Er – older.'

'Married?'

'Oh, er, yes.'

'Children?'

'Er – what's that?'

'Has she any children?'

'Yes.'

'How many?'

'Er – two.'

'Boys or girls?'

'Two boys.'

'How old are they?'

'Oh, er, young.'

I gave up. To probe further seemed an impertinence; neither did I particularly want to know about Gerald's background. Did he return my feelings? That was all that mattered then. Now, in the few weeks before Helen's arrival, I began to make slow but certain headway, especially regarding his war years, which he talked about comparatively freely. Pieced together, the picture rounded out nicely:

'When was I called up? Oh, er, in nineteen-forty with my age group. I was passed medically A1 fit at the first medical; at my age that meant combat training and front-line fighting. When they get you in they give you another medical. This time they didn't pass me A1. They put me in Group 3 – said I had a condition known as disordered action of the heart and I was excused all duties until I was posted. No, it wasn't serious, they said, but I should avoid physical strain. They weren't awfully precise about it. Yes, my dear, I'm satisfied it's nothing to worry about.

'Being excused all duties is not as good as it sounds. I was delighted at first – no parades, no chores – but after a while it became boring. There was one person far more put out by all this than I was and that was my sergeant. What a swine! One of the many, I suppose. This sergeant, you see,' – a wry smile crinkled his face – 'he couldn't bear the fact that I'd been excused all duties. He couldn't get his hands on me at all, you see, drill me or put me through it with all the other poor blighters.

'He made the mistake of thinking I was a bit of a physical weakling, just because I'm so lean. Actually I'd been quite an athlete – cross-country running, sprinting, boxing, and of course cricket. Sergeant Tapper – yes, that was his name, the bastard – he used to vent his frustration on me by suddenly hurling his rifle at me as I stood at the door of our hut. He'd be walking past, you see, and suddenly without warning his rifle would be hurled straight at me with terrific force. He was six-foot-two and as strong as an ox. Do you know how heavy a rifle is? Heavy enough to do plenty of damage if it landed on some-one. It could crack your skull; no doubt Tapper hoped it would crack mine. Luckily for me I used to play wicket-keeper. I always managed to catch the damned thing. That made him hate me even more, of course. In the end he got tired of it and gave it up.

'His other little trick was emptying a bucket of cold water over me in bed in the morning – I never was very good at waking up. That's an old one, of course. Report him? My dear, army life's not like that. They would only get back at you all the more if you did, and they all defend each other up to the hilt. You'd never make the charge stick. There are ways round things like that …

'They kept me hanging about that camp for six months doing absolutely nothing. Eventually my papers came through. Posted to Wales for clerical duties. That was going to be my lot for the dura-tion, a routine office job any schoolboy could do.

'Even worse than that was sharing the barracks with those disgust-ing men; my dear, you've no idea how disgusting a group of men can be, filthy language, filthy habits; I wouldn't dare repeat it. Then there was the revolting food, the parades, the cleaning of one's kit – I'd no taste for that sort of thing. My mother always did everything for me, of course, cleaned my shoes, everything. I used to send her my laundry every week by post; within a week it was always back. Pretty good going, eh! Well, can you imagine me washing my smalls?

'There was only one thing to be done, and that was to get promotion; so I worked for it, I'd made up my mind. Within a year I'd been promoted three times and then I was appointed orderly-room sergeant. What is the orderly-room? It's the administrative office of the company concerned. All the records are kept there, paperwork to do with pay and allowances, leave, postings, all the day-to-day running, contact with the War Office, that sort of thing. The orderly-room sergeant is in charge of the office and he's responsible to the adjutant. Ours was a very large training depot. New conscripts and recruits came for training – about three to six months – and then they were posted. You can imagine the records and paperwork for such a large changing population. I had staff, of course. Well, before long I was nicely settled in. The adjutant was a marvellous chap – in fact he was an Oxford don, and of course when we heard of his appointment we all thought we were going to get some bumbling impractical officious ass. Nothing of the sort. The chap, Professor Frost – he was a history professor – had a brilliant brain, was a wonderful organiser. Never seen anyone so quick on the uptake.

'I conducted him round the office, about fifteen chaps, all sitting at their desks smirking at this learned-looking little fellow with wild bushy hair and great horn-rimmed spectacles, owlish looking. Of course, each of them thought he'd never grasp the routine clerical procedures they'd mastered slowly by constant repetition. I noticed right away the keen look in his eye, the incisiveness, the way he listened intently as each one of them outlined their duties; I had to explain mine, too, of course. Well, sure enough, in a few days – only a few days, mark you – he'd grasped everything there was to know about the place.

'Before long he saw that he could safely leave everything to me and he did just that. I worked, in effect, alone. He had to sign everything, of course. In the end he used to sign without reading first

75

and he'd never have done that without being sure of me. He gave me a wonderful testimonial when I was demobbed – you've seen it. He stretched quite a few points for me. I even shared his batman. I had my own quarters and I got him to excuse me all parades on the grounds of pressure of work.

'The next thing was they wanted me to take officer training. I wanted to do it, of course, but I knew, I knew it was no use. In my medical category I could never have been passed – it's one of the stipulations, to be an officer one has to have a certain minimum medical category. They pestered me for ages before they finally took my word for it that it was hopeless and left me alone. You see, I was something of an expert on King's Regulations by then; that was how I'd got my promotion.

'Eventually they realised how much I did know about King's Regulations. Even the CO, if he wanted to know anything, he'd call me in and ask me rather than look it up. He'd act on my word without bothering to verify it; sign anything. It wasn't just a question of memorising, of course; it was a question of application, precedent, and so forth. Officers' pay and allowances alone was quite a subject – you'd be surprised! I don't know how I did it myself. Somehow I just couldn't help remembering. Of course, I've always had a pretty retentive memory. It was amazing, I practically knew the whole book off by heart.

'Then, as regards the day-to-day work, without trying I seemed to remember the contents of hundreds of files, the names of the men, where they'd come from, what training they'd had, where they'd been posted to. The trouble was I took on too much work, of course. I began to worry about everything. I would check everyone's work instead of leaving it to them. Unfortunately, I knew more about all of their jobs than they knew themselves. I worked twelve hours a day, seven days a week. Occasionally I went on leave; sometimes I didn't bother. Apart from leave there was no opportunity to spend my pay except on cigarettes. I just allowed it to accumulate.

76

'Then there was the half-pay I was getting from my firm, too. Didn't I tell you about that? Before the war I was employed by one of the big building contractors; cashier on a local building site, a very large housing estate. I had a jolly good hut as an office, I had the use of the firm's car, I was pretty well off. I liked the job well enough, knew where I stood with it; everything was cut and dried; I like it that way. Like lots of big firms they kept a lot of their staff on half-pay after their call-up, the idea being that we returned to work for them after the war. So there was my half-pay going into the bank every week as well. When I was demobbed in 1946 I had over two thousand pounds saved.

'It wasn't until I was back home, actually finished with it all, that I realised how dog tired I was, just wanted to sleep and do nothing in particular. Only then did it dawn on me how much I'd been overworking for years. All right, I thought, I need a rest, I'll have a rest. One gets three months' demob leave on full pay, you know. So I thought I'd enjoy them to the full. It was marvellous to be home again, creature comforts and so forth. I dismissed King's Regulations from my mind. Amazing how all that mass of information I'd been using every day for years seemed to vanish as though it had never existed. I thought I'd go out sometimes, or stay at home, just as I felt; might get a girl or I might not bother. Get some new clothes when I could bother to get round to it – I'd outgrown all my others.

'I'd forgotten just one thing: my mother. Now my mother is what she is. Aren't we all? She can't help it. She's very limited, of course, poor dear. Nothing will change her; she could never see another point of view. She's had a hard life. As a girl she used to work on her people's farm, and I've a good idea just how hard she did have to work. When she married she had a drunken husband to contend with and a large public house and two children to look after. A creature of habit, of course; lives strictly within her code and can't recognise any other. But she means well.

'I'd been home a fortnight – only a fortnight, mind you – when she suddenly said to me – I shall never forget it, "Well, what are you going to wear for work next week?"

"Next week?" I said. "What do you mean?"

"Well, you've had a fortnight, haven't you."

"A fortnight?"

"Yes, you've been home a fortnight. You've got to go back to work now, haven't you."

'Then I realised all too well what she was getting at. No point in saying anything; no point in arguing. I could have pleased myself, of course, could have ignored her. But what was the use? If I'd asserted myself I'd have felt guilty at letting her down and my peace of mind would have been ruined. I couldn't have enjoyed myself any longer. My mother just can't be ignored. She has to have things her way, otherwise she's so upset, poor thing. She can't help it. I held out for another fortnight then I gave up, thought on the whole I'd be better off at work. So back I went …

'What was the point about the fortnight? The point about the fortnight, my dear, is that my mother, as I've said, is a conventional creature and her experience of life is very limited. She's never heard of anyone having more than a fortnight's holiday. If she had she'd regard it as vaguely immoral; it wouldn't be right, certainly not for people like us.

'There was no work in my area at the time so the firm asked me to come and work at Head Office pro tem. So there I was, commuting to London by train, marching into a bloody great office block and sitting all day in a room with about fifty desks in it, all in straight rows. I didn't like any of that but I tried to make the best of it. They'd been very good to me. They said I needn't stay there permanently if I didn't want to; they'd find me something else in due course.

'The trouble was, I couldn't work, couldn't concentrate. Dozens of disconnected thoughts kept flitting through my mind all the time. That was when it started, of course; tremendous effort to remember the smallest things about work, or get anything done at all. Then the insomnia started. Mental activity all day, then at night it seemed to get worse than ever. In the end I gave up even trying to get to bed till about four in the morning. I'd sit on the bed, reading and smoking, making notes, looking things up; you know, one thing leads to another; I mean, ascertaining one point often leads to enquiring about another, and so on. I used to be quite busy!

'Then I began to get very tired in the day, couldn't get up in the morning, would doze on the train; once I missed the station coming home. Then one morning I got to work, I was just going to sit down at my desk, when I damn well fainted. It seemed such a ridiculous thing to do!

'The firm were wonderful. Treated me like a war hero; sent me home in a firm's car, told me to see my doctor, not to come back till I was really better. Mitchell diagnosed neurasthenia, said I was to rest. They kept me on full pay; very decent of them, wasn't it. Yes, they were a very good firm. My mother, of course, was very upset. Not because I was ill but because, poor soul, she didn't like having to tell the neighbours that I was ill. It wasn't as if it was a respectable illness like stomach ulcers or something. She was ashamed of it, and of me, of course! Why the hell wasn't I at work like everybody else? She couldn't understand it. As far as she was concerned there was nothing really wrong with me.

'The insomnia didn't get any better. Worse, if anything. Mitchell gave me pheno-barbitone. I still never got to sleep before about four or five in the morning but I began sleeping on longer. I trained my mother to bring me in my breakfast about eleven. I didn't argue with her about it or try to explain why I wasn't going to get up at a normal time, just instructed her – it was easier for her that way.

'I began to get very depressed: the effect of the pheno-barbitone, of course. Eventually I went to see Mitchell and told him I wanted to see a specialist privately. He recommended someone in Harley Street and made an appointment for me.

'Harley Street! My God! What a farce that was! You can keep all of Harley Street!

'What happened? You may well ask. An imposing place, of course! You know, like something out of a plush film set. As soon as the door opened you were in this cushioned atmosphere: soft carpets, soft chairs, soft couch, soft lights, soft-voiced secretary. It's a wonder they didn't have soft background music as well. His name was – let me see – what was his name? Ross-Walker, that was it; hyphenated of course! Another bastard. They come in all kinds, don't they. This one was as smooth as a confidence trickster. I suppose he was a confidence trickster of sorts, so urbane with his silk shirt and tie and his Savile Row suit. I bet he had twenty of them in his wardrobe. He should have. I'm sure he could afford them.

'What did he do? He didn't do anything, my dear, that was the point, not a damned thing. Didn't listen to me, didn't look at me, didn't care about me. Just wasn't interested, that was all too obvious. Oh, he went through the motions, all right, oozed charm and courtesy, had me stretched out on a black leather couch as soft as Joan Blondell's breasts in no time at all; made a few notes, asked a few questions.

'Of course, he had to put up a show. But he kept glancing at his gold watch and I knew by the way the questions were going – very slowly, I can tell you – that he'd mentally enrolled me as probably good for at least a year or two, half an hour a week at five guineas a time. Yes, of course, it's much more than that now. The only time his voice took on a note of sincerity was when he was ushering me out and he said, 'Don't forget to see my secretary on your way out and make another appointment.' Needless to say, what they were after as well as the next appointment was my five guineas, which she more or less held out her hand for. Well, I gave it to her but I didn't bother about the next appointment.

'Yes, it was a bit of an anticlimax, to say the least. I didn't know what to do next. I didn't complain to Mitchell, of course. There'd be no point; they all hang together; merely said I wouldn't be going back. He thought he was being awfully tactful in saying no more about it; just wrote out a prescription for more pheno-barbitone.

The insomnia still got no better. It could hardly get worse. Another three months went by. God knows how I stuck it. Thought of suicide, of course, but I'm not the type. I won't give in. I thought drink might be a good idea, might stop me thinking. I tried it, but all it did was make me sick, repeatedly. I had to give it up. Obviously I haven't my father's stomach.

'Meanwhile the firm had been enquiring about my progress from Mitchell and they suggested a rehabilitation centre.

'What is that? You may well ask. Definitely not a lunatic asylum, my dear, nor anything as drastic as a mental hospital. Strictly for war-time casualties – mental casualties, of course. A large country house in Sussex, scores of patients, men and women, all sorts, all ages, and about three – yes, three – doctors between the lot of us.

'Fortunately, I liked mine. Fletcher, his name was; yes, Don Fletcher. Delightful chap. We used to have two half-hour talks a week. Can't get very far on that, can you. Still, it's harmless, I suppose. Not that I ever expected to get very far. It's all too obvious these chaps haven't much of a clue: just feeling their way in the dark. Of course, there was the faint hope that they'd penetrate one's mind, guess what was going on and come up with some magic formula that would wipe the whole slate clean. A very faint hope, I might add, which I never entertained for very long.

'It was January when I arrived there; January '47. My God, what a winter! Do you remember it? The worst for I don't know how many years. Very little fuel anywhere; the place was freezing. I didn't know much about it at first. They put me to sleep – sodium amytal, marvel-lous stuff; seventeen days and nights. Oh, they wake you up during the day for feeding, washing, and so on; another dose, and off you go. Yes, I felt a little better after it but not much. Refreshed, of course, not so damned tired, but that didn't last long. The damned activity started again immediately; no let-up; well, perhaps it had slowed down a little but it was still there, very much so.

'What did we do? That was the devil of it, to pass the time. My mother came to see me twice. The first time she had a ghastly train journey in the snow, delays on the line, bitterly cold. Later I was allowed to go into the town for tea and the occasional cinema. There was a girl, of course; Edna. Yes, she was attractive, but not nearly so attractive as you, my dear. She became rather difficult towards the end; left before me, wanted me to promise to go and stay with her people. I didn't go. Kinder not to.

'Altogether I stayed six months. At the end of it I was precisely the same as I was at the beginning. Perhaps a little more rested, though I doubt it; the conditions, you see; having to share a room, the community life. I'd had enough of that in the army. I returned home supposedly cured and went back to work in London. It was intolerable. The journey into town, the long day, having to get up when I'd barely fallen asleep: yes, I still had the insomnia. The work was humdrum, to say the least. I did try hard to stick it because they'd been so good to me but it was hopeless. After a few weeks I asked if there was any chance of a transfer. The only cashier's post available then was on a new housing estate in the wilds of Scotland. I couldn't face that either, being so far away from home, digs, and so on – just like the army all over again. I hated doing it, but I handed in my resignation. I thought the only thing to do was to stay home and find another job locally.

'For a week or two I looked for a job; got the local paper, went to the labour exchange. There was nothing doing, no jobs going at all. Then I saw a pile of leaflets about farming camps and took one home with me. I realised that I was still damnably tired. It seemed a good idea to go to one of these camps – plenty of fresh air, a chance to recuperate. I sent off the application form for the place in Suffolk, an ex-RAF camp, and a week later I got an answer. I packed a bag.

'The next morning, at noon, that is, when she brought my tea my mother saw the bag.

"What's that for?" she said in that sharp way of hers.

"I'm going away," I said.

"Away? Away where? What for?"

"I'm going to a farming camp. In Suffolk. Get some fresh air, a sort of cheap holiday. I'll write to you."

"But you can't."

"I'm going."

'She knows it's no use arguing when I've made up my mind. I had breakfast, got up and slipped away. She held open the door for me without a word. I felt very sorry for her but I had to go.

'The trouble was, I couldn't do the work, potato picking. You need lots of energy, as you know, and I was incredibly weak. We were just getting into the lorry to go back at the end of the third day when I fainted. That's where Mrs Palmer came in. You remember her, the manager's wife, nearly old enough to be my mother, I know, but for some reason she seemed to be fond of me; well, yes, I suppose she did have a sort of crush on me. She wouldn't hear of my leaving, said I could go on the staff and do light work, washing up, serving meals, you know the kind of thing. In fact, the other women on the staff were all marvellous to me, I hardly did a thing, sat in the staff room in the afternoon listening to the Test Match. The girls brought me tea. I had that small bedroom to myself.

'I'd been there two months when you arrived.'

Ten

What, if anything, was to be said about Gerald? Helen's train was due at any moment and I had still not been able to decide. She knew me too well not to guess right away that something was wrong. But if I did defy Gerald and speak out, what if later on a chance remark gave us away? What would he do? Leave me? The threat was always there, like living in an earthquake zone.

The train was approaching. Say as little as possible, that was the safest. If only I could just enjoy seeing her again! If only there was nothing to tell, nothing to hide.

Exuberant kisses on cheeks. Warm hugs. I clung to Helen's fragrant shoulder (Elizabeth Arden Blue Grass, her favourite perfume).

She drew back. 'Let me look at you.'

The old affectionate smile, the absence of restraint, brought me near to tears, and I quickly bent down to pick up Helen's bag.

'It's so good to see you.' I took Helen's free arm. 'It's not far to the bus.' I walked on in silence for a moment. Helen's happy face had triggered a glimpse of my own face frowning back at me from the mirror and I wondered when I had last looked as happy as her. But, more immediately, what was I to say about Gerald? Helen was already eyeing me with concern.

'How's your new flat?' I asked.

She smiled. 'It's very nice; especially having lots of space.'

Lots of nice clothes, too, I thought, glancing sideways: tailored cream wool suit, probably Jaeger (the name wafted me back to lunchtime window-shopping in Regent Street); expensive black accessories, silk blouse, leather shoes and bag and gloves. An outfit probably costing more than my total expenditure on clothes in the last five years. Wonderful for Helen, of course, especially after wartime clothes rationing and the years on a low income, her husband Alan studying on a grant. But he was making up for it now. Naturally they both thought me idiotic to tolerate a husband with nothing to offer but a talent for inflicting misery. 'What a blind fool that girl is!' I once overheard Helen complaining to Alan, 'What a blind fool!'

I put down Helen's bag at the bus-stop.

'So it's goodbye to bedsitters at last,' I said.

'Do you remember our old rooms?'

'Of course I do!' The memories were intact: ardent midnight discussions, music, radio plays (*Mrs Warren's Profession* and Helen's amazed comment later: 'I don't think you know what Mrs Warren's profession was!') And neither had I, not till years later. Annoyingly, people only laughed at confessions to incomprehension and refused to enlarge, perhaps wishing to preserve a shining example of their own lost innocence – or were they merely intent on refusing admittance of the outsider to the inner circle? Gerald alone had always been ready with precise information on impersonal matters. A certain amount had been gleaned from Gerald.

In the bus, after a short silence an explanation was demanded for my wan appearance.

'Well,' I said, rather relieved now that the moment had come, 'You won't tell anyone, will you?'

'No – not if you don't want me to.'

'Not even Alan?'

'All right, if that's what you want.'

'Well, you see – you see – Gerald's been mentally ill.'

'Ill? In what way? What do you mean?'

'Well, it's rather hard to explain.'

'I'm listening.'

'Well, it's nothing serious,' I said, possibly by way of reassurance to myself as well as to Helen. 'It's just – it's just that when he forgets something quite ordinary as we all do, like, say, the name of an actor, or something we've read, or the title of a film, well, instead of letting it take its time to come back, as we often have to, don't we, he has to worry away at it until he's remembered. He can't let it go.'

'Why not?'

'Well, he just can't; that's the problem. But don't worry, he's going to see a specialist. He's got an appointment. The trouble is' – I bit my lip – 'there's something else.'

'What's that?'

'Well, it isn't his fault, of course, but he hasn't got a job yet.'

'Not yet? You mean, all the time you've been down here, what is it, more than two years?'

'Yes, that's right.'

'My God! Do you mean to say you're putting up with all that?'

The remark seemed to me unfair and unwarranted. Sympathy and understanding were needed, not indignation. And why regard me as the injured party when it was poor Gerald that was suffering?

'You don't understand,' I protested.

Helen was annoyed. 'And what started all this off?'

'Oh, it was overwork during the war or something. But he'll soon be better. Now you're not to worry; you can just act naturally with him. I don't think you'll notice anything wrong.'

Helen noticed first the bare floorboards and shabby furniture. But despite Gerald's failings as a provider, and placated by courtesy, if not charm – for she was immune to Gerald's brand of charm – she seemed to find nothing wrong with him personally as he showed her on the map all the lovely places we were about to visit, passed her his prized binoculars for bird-watching, and had her sharing his excitement when we saw our first sparrow-hawk as it glided swiftly over a hedge.

Helen was impressed by Gerald's elaborate precautions on approaching a wren's nest he knew about, keeping us waiting a few yards off while he walked nonchalantly past the spot in case anyone of evil intent should suddenly appear and discover the location. Once certain that no one was about he beckoned us on, thrusting his hand into the hedge where the nest was so cunningly concealed. Out came his hand, cradling a tiny blue speckled egg which Helen was allowed to hold in her hand for one precious moment before it was tenderly replaced in its home. Then she found herself gazing in wonder at the intricate conical nest. 'Put your hand inside,' Gerald said, 'just here; gently.' She was awestruck at the incredible softness of the layered lining of tiny blunt-ended feathers. Checking that no telltale gap was left in the hedge, Gerald again kept us waiting while he meticulously patted twigs and leaves into place before we walked away, curiously elated.

On the moors Helen was shown wheatears and missel-thrushes and the majestic slow-flapping buzzards and was captivated by the wild ponies and tales of toy white lambs. Another time we took a bus to a favourite large estuary to show her oystercatchers and ringed plovers, dunlin and turnstones. Yes, the scenery and wildlife were wonderful, she agreed, but didn't we miss the London theatres, not to mention my beloved concerts?

'All this' – I waved a magnanimous hand at the outdoors – 'is more than enough compensation. I'm amazed how thoroughly I've forgotten London. I honestly don't think I'll ever miss it.'

'Well, you will come and see me soon. Let me know when you're coming and I'll get some tickets.'

'Well, I have got another week's holiday due. We'll see.'

Despite Gerald's courtesy, Helen looked uneasy when it was time to say goodbye. Returning her farewell wave, I reflected that it was just as well I had said very little about Gerald. What if she had known, for instance, how he had agonised over the purchase of our binoculars? Was he justified in spending the money? Was he wrong to insist on the best make and not settle for a cheaper one? Which model to buy? Yet it was so good to see him smiling and eager, I couldn't begrudge him his pleasure, despite the tedious weeks of scanning and re-scanning catalogues and leaflets, the endless debating of the relative merits: the maximum weight that could be held steady; the right balance between light-gathering power and magnification ...

Typing the letters to the suppliers in London added to the complications, typing letters for Gerald being an ordeal in itself. Didn't I know, he once asked, to my amazement, the difference between an abbreviation and a contraction? That Mr and Mrs and Messrs were all contractions and therefore not to be followed by a full stop? The habit of years of typing dates and names and addresses full of these unsuspected traps counted for nothing; a disfiguring rubber must never be used, but regardless of pressures of time or fatigue, a fresh start must be made.

Had she been able to guess at half these secrets, Helen could only have demanded angrily that I leave him. As for other prospective confidantes, his mother's attitude had been made clear when I was once upset at some lapse on his part: 'He's always been a bit queer – take no notice; we don't.' And I could well imagine the silent bemusement of my own mother, or the scathing comments of my ex-teacher sisters Joan and Nancy, both busy raising families: 'Mental problems? What are you talking about? Load o' twaddle! Let him get out and do a good day's work, that'll soon cure him. Big sister Elaine trying to be clever, talking about mental illness, whatever that's supposed to be, pretending she knows something we don't; just as she pretends to like all that classical music; putting on airs; just a pose, mixing with a lot of snobs, pretending they like that racket.'

Our new friends had not been mentioned to Helen. I wasn't going to discuss my feelings about Roger, though precisely what those feelings were was far from clear. I loved Gerald, was surprised that I felt no shame at being attracted to another man, and was further surprised not only that it was happening but that I wanted it to go on.

Eleven

'I'm not going,' Gerald said.

His voice sliced the air with the precision of a master stroke at Wimbledon. I looked up in alarm – I had been repairing the torn hem of a skirt. His face was aloof, detached, almost as if he were not personally involved.

'You don't mean it,' I stammered. 'Of course you're going.'

'I'm not.'

His coolness, his decisiveness, were frightening. I felt as if I were going to collapse on the spot and never recover. He meant it, of course he did. His mind was made up and was not going to be deflected, not Gerald's mind. So there was no arguing with it. Only I had to argue, I had to put up some sort of a fight, try to find a way round it even while my heart was saying there was no way.

I spoke in a controlled level voice. 'But we talked about it only the other day. You said you wanted me to go with you. I've got tomorrow morning off.'

At this he looked suspicious and I added hastily, 'No, of course I didn't say what it was for. I said I was going to the dentist.'

Lying for Gerald had become at times an unavoidable necessity. I was getting quite good at it. I introduced a practical note: 'I'll put the alarm on for seven-thirty, shall I?'

'Do as you like. I'm not going.'

His face wore the old stubborn air that brooked no argument. He looked at me with scorn, then quickly away again as if I'd been a fool ever to have thought he would go. So this was final. Final, the end. Gerald had spoken and there was nothing I could say or do about it. Still, I had to make the attempt, steady myself and try again.

Head down, he had slumped back in his chair.

I kept my voice low and reasonable. 'Why don't you want to go?'

He looked up with a sigh, grudgingly allotting me a fragment of his attention snatched from weightier matters.

'There would be no point in it. They could do nothing for me.'

'But we've discussed this so many times. You said you wanted to go.'

'I've changed my mind.'

'But you don't know for certain that nothing could be done.'

'I'm certain. It's incurable.'

'But there'd be no harm in trying.'

No reply. His head was down again.

'Won't you go for my sake, then?'

His head didn't move. 'No.'

I was losing the battle. Fighting back tears, I tried again.

'I don't ask very much of you. Surely you could do this for me?'

He looked up; his face softened. 'I'm sorry, my dear, I can't go; I just can't.'

The new placatory tone helped to ward off the tears. Laying my sewing aside I sat on his knee, hugging and kissing him. After a moment or two, I drew back.

'Darling, it's ridiculous not to go. You might be able to get rid of all this misery, just like that.' With my free hand I made a useless gesture. I'd never been able to master the trick of snapping my fingers, and the small failure brought the tears welling up again.

'What could they do?'

I stifled a groan. 'There's no point in asking me that. You know I know nothing about it. There may be all sorts of things they can do.'

'There is nothing, I know.'

His authoritative tone was convincing until I reasoned that had he been quite certain that nothing could be done he would not have considered going in the first place. Or had he enacted the charade of consulting the doctor merely to appease me?

'It's years since you last had treatment,' I said. 'They may have discovered all sorts of things since then. Besides, don't forget you never told them what was wrong with you.'

No answer. I felt him stiffen. He was impatient to get back to his interrupted thinking.

It was my turn to become impatient.

'If you really wanted to get better you'd be willing to try anything.'

Silence. I gave his shoulder a little prod, wanting to shake him, batter out some sort of response. But what would that achieve?

'Darling, please answer me. I must have a reason why you don't want to go; just one reason, please.'

'I'm sorry, my dear, I can't give you a reason, but I can't go.' He spoke as if the decision had somehow been made for him and there was nothing he could do about it.

'But what shall we do?' My voice shook a little.

He patted my head. 'Never mind, my dear, all will be well.'

The unprecedented little show of sympathy finally brought tears, and I fumbled in the sleeve of my cardigan for my handkerchief.

'We can't just let it go on; we've got to do something.'

He was stroking my hair. 'All will be well.'

'Why not let me go for you?'

'No, I won't have that.' He snatched his hand away.

'You couldn't stop me going if I wanted to.'

'If you did, that would be the end of us.'

He meant it. What should I do? All the days, weeks, months, of waiting and hoping – all to no purpose.

It was amazing how quickly Gerald could fall asleep when trouble was afoot. But my tears were unstoppable. It was an end to hoping that at some point the nightmare was going to end. And if there was no hope, how could we go on together? Gradually the tears waned, exhaustion did its work and I was dragged off to sleep.

The next morning my head throbbed. The bathroom mirror disclosed hideous red-rimmed eyes, the eyes of a fool, I told myself, bathing them repeatedly in cold water ready for the office in the afternoon. The frightful new implications didn't bear thinking about. I was tired of worrying about Gerald, tired of helping him, tired of hoping for a miracle, tired of sitting up with him at night. Well, that would stop now. What a waste of time and effort it had all been. If he refused to let the doctors help him, I wouldn't help him either. At least I'd be relieved of that burden. I had done my best. I could do no more.

The musical evenings with Roger had become a regular weekly event, Muriel and Gerald retreating to chat in the dining-room – Gerald, I gathered, chiefly listening while Muriel, glad of an audience, complained about the deficiencies of country life, a particular bugbear being the round of dinner parties with several other 'medical' couples, each in turn acting as host. 'So bloody boring,' she said, re-crossing her legs to give Gerald a flash of slim white thigh. 'The men talk nothing but shop, the women witter on about their obnoxious darling children …' Neither of the two, I noted with a certain relief, was particularly attracted to the other, nor had they much in common.

Sunk in a comfortable brocaded settee, I began to find Roger's presence a distraction from the delights of Mozart. Reminders that he was a married man, and, I'd now learnt, the father of four sons, went unheeded. The two polite teenagers remained conveniently occupied in their rooms, the two younger boys, aged two and four, were already in bed when we arrived. The atmosphere in the large comfortable house seemed relaxed and orderly, Roger's relations with his wife smooth and uncomplicated. Muriel was very attractive, no denying that, fairly tall, a shapely body slimmer than mine, short glinting auburn hair, plenty of make-up on a small doll-like animated face; both she and Roger were several years our seniors.

The astounding decision that he would prefer not to attend any more of these evenings was made by Gerald some weeks later. 'Why not go alone?' he suggested.

Was this some kind of trap? No, I should have known. Gerald trusted me completely, he thought me as incapable of duplicity as I had thought myself. He must have decided that this was a chance to wrestle undisturbed with his current problems. A sickening thought, but I could do nothing about that. Music. And the exquisite relief of speaking spontaneously, no questioning what to say or what not to say, how to say it or how not to say it. My heart danced a little jig as I walked down to the village with a curious sense of freedom, hardly daring to think about being ferried home alone by Roger.

The new arrangement was accepted as nothing unusual, Muriel pleasantly absenting herself from the music, casually bringing in coffee and leaving us to it. And then I began to long for Roger to sit next to me on the settee. Crazy of me. What should we do? Hold hands? What of Muriel's sudden re-entry? What if Roger had no wish to be near me, let alone hold hands?

Alone with him at last in his car, I became an expectant schoolgirl out on her first date. But Roger merely switched off the engine and bade me a friendly goodnight.

I stumbled up the steep steps to the house. What was I thinking of? I loved Gerald and no doubt Roger loved Muriel, was a perfectly happy and contented husband and father. And what of the danger of a liaison between doctor and patient? I was mad, mad to live for these weekly meetings. But the madness continued.

On the fourth occasion alone in the car all doubts were resolved when Roger switched off the engine. I dared to wait a moment before moving away, and he leaned over and kissed me softly on the lips.

A moment later I heard my voice repeating his whispered 'Goodnight', then I was mounting the steps to the house, glancing back to see the red tail lights of the car dissolve into the dark. I stood there in the mild October night, reinventing the kiss. The air was still, no sound but the faint stirring of leaves. And the loud insistent pumping of my heart.

I went inside. How to face Gerald? How could he fail to read signs of treachery? I who had always been honest and straightforward, blurting out truths, disguising nothing except in his interests. How could he fail to notice the change?

He was immersed as usual in his open notebook, and I recoiled away from his cold concentration. Was this a real live person well known to me? Then I was moved to pity for his isolation and went over and gave him a little kiss on the cheek.

'Hello, darling.'

A quick glance, a muttered 'Hello'. He returned to his notes.

'Would you like some tea?' I longed to be lying in bed in the dark, thinking about Roger.

He looked up with a quick smile. 'Yes please, my dear.' I went into the kitchen. How to wait a whole week to see Roger again?

It seemed only natural to end future evenings with more, and lengthier, kisses. We didn't speak about it; we both knew the truth of what was happening and accepted it gladly as a bonus, expecting nothing more. I thought only about when I'd see Roger again; the week of waiting stretched ahead endlessly and I longed for the occasional encounter in the village. His nod or smile from across the street when he was engaged in conversation, or the greater thrill of an actual exchange of pleasantries, even if Gerald happened to be present, made the day, easing the time before our next meeting.

Too early in the year to be crowded out by holidaymakers, a mild Sunday in March was an ideal choice for Roger's proposed trip to the coast.

Muriel had planned for four adults only. The two older boys were spending the day with friends. 'Of course, we don't take the little ones with us,' she said. 'Betty and Doris always look after them.'

We'd met Betty and Doris, two kind sensible village women with grown-up children of their own who in turn acted as household helps and cared for the children.

'At the weekends as well?' I said, hiding my surprise and disapproval.

'Of course!'

'Do let them come too,' I pleaded.

'Do you really want them?'

'Yes, why not?'

Muriel gave a curious doubting look. 'All right then, if you're sure.'

The day was enjoyed by all: Roger and I were happy to be together, Gerald was at the place of his choice, a distant resort in East Devon we hadn't yet visited, Muriel was indulging her mood of the moment, and the two small boys were enjoying a rare outing with parents including a picnic and ball games on the beach.

Betty's and Doris's cottages had become their second homes. At eight each morning, one of the two helpers came to wash, dress and feed the two youngsters and take them away for the day, returning them in the evening already fed, to be bathed and put to bed after a quick parental goodnight kiss. The two pleasant easygoing women were fond of their charges and Muriel's needs ensured Roger's complicity in this heartlessness.

'I met her when I was lodging in her father's home at the start of my medical training in London,' Roger told me one evening. 'Her father was a widower. A year later, Muriel was pregnant and we got married. Luckily, her father let us stay on there after David was born, and after another year we had Michael.

'She's never liked it down here. I suppose she wouldn't mind it so much if I was a business or professional nine-to-five man. She doesn't want to be bothered with the practice. She hates taking telephone messages, especially if it's an emergency when she's ready to go to Plymouth. We go most afternoons. What for? Well, we love hunting out antique furniture. And Staffordshire china. Then there's the weekly hairdo; or clothes – Muriel loves clothes. No, she'd never go by bus. What would the villagers think? Besides, Muriel doesn't like waiting. If I'm not home by one for lunch she doesn't like that, either. Even if I am, I never know what I'm going to find.' He shrugged. 'If there's a fly in the sugar, Muriel's day is ruined.'

He seemed to take Muriel's moods fairly lightly, I thought. When the four of us met by chance outside Dingles in Plymouth one Saturday afternoon, Muriel suddenly interrupted our chatter to remark with disarming frankness, 'I'm a manic depressive, didn't you know.' There was a puzzled silence. 'I won't be long,' she said, turning quickly to disappear through the revolving door.

'It's nothing serious,' Roger explained reassuringly, 'just sudden changes of mood. Muriel's usually on a high, or a low. We're used to it. She has drugs for it, of course. Most of the time she's a most delightful companion.'

The term 'manic depressive' was new to me. I felt vaguely uneasy, but I couldn't help liking Muriel: charming, witty, vivacious, intelligent, an excellent cook. Household shopping for food and incidentals was enviously easy for her, a list taken to the village by one of the helpers and goods promptly delivered to the door.

'She's insatiable in bed, too,' Roger added with a twinkle.

Did this explain his avoidance of new sexual commitments? Was he too worn out to insist? Not that I minded this too much, though I did dream of illicit weekends and afternoons in bed. But whose bed? And what of his medical reputation? Parked by our house for any length of time the doctor's car would be sure to attract a passing spy and the resulting local gossip. The doctor was a person of importance, not to say near-reverence. Caps were doffed upon his approach. He was known to be a collector of Staffordshire china, and his glance at an interesting example on a farm labourer's mantelpiece received the automatic response: 'Do you like it, doctor? It's yours, then.'

Our abstinence, frustrating though it was, in a way simplified matters, dispensing with the lying and deceit which would probably follow deeper involvement, and also averting the danger of finding it all the harder to stay apart. And the back seat of a car was no substitute for bed. With embraces from Gerald a scarce commodity, Roger's passionate kisses and caresses brought satisfaction enough for the moment.

Twelve

'Have you seen this?'

I held out to Gerald the *Western Morning News* folded back at 'Situations Vacant'.

He glanced up from a re-examination of Fowler's 'Will and shall'.

'Yes, I've seen it,' he said quietly. He returned to Fowler.

'Well, have you applied?'

He barely looked up. 'No.'

'But you're going to, of course. Isn't it wonderful! Imagine it! Right on our doorstep, the perfect job for you. You're bound to get it. There aren't many experienced office managers round here. Just imagine, darling, first-class salary, it says, and a car, too.'

The long-awaited opportunity, and an unexpected one: a national company hiring out agricultural machinery wanted a manager for a new branch to be opened right here in our village. Not that Gerald knew anything about agricultural or any other kind of machinery; he wasn't interested in how things worked. But he had excellent references and was a good organiser, an asset to any company, my office experience told me that. And being left alone in charge of a small quiet office would be ideal for him.

Loving Roger had not affected marital concerns. Roger was inaccessible, on a plane apart. Here, on this plane, the job would be our salvation. My mind was leaping ahead, listing dozens of out-of-the-way places we'd be able to visit in Gerald's new car, whisked away on a magic carpet.

'Darling, it was brilliant of you to have kept up your driving licence all these years. I don't mind admitting it, I did think it a bit of a waste, paying out that seven-and-sixpence every year. There seemed no chance of ever getting a car. Still, you never know your luck.'

Gerald stayed with Fowler.

'Do say you're a little bit excited.'

He looked up. He wasn't smiling.

'There's nothing to be excited about. I'm not going to apply.' His tone was flat, precise, final.

'But of course you are! Now don't tease me. Isn't it lucky it's Friday? You'll have all tomorrow to do it. If we post it on Sunday they'll get it on Monday. Or we could walk down to the village and drop it in.'

His voice stayed flat. 'I'm not going to apply.'

My smile vanished. 'Stop it, the joke's gone far enough.'

His voice softened. 'It's no joke,' he said.

'It certainly isn't.' I flared. 'Really, why do we have to have these nonsensical arguments? I think you enjoy tormenting me.' I stalked out of the room, banging the door behind me.

Sweet relief, after years of endlessly placating, to lose my temper. The unaccustomed sound of the door banging brought exquisite satisfaction. But in the kitchen I found I was trembling. It wasn't so satisfying after all. What the hell was he playing at? I sat down heavily on the chair, staring down at the scrubbed floorboards.

I had learnt painfully never to expect Gerald to come to me when I was upset. Whatever the problem or the degree of distress, I had always been left to recover myself and come sheepishly to him.

For once he came to me. To my surprise the kitchen door opened and he stood looking down at me with an affectionate smile.

'I didn't know you had a temper.'

I didn't look up. 'There are limits, you know.'

A short silence. 'My dear,' he said, 'I can't apply for that job. They want handwritten applications.'

Gerald's riddles really were too tiresome at times. I looked up with unconcealed irritation. 'Well, what's wrong with that?'

He hesitated a moment. Then he said, very quietly, 'I can't write.'

'You can't write? What on earth are you talking about?'

'That is so, I can't write.' Slowly nodding his head, he gave a rueful little smile. 'I haven't been able to write properly since – since –'

I drew a sharp breath. 'Do you mean – you don't mean since you were first ill?' And I immediately wondered why I had been stupid enough to say that, because of course it couldn't possibly be so.

'That is so,' he said, 'but it –' He stopped, looked away.

About to protest that I had seen him write because it seemed impossible not to have seen him write in five years, I realised with a shock that I never had. Except, of course, for scribbling his notes; and signing his name on the marriage register. The letter he had sent me from Suffolk, the only one I had ever received from him, had been very short. The writing had been tiny and spiked and barely legible. And for some obscure reason, he had used a pencil. 'The pencil is mightier than the pen,' he had written, and I'd wondered what he meant but didn't like to ask. But it was incredible, one didn't forget how to write.

Something occurred to me. 'Is that why you wouldn't go to the labour exchange, because of filling in forms?' I scolded myself for immediately believing the unbelievable.

'Yes.'

The unbelievable when applied to Gerald was apt to become hard fact. I led the way back to the sitting-room, sat on his lap, straightened his hunched shoulders and kissed him.

'Why didn't you tell me?'

'I wasn't exactly proud of it.'

I pondered this conundrum in silence for a while.

'It's impossible that you can't write. Come on, I'll prove that you can.' Moving his little pile of books to the floor, I drew the small battered coffee table up to his chair and fetched a clean sheet of note-paper from the bottom cupboard of the kitchen cabinet, our only downstairs storage space.

'Now you're going to write a word, any word.'

He picked up his propelling pencil and I watched him bend over, then I snatched the pencil from his hand as he was about to begin writing. 'No, not like that. You're gripping the pencil much too hard. Now take it gently; gently. Don't hold it so near the tip; higher up – that's right. Now try again.'

Once more Gerald's grip tightened convulsively on the pencil.

'Just a minute. I've an idea. Put the pencil down a minute; lean back and do this.' I flapped my hands vigorously up and down, a device I often used to relax aching hands after long spells of short-hand and typing. I kept him at it for a minute or two. 'Now drop your hands down to your sides and relax.' I straightened his drooping shoulders. 'Good. Now I think you can try again.'

He leaned over obediently and presently held the paper out to me. 'Dear Sir,' I read in small, even script.

'Well, what's wrong with that?' I thrust the paper in front of him. 'Surely you can see there's nothing wrong with that. It's perfect writing.'

'I don't know if I can keep it up.' Taking the sheet, he again bent over.

Confident that another minor problem had been solved I went to put the kettle on, returning to find him collapsed over his knees, chin in hand. I put the tea down; he tried to hide the paper with his arm as I made to pick it up.

'Come on, darling, you don't mind me, do you?'

He handed me the sheet. Across the top a single line of writing began: 'Concerning your'. The rest of the line degenerated into a series of sharp strokes where the pencil had bitten deep into the paper. Not a single word more, not a single letter was legible. I stared at the paper for a minute before putting it down, then turned to hug him, looking blankly over his shoulder.

Was all this really happening?

'Now darling, you're not to worry. It's only a matter of practice.'

'I shall never be able to do it.'

'Of course you will. Your hand is stiff and tired, naturally, after not writing all this time. You'll see. All you need is practice.'

If only I were half as confident as I sounded.

He looked up despondently from a litter of discarded sheets of paper when I returned from the village the next morning.

'It's no use,' he whispered, barely able to speak. 'I'll never be able to do it.'

I drew his head to my breast, stroked his hair.

'I expect you're starving,' I said after a while, moving away to the kitchen.

When I brought in lunch I glanced at more of his efforts. Dozens of sheets headed with address and date began, 'Dear Sir'. The next line mostly ended at 'Con –' The furthest he had got was 'Concerning your advertisement'. Each time the writing tailed away into a jerky line like a section of an electrocardiogram. I put the sheaf of papers down.

'I'm sorry,' he said. 'I did try. I wanted that job.'

I forced a smile. 'Don't worry, darling. It can't be helped. Something else will turn up.' I didn't believe that. Such openings were practically unheard of hereabouts.

The fiasco brought an unexpected benefit. After further weeks of practice Gerald declared himself nearly ready to go to the labour exchange. His refusal to claim his much-needed unemployment benefit had not been mentioned since our early months in Plymouth. Distressed and puzzled as I was at the time, I knew that when Gerald had made up his mind it was pointless to argue.

'How is the writing now?' I asked.

'A little better.'

'Well, don't worry about it. I mean, when you go, if you find you can't write well enough to fill in the form you've only to walk out again. No one's going to compel you to do anything.'

'I may go tomorrow.'

His face when I arrived home from work the next day gave nothing away. It was impossible to tell whether he had been or not. I fumed at his trick of keeping me guessing.

'Well, did you go?'

'Yes.'

'Well, how did you get on?'

'All right.' He sounded offhand, and slightly impatient at being pestered unduly. He nodded casually towards some notes and silver on the table. 'I'm to get thirty-six shillings a week.'

With an effort, I resisted calculating thirty-six times the number of weeks he had been out of work.

'Well, that's wonderful! You did it! Did you have to write much?'

'No, not much.' His face was folded in concentration.

'Have you forgotten something again?'

He glanced up impatiently. 'There are scores of points.' He turned away, back to his conflict.

I went to make the dinner.

There were days, sometimes consecutive ones, when I began to forget about Gerald's compulsions. Not many, though thinking about Roger helped me to exist for much of the time in a haze of anticipation, willing away the time that kept us apart.

Thirteen

'I don't mind applying for a job through your personnel office in the normal way.'

It was some weeks later. Having long ago despaired of anything half as positive from Gerald I was caught unawares, but I kept my face impassive. You never knew what harm the wrong expression might do.

'Of course,' he added, 'I'm not sure yet about being able to fill in the form.'

The company where I worked as secretary to the General Sales Manager made components for the fast-expanding motor industry, some key staff having relocated from London. About two thousand former farmers, builders, butchers, bakers, shop assistants, insurance agents, milkmen and the like were earning relatively high wages in the factory or in routine office jobs, a big problem for the company being the shortage of experienced office workers in a rural area.

Mr West was hard-working, proficient and progressive, unlike most of my former bosses for whom real work often came a poor second (in the time left over from protecting their egos and their perks – expenses, company car, free two-hour meals in the managers' canteen, pretty secretary, imposing office-desk, padded swivel chair, quality carpet; most important of all, position and status as ruler of a little empire, maintained by the cunning use of powers of delegation), the real slog, the day-to-day grind with its hidden responsibilities, being done by underlings, which after all was what they were there for.

Although he valued efficiency in his secretary even more than looks, Mr West was known to be no saint when it came to extra-

104

marital romance, ideal candidates being those most likely to be free to take business trips, usually single girls or young wives of servicemen stationed abroad. But all that was before becoming the proud father of a perfect little girl. My own arrival round about that time, and the fact that I was shrewdly judged to be not quite the right type for nonsense, helped to set Mr West on a new path of virtue, his face shining with pleasure when an urgent call from his wife interrupted a board meeting to remind him to bring home another pack of Paddi-Pants. 'Does that baby pee!' he'd announce, flushed with pride, to an embarrassed audience; with a nod to me, taking the minutes, 'Remind me, Elaine –'

His brisk, often brusque, exterior belied much kindness, and I had long ago suggested that Gerald apply to him for a job; in view of the serious staff shortages, I said, he would be doing Mr West a favour.

Gerald refused outright. When he got a job it would be entirely on his own merits, without the demeaning intervention of a wife. His jaw was set, there would be no further argument.

'What I could do perhaps is,' I schemed aloud in response to Gerald's unexpected turnabout, 'er – let me see – perhaps I could get hold of a few application forms and bring them home. Then you could fill one in in your own time.'

'Could you really do that?'

'Well, it might be a bit awkward.' Why did I rashly commit myself to these difficult assignments? Gerald's face was unusually eager. 'I'll manage it somehow,' I said.

'Clever girl! You'll think of a way. You're my good angel, you know.' He patted my head. We kissed. He took my face in his hands and gave me one of his approving smiles, the unfailing spur to greater efforts.

It was more than a little awkward. The constant stream of new applicants was processed with conveyor-belt efficiency by the personnel manager, ex-naval Commander Smith, running his first tight ship in the world of industry. From the adjoining office, his number one,

Mr Johnson, handled the initial enquiries via a hatch giving on to the personnel waiting-room, where new job-seekers filled in a lengthy application form to be passed on to the Commander. If there was no suitable vacancy, Johnson filed the form against possible future needs, whereas a likely vacancy meant an immediate preliminary interview with the Commander.

I discarded dozens of ideas before forming a plan. At the first free moment I went downstairs and peeped through the open hatch to ensure that Johnson was alone before knocking. The young man sprang up. Secretaries of executives were treated with a respect amounting to deference.

'Good morning, Mrs Gardner.'

I smiled sweetly. 'Could I have a few application forms, Mr Johnson? Mr West wants to have a look at them.' The lie came without a blush, but my heart was hammering as though I were robbing the Bank of England.

'Certainly, Mrs Gardner.' Reaching over to a shelf, Johnson handed me a wad of foolscap forms.

'Thanks.'

A tireless innovator, Mr West was known for making sweeping changes to a very imperfect stodgy administration. Johnson, a former naval wireless operator glad to have found a safe post-war niche, must have wondered in passing what was afoot, but with his own position secure he could afford to dismiss the matter with a shrug.

Safely back in my office, a criminal hiding her booty, I slid the pile of forms into a large envelope, placing it out of sight in my shopping bag. Nobody but the managing director ever questioned Mr West's activities and it was fairly safe to assume that the forms would not be mentioned.

The prize was borne home. Now Gerald could take his time about filling in the form regardless of how many were wasted. He had agreed to come to the personnel office with a completed form rolled up in his inside pocket, ask for a new form and pretend to fill it in and then hand in the already completed form. With constant practice his handwriting was steadily improving and we were trusting that any forthcoming job would entail little or no writing. And returning to the mainstream of life would surely hasten a final recovery.

It took Gerald a week to fill in the form and another week to present himself in his best brown barathea suit at the factory.

Thankful that no sudden business trip had interfered with my plans, I went into my boss's office with the morning post.

'Good morning, Mr West.'

'Morning, Elaine.' He looked up from his desk, a pleasant-looking fresh-faced man in his forties, confident in himself on both the personal and business fronts and needing to prove nothing.

'I hope you don't mind my mentioning it, but my husband's coming to see Commander Smith this morning.'

'Yes, Elaine.'

'Well, you remember you were thinking of starting up a market research department?'

'Yes –?'

'Well, er, I wondered whether you could maybe make use of my husband.'

'You mentioned him to me once before, didn't you? Wasn't he going to come and see me?'

'Yes, you did say he could, but –' Annoyingly, I blushed. 'You see, um, he didn't want any special favours. He insisted on being treated purely on his own merits.'

'I see.' Mr West produced one of his warm smiles rarely seen during business hours. 'Well, tell the Commander to wheel him in when he arrives and we'll have a look at him.'

'Thank you, Mr West. I do appreciate it. May I – may I ask you not to mention that I've spoken to you? Do you mind?'

'Of course not, Elaine. Leave it to me.' A further warm smile gave an encouraging feeling of security. 'Now, what's in the post this morning?'

I danced out of the office and rang Commander Smith.

By lunchtime, our future was gloriously settled. Gerald was to start work immediately as the first member of Mr West's new market research department, an innovation viewed by the management, with deep mistrust, as a cranky idea and a waste of money. But Mr West was persuasive. Gerald's salary was to be a generous eight pounds a week, two pounds more than I was earning and more than other men on routine clerical work. 'I don't believe,' Mr West told me with a wink, 'in a man earning less than his wife. It isn't good for either of them.'

Thus went the fifties legend.

I was amazed, grateful, overjoyed. For our relatively modest duties we would both be earning top wages in the area, only about two-thirds of London rates, it was true, but a price well worth paying to live in the country. I sat on the evening bus in blissful content, beaming through the window at the promised land, ours at the end of a long journey.

The work situation revealed a new Gerald, a popular social crea-ture, and, I gathered from various comments fed back to me, an adept flatterer of women. A look or word from him was enough to convince the plainest female, young or old, stupid or intelligent, that if not actually beautiful, she was certainly more attractive than she had ever imagined. His large brown eyes, earnest or approv-ing, never failed to raise, if not actual flutters, then an appreciative smile. 'You're certainly looking your best today' gladdened the heart of dumpy Mrs Rose in the filing department. A door held open with a beaming 'I like your hair today', and office-girl Sally bringing in the tea temporarily forgot her worries over a nondescript face and sallow complexion. 'Have I seen that dress before? It certainly suits you' did wonders for the managing director's secretary, stout middle-aged Miss Jordan who had been diplomatically chosen to spike the guns of a jealous wife. Making his rounds in the course of compiling his records, Gerald left behind him a trail of elation and hope. Unlike the usual crude womaniser, Gerald had style. 'He's such a gentleman,' Sally enthused. 'Everyone says so.'

Equally popular with the men, his trick here was to listen gravely to every commonplace observation with an air of rapt attention. His earnest 'Yes, I think you're right, old man' held just the right touch of insightful surprise, as if the matter had been revealed in a new light, or had just come to his attention for the first time, raising every trivial utterance to the level of a profundity. I once witnessed him leaving doddery old Mr Simms in the order department scratching his head, obviously thinking that perhaps he wasn't quite such a fool after all. And Gerald's manner of listening, I noticed, was automatically adjusted to the intelligence, experience or background of the person concerned, this having already been unerringly assessed.

Little could any of the recipients of this largesse, male or female, have guessed that behind the polite facade he himself was inwardly pursuing quite different – to him far weightier – matters. Mr West took a great liking to him and began to offer the occasional lift home, since he lived on our route; and when his wife and daughter were away visiting relatives he invited us both out to a country pub for an after-office drink, an unheard-of honour. There was no attempt to flatter Mr West, I noticed. Gerald knew better than that. He merely listened to good effect.

My heart began to sing a new kind of song.

But I still loved Roger. That was unalterable, though loving Roger for himself was one thing, loving a married man, a devoted husband and father who was also a doctor, quite another. The role of wife of Gerald with a job drew me back, in some measure, towards sanity.

We made friends at work with Jill and Robert, a young couple who shared our lunch table in the small café near the factory. The food was tasty and wholesome but twice the price of the canteen meals, which had very promptly been rejected by Gerald's oversensitive stomach, and the café became one of life's little luxuries we could now afford, though given a choice I would have suffered the canteen and saved the extra money towards some much needed home comforts.

It is not often in life that one comes face to face with a really beautiful young woman. I found it hard not to keep staring at Jill across the small glass-topped table: silky rosy skin over high cheek-bones, large lustrous sea-green eyes, long tawny hair, tall willowy figure. Intelligent, too, as well as artistic, employed, improbably, as a draughtswoman in the factory but earning more in her spare time designing advertisements freelance for national companies. We had seen her impressive portfolio. As well as agreeable, it was conven-ient sharing a table with a congenial couple, since Gerald's stomach would have rebelled against the close proximity of most others in the crowded café. He would literally have felt sick and unable to eat.

As so often happens, for a young woman as gifted and accom-plished as Jill, Robert seemed an unlikely choice as a husband, a gauche lanky country lad who, for want of better material, had been taken on to train as the product manager's personal assistant. But there had to be more to him, since he and Jill were devoted.

When Gerald approved of innovating something of a social life by inviting them to dinner, I was delighted. The evening went well, the simple meal of roast lamb was a success, conversation flowed and bubbled. Flushed with pleasure, I carried the coffee tray into the kitchen, and heard through the open door the sounds of excited chatter, a loud burst of laughter, more talk … I stood there listening to another burst of laughter and suddenly realised, with something of a shock, that it was a sound not previously heard by me in that house; nor, until that instant, had I known how badly I needed to hear it. The memory of that moment is strong: a younger, slimmer version of myself standing in the kitchen doorway whispering with fervour into cupped hands, please let it go on, please let it go on …

The writing needs of Gerald's job were fortunately minimal, mostly jotting down figures and making notes. Hearing that he could type, Mr West immediately allocated him a typewriter for his reports and schedules. Gerald was the first male member of staff to be so favoured and the subject of much comment and envy. Evenings found the jumbled little black notebook still much in evidence. 'Yes, it's still going on' – the admission came with a wry smile – 'but it's all right; I can easily manage the work.'

In our carefree new world we shared Robert and Jill's small car on a Saturday shopping trip to Exeter. The men went off to find a car tool for Robert, leaving the women to window shop, and we were gazing at some clothes when I suddenly exclaimed to Jill, 'Isn't it wonderful, being married!' Until I saw her look of surprise I had no idea that I had said anything unusual, that the blessings of a happy marriage could be accepted as an agreeable but unremarkable gift of the gods. All Jill needed was a home of her own; she and Robert were sharing her parents' small bungalow, as well as their car, whilst saving for a deposit on a house.

Household goods, furniture and clothes could now be realistically budgeted for. It should take about three years, I calculated, to achieve a modest standard of comfort, then I could think about leaving work and starting a family.

Uncertain of Gerald's attitude to fatherhood, I one day received a pleasant surprise. We were walking along a lane when he suddenly turned about. 'Come along, Melanie,' he called, 'don't dawdle.'

I was puzzled. 'Who's Melanie?'

He smiled boyishly. 'Our daughter, of course!'

'How do you know it will be a girl?'

'It's going to be a girl and her name's going to be Melanie.'

So he did want a child! Smiling, I took his arm. But what if it should be a boy? Best not dwell on that. When the time came, if it came, he would surely be glad to accept what the fates had to offer.

Gerald's bureau-bookcase still remained undisturbed in his bachelor bedroom, and when he offered, unprompted, to visit London to pack this treasure and have it sent with his books to Devon I was overjoyed.

A weekend spent with Helen and Alan while Gerald went on to Beston alone was a celebration. Helen was doubtful about the cancelled psychiatric appointment but relieved at the news of the job. Perhaps Gerald was getting better. She could see that I seemed better, without knowing the true cause of my flushed cheeks.

Helen's ground-floor flat was in a spacious detached house with a large garden in an expensive residential area of North London popular with minor diplomats, thriving businessmen and established professionals. It was luxuriously furnished and equipped: Wilton carpets, soft settees, comfortable beds, Merino wool blankets, fine Egyptian cotton sheets, huge thick towels, elegant Scandinavian glassware and china, a superb kitchen with the latest stainless steel and expensive Italian tiles. Transported to this finery from Paddington in Helen's big new Rover car, I felt outclassed and outmoded.

But the friendship was unchanged; laughing over old times: Helen during the war mistakenly using her week's ration of two ounces of butter instead of margarine to fry some onions. 'Don't those onions smell wonderful,' she remarked, then was appalled when she recognised the delicious taste. We looked at each other open-mouthed before collapsing into helpless laughter. The lavish production of *Tosca* at Covent Garden was a wonderful treat, a great improvement on wartime restraints. But did I still crave the constant opera-going and concerts we'd enjoyed throughout the war? Boosey & Hawkes, the benevolent music publishers where I worked as secretary, had very kindly provided staff with regular free tickets, always two. Usually Helen came with me and we revelled in the marvellous opportunity to establish lasting musical tastes. But being in the swim of musical activities, feeling obliged to keep up with all the latest performers and conductors, and being knowledgeable about modern works, can become compulsive. Helen and Alan still keep it up now, after fifty years, but once away from London I found

I didn't miss the music nearly as much as I had expected; there were other compensations.

We'd been surprised to hear our rural joys denounced as worthless by certain office workers who had moved to Devon with the company and subsequently, after much heart-searching and despite the loss of jobs and homes, decided to return to London. 'It's no good,' they moaned, 'the country's all right for holidays but not to live in. There's nothing here, nothing to do.'

The answer to 'What do you miss about London?' was vague: 'Oh, theatres and all that –'

'Did you go to the theatre much?'

'Well, not really, but they're there, aren't they, if you want them.'

It took a while to discover that what they really needed was the reassurance of a familiar environment. Without it they were lost, strangers in a foreign land.

'Are you sure you're all right?' Helen asked when I was leaving.

'Yes, of course I am.'

Helen was reassured, up to a point.

At Roger's suggestion we were all four to attend some summer chamber concerts at Dartington Hall, fifteen miles away, an undertaking impossible without a car. Programmes were eagerly scanned by Roger and me, tickets for the first concert, by the Amadeus Quartet, were booked and the outing was celebrated with the special treat of dinner beforehand in a Totnes hotel. But in the car on the way home, Muriel, in the front passenger seat, unexpectedly turned round to say to Gerald, 'Boring, really, don't you think?'

Silence greeted this blasphemy, mine disapproving, Roger's amused.

'I agree,' came from Gerald.

I thought of all those First Performances at the Wigmore Hall (Bartok, Britten, Schoenberg …) – nothing like the Brahms, the Beethoven, the Mozart, the Tchaikovsky rounding out the spaces of the Albert Hall. My ears protested, my eyes darted furtively sidewards testing the reaction of other more seasoned ears: not a move, not a wriggle; only rapt attention. This kind of thing, then, this jarring tunelessness, must be all right, must have hidden qualities; it was only that I, the stupid ignorant Eastender, needed educating, like training the palate for wine, like learning to read all over again when it came to modern novels after the lucidity of Jane Austen. Years later, my ears, to an extent, had tuned in – had sorted and selected, had even dared to reject. The process slowly continued.

The car drew up at our gate.

'I think,' Muriel said, 'that if there's to be any more of this concert-going, then Roger and Elaine should go alone, don't you agree, Gerald?'

'Certainly,' came the reply.

'That's settled, then.'

Alone with Roger for hours at a time, free of spouses! I debated feverishly what to wear, bought three new dresses in the last of the summer sales, parading secretly – when Gerald was in the bath – in front of mirrors. It was inconceivable that this chance to be alone would not result, somewhere and somehow, in passionate lovemaking. There was a temptation to buy new underwear in the certainty of undressing before Roger, or, I prudishly hoped, being undressed by him, but I dared not risk raising Gerald's suspicions.

A lovely summer evening saw us, just the two of us, seated in the majestic Great Hall at Dartington, awaiting once more the pleasure of the Amadeus. We had arrived early, and there was time before joining the throng in the small foyer for a turn round the lovely ancient quadrangle, and we strolled a little apart in the warm air of the August heatwave, not quite touching, not quite alone after all but dangerously open to public scrutiny, to possible prying eyes. The luck of some women, free to walk arm in arm with lovers or husbands. It had seemed more than enough to come here alone with Roger, to speak freely and snatch secret smiles, sit close together, drive home alone and kiss with abandon. But here I was, wanting more. I should have been ashamed. But I wasn't ashamed. I did want more.

I looked around the towering hall; long windows giving on to rolling greens and reds; an audience refreshingly different from their London counterparts, families with attentive, often quite small children, unstudied informality, summer dresses, open-neck shirts, bare brown legs in sandals; young and old reliably musical – no chance here of blundering applause in mid-work.

My pleasure halfway through the music was marred by a sudden desperate need to feel Roger's hand on my bare arm, which was separated from him by an unbridgeable gulf of a few inches. The temperature had simmered down from a scorching ninety Fahrenheit to a sticky seventy-five. I was wearing my new sleeveless lawn dress with a demure Peter Pan collar – lemon/green narrow stripes on a white background picked out in thin gold thread which I hoped caught the gold glints in my hair. The gleam in Roger's face when I appeared at the front door confirmed that the rather high sale price had not been wasted.

My arm suddenly seemed to have acquired an identity of its own. It ached with a terrible insistent longing so acute, I didn't know how to deal with it. Roger seemed annoyingly, stodgily, unaware of anything amiss, sitting there, tall, broad, rock solid, acutely desirable, unattainable, immersed in the music, content to cast a sweet smile or two in my direction. Damn Muriel and her ceaseless sexual demands! Roger was maddeningly a man more or less drained of sexual desire. But not wholly drained! That much had been apparent all along. And at that moment a plan formed in my mind. However, for the present there was nothing for it but to sidle up to him as close as I dared and allow my bare upper arm to make contact with the rough sleeve of his tweed jacket. Surreptitiously we contrived once or twice briefly to hold hands, but although we were some way from home, Roger was known to many and care was essential.

Throughout a steaming August we attended two concerts a week,

115

Roger frustratingly less alive than I to the new opportunities for intimacy. I could only fit my mood, if not my needs, to his. And there was the compensation that our arrival home could not be timed and we could take a little longer than usual for kissing and embracing in the car. Then slightly crestfallen and no longer worrying about hiding telltale creases or dreaming of lacy underwear, I was once more home with an abstracted Gerald. But there was the next concert to look forward to – and my plan.

I had gradually learnt about Muriel's dependence on drugs for her 'moods', and her violent outbursts of anger against Roger or the children or the daily helpers. And, more embarrassing though likewise dismissed by Roger with an indulgent smile, her tirades against village shopkeepers – regardless of the presence of shocked bystanders – for perhaps a trifling mistake in an order; or even worse, the occasional invasion of a surgery consultation because of lurking unfounded suspicions of a particular female patient. I wondered that I myself never came under suspicion, but Roger and I continued to be trusted without question.

The day of the last concert was a Saturday, still sultry, ideal for my designs, as long as the threatened storm kept off. I bathed in the afternoon and dressed with care, the same gold-green dress, my coolest, buttoning, conveniently, down the front, no stockings, white high-heeled sandals, comfortable enough except for much walking. Face carefully giving nothing away, a casual 'Bye, darling', Gerald already deep in the *Radio Times*, his notebook and reference books to hand.

Roger's car drew up on time at our gate, his smile saying all that was needed. For this one evening, these few hours, he would be mine. No qualms, not one. I didn't feel guilty, didn't feel bad or wicked or in the wrong; another surprise, but a welcome one.

'We're not going to the concert,' I told Roger as we drove off.

He didn't look at all surprised. 'We're not?'

'No, darling.'

The car turned right from the lane on to the main road.

'Have you got that picnic blanket of yours in the boot?'

Eyebrows raised, half smiling, Roger glanced sideways at me. 'Yes, I have.'

'Good!'

'Where shall we go then?'

'I'll leave that to you, darling.'

I never did discover where he took me. Well away from Stowbury, somewhere near Dartington. 'This looks promising,' he said, turning off the main road down a deserted lane. We came to a wide gateless opening into a golden harvested field lit by the evening sun. Roger bumped the car inside and parked a few yards on in the shelter of a thick hedge. We kissed and embraced. 'I've been waiting for this,' he said. 'Come on, darling.' We got out of the car and he opened the boot for the rug.

The next two hours were not just a matter of exhilarating, satisfying sex. They were everything I had ever imagined and more, an initiation into real, natural affection and passion on another plane from Gerald's mechanical performance.

We donned our discarded clothes slowly, shaking out shreds of grass. I brushed my hair, applied lipstick. I wasn't sorry. You couldn't be sorry to be alive.

The languid August days ended with violent thunderstorms, and a resumption of our musical evenings at Roger's. Some of the hunger was assuaged. Be content with that. Gerald's job was going well. I was saving money, and taking the bus alone into Plymouth on a Saturday to enjoy modest shopping sprees for extra food or sale bargains. With its sea air, the town was exceptionally clean and inviting. Extensively bombed during the war, an impressive new centre had been built with straight wide tree-lined roads and imposing new stores faced with local white stone.

As Christmas approached, I found that I had missed a period. It had never happened before. I must be pregnant.

Fourteen

The monthly 'Safe Period' was never foolproof in the past any more than 'The Pill' is foolproof today unless all the relevant rules are strictly obeyed. With Gerald safely in a job I must have become careless in observing exact dates. I came out of the bathroom in a panic, wondering if Roger was the father. When he and I had made love in August I hadn't bothered about the date, the time of month. How could I have been so rash? But at the time I hadn't cared about consequences, perhaps had half wanted to get pregnant by Roger and settle matters that way. But only half wanted it.

My legs felt suddenly weak. I sat down heavily on the bed. Then I began counting on my fingers, and sighed with relief. It was now December. So the baby was undoubtedly Gerald's.

Was I glad or sorry? I felt relieved rather than glad that marital rights had stepped in and neatly resolved the issue. But sorry – more than sorry, dismayed – that my relationship with Roger would have to end, for I could not be both mother and mistress. I would somehow have to bear it. Having a child would help, and there was Gerald, too. I still cared deeply for Gerald, wanted to make him happy; and here was the perfect opportunity. A child would change him, would give him a new outlook.

Two months later there was a certain quaint humour in having the pregnancy confirmed by none other than Roger himself. Gerald's initial reaction had been disheartening: a solemn nod, a quick non-committal glance; no anticipatory gleam, not even an encouraging pat on the head, but rather an avoidance of the subject, and of my eyes. Did this mean that he was concerned about something other than the prognosis itself, something – dared I think this? – connected with his ultra possessiveness about that most inalienable property of his, my body? The ugly suspicion seemed hardly worthy of consideration. On the other hand, where Gerald was concerned …

'Aren't you pleased, darling?'

I should never have had to put such a question.

'Yes, of course I am.'

But he didn't look pleased. He looked worried, though certainly not on account of any fears for my well-being. Trust Gerald to produce some devious complication of his own. I shuddered. Someone walking over your grave, my mother would say.

He insisted on coming with me to the surgery, but not into the examination, and I found him afterwards still hunched over his notebook. Without a word he fussily stowed the notebook and pencil away in his inside jacket pocket and followed me outside. And in the sunny village street my vague fears suddenly seemed groundless. With a sense of reclaiming husband, rightful lover, father of my child, I took his arm.

'I'm definitely pregnant,' I said, my mind fixed on a happy outcome.

A grave nod. 'I see,' he said thoughtfully. No sign of joy, no exuberant hug or kiss. I grew annoyed. He might have managed a little squeeze of the hand, a smile. But, far from smiling, he was concerned – very concerned – about something, something of his own, some piffling little worry. I bit my lip and clenched my fists, hardly knowing how to contain my anger and disappointment.

Passing the dairy, I felt nausea at the thought of cream. The garage was abuzz with cars entering and leaving, people were walking up and down, in and out of shops, chatting, smiling, life going on normally – the life of normal people. I glanced sideways at the strained immobile face. Why, especially now, could he not act naturally? Why not just turn with a smile and grip my arm, and rejoice, rejoice!

Just past the garage he suddenly stammered out, 'How – er – that is – how did he …?'

'The examination, do you mean?'

He nodded, frowning, deeply anxious.

So I'd been right all along in thinking that he might be concerned at some such trifle. But there was too much at stake for anger.

'Well –' my tone was deliberately even – 'when I said I'd missed three periods and kept feeling sick I had to lie down on the couch.'

He looked even more anxious.

'It's all right,' I said, my scorn hidden behind a matter-of-fact air. 'Nothing was revealed. They've obviously got it all worked out. You lie down and they put a blanket over your legs up to the part they want to look at.' Another anxious look. If only he had known the difference between Roger's loving eyes and his own morbid possessiveness. I indicated the right-hand side of my abdomen. 'Don't worry, he only wanted to examine the area of the womb. Apparently after the third month they can feel it very slightly raised.'

'Really!'

'Yes, I was surprised.' The marked relief in his face made me uneasy. I added, 'I'd not heard of that as a test, had you?'

'Can't say that I had.' (Still no sign of a smile.)

'Anyway, that's over, thank goodness.'

Something else was over, too, as I had known it would be, but not the manner of it. Taking my hand, Roger had given me his blessing with a wry tender little smile.

'You're definitely pregnant,' he said. 'Best of luck with it, my darling,' and it suddenly seemed easier not to want to kiss him quite as badly as before – a nun righteously clinging to her vows. A warm handclasp and exchange of glances seemed about right.

'Of course,' I said to Gerald, 'I hadn't the faintest idea what kind of examination it would be, had you?'

'No, but I did wonder.' His eyes still avoided mine.

I bet you did, I thought, dismayed that he could go on fussing over one of his trifles at such a time. 'I've got to go and see him again next week,' I said, clinging to practicalities, 'and I've got a prescription for some pills, vitamins, I think; or did he say iron? They're all routine, anyway.'

'Why do you have to go next week?'

'Haven't the faintest. Never mind, it's probably just routine.'

If only he were less concerned about these minor details and his own obscure worries and more interested in looming financial difficulties. With only one instead of the three years of planned savings, and with floors still uncovered and rooms and windows bare, drastic revision of budgeting was needed. Once I had left work there would be no money left over for furnishings.

'I shall have to go on working until six weeks before the baby's due,' I said, looking up one evening from my lists and calculations.

'Really!' Gerald barely glanced up from his book.

'Yes, don't worry. It'll probably work out all right.'

He continued reading.

'I'll have to go to town on Saturday.'

He looked up vaguely. 'What's that – ?'

'I'll have to go to town on Saturday, to find out about baby things, how much they all cost, that sort of thing. Do you want to come?'

'Saturday? I think not, my dear. You can manage alone, can't you?'

'Yes, of course.'

Silly to think it would be nice if just this once he came with me. He wouldn't even bother to buy his own clothes, was reluctant even to go and try on a suit or coat or a pair of shoes. Everything else I was obliged to buy for him. 'You know what I like,' he insisted. 'Don't bother me, my dear. Anyway, I don't need any more clothes, do I?' Gerald's idea of an adequate wardrobe was to possess one, at most two, of any one item.

I wrote my news to Helen and received an unexpected reply. 'Snap! Have just discovered that I'm expecting, too. What a scream! Both of us at the same time. I think I'm a month or so behind you;

121

pity, really, because now I won't be able to come and see you next summer. Never mind, we'll have babies the same age, which should be very handy.'

Lovely for Helen, of course, but disappointing not to be able to meet for such a long time. I was surprised at the depth of my disappointment. Why should I so badly need to see Helen now?

Unexpected reactions came from fellow workers: sly looks and sham congratulations as though I had somehow behaved reprehensibly; barely concealed glee from established parents that two who had 'got away' with it for so long were now justly recruited to the ranks of the long-suffering. Only Jill and Robert, and Mr West, showed genuine pleasure, the latter with sporting goodwill at losing his secretary, though from a certain gleam in his eye I suspected that he was now ready to welcome the change. Even more astonishing was the avid interest of local people to whom I had never spoken a word, complete strangers closing with me in the village street with furtive sidelong looks. 'So you're having a baby, then?' – I had achieved a kind of fame.

Roger had recommended that the baby be born in hospital. 'It's thought best for the first one,' he said, handing over a form. 'You just need to go along to the antenatal clinic Wednesday afternoons at two o'clock.' This was convenient; possible embarrassment to Gerald over examinations would be avoided and Roger would still be available, medically speaking, in case of emergency.

The process of human reproduction may be viewed, particularly by childless people, as an unremarkable event, but when that same event occurs within one's own humble body it is promoted to the status of a miracle. My own miracle acted as part compensation for Gerald's aloofness, which surely could only be due to anxiety about the outcome. Just let it be born healthy.

I was finding it more and more difficult to keep awake during the weekly examinations. Left lying on the couch, decently covered with a crisp white sheet, the growing mound, smooth as marble, exposed,

122

awaiting the doctor's pleasure, I immediately became compulsively sleepy, dozing off, if only for a minute or two while waiting, and even between sundry proddings and murmurings. I had relented in the matter of Gerald's late-night sittings and now they were taking their toll.

'We shall have to X-ray you later on.'

A brisk male voice had penetrated my torpor. I roused with an effort. A dark-haired good-looking young doctor was regarding me speculatively. 'We can't do it yet, it isn't good for the baby, but there's a possibility that you may be having twins.'

Wide awake now, new problems cascaded about me like a sudden snowstorm: the risks, the extra expense, managing two babies; worst of all, the possible unfavourable reaction from Gerald. But it might not be twins; no need to worry him yet.

Weeks later the same cool voice roused me.

'Your blood pressure's up a bit. It often is at this time. I'll give you a prescription and I want you to take one of these twice a day.' The young registrar was scribbling on the label of a small bottle, which he handed over with an admonitory air. 'Now you are resting for two hours each afternoon with your feet up, aren't you? It's absolutely essential that you do that.'

'Yes, doctor.'

Hadn't these people heard of work, of money problems? The lie made me feel like a naughty schoolgirl. I was glad not to have blushed. Put your feet up, indeed. All I wanted was to air my vague nagging fears about Gerald.

But what, precisely, did I fear?

Fifteen

The annual staff outing, a trip to the coast, was a welcome day off work and rare social event to be shared with my husband.

The May weather was exceptionally warm, and it was already hot and sunny when the coach picked us up at the top of the lane. I took my seat with relief. Standing even for a short time in this weather produced painful swollen ankles.

Visibility was good, the sky a lovely clear blue. I was admiring the changing colours of the brilliant velvety patchwork, and was just fancying that the curving hills resembled the outlines of a shapely woman, when I became aware of great heat rising from the floor of the coach. We must be sitting over some part of the engine. In the sixth month of pregnancy, heat had become a menace. I tried to ignore it but soon my ankles and feet became painfully swollen. I tugged at Gerald's sleeve.

'I'm afraid my feet are swelling in this heat. We'll have to ask someone to change seats with us. They won't mind,' I added placatingly, sensing an unexpected resistance.

His face had instantly darkened. 'No, no, no, you can't do that.'

I was astonished; and perplexed. A warning light flickered, giving notice of yet another obscure Gerald difficulty. But why should he object? Nobody would mind changing places. We had only to ask.

'Darling, my feet really are painful.'

His face stayed darkened. 'Don't say anything,' he hissed. 'We'll soon be there.' His petty concern at being overheard increased my exasperation as he turned to the window, detaching himself from his wife and her awkward private problems.

The journey to East Devon would take another two hours. My

feet swelled more and more until they were about to burst. The sun rose high, targeting my face as if conspiring with the floor in some hideous new form of torture. Flat-heeled sandals which had started the day comfortable now seemed several sizes too small and had to be removed. If only my feet could have been raised up. But in the confined space they could only move a few inches from one tormenting hot spot to another. If only we had sat on the other side of the coach, away from the sun, which I normally loved.

Why was Gerald being so churlish? He simply couldn't bear us to be exposed to public censure, that must be it. Whatever the circumstances, no fuss must be made in public. I thought of a cinema visit after work one evening when the waitress in the café forgot our order of tea and toast, and rather than signal her during a ridiculously long wait, Gerald insisted on leaving without our tea. He wasn't going to make a fuss, or risk being late for the last performance. For twenty minutes the waitress had stood at the pay desk in the almost empty café chatting to the cashier. Perhaps she was in love. For whatever reason, she'd forgotten us, and my tentative offer to intervene met with a horrified refusal, as I half expected it would; the man must take charge in public.

A very peculiar look was directed at us as we left, Gerald marching me out without noticing, but I surmised that the waitress must have mistaken us for another couple who were lingering on after finishing their meal. She must, then, have thought that we'd not paid our bill!

At ten-thirty I left the cinema, as I had known I would, with a severe migraine-type of headache which lasted well into the next morning.

The nightmare journey ended at last. Half pushing my feet into sandals, I braced myself to stand and hobbled away leaning heavily on Gerald's arm. Fortuitously, like a rescue-ship on the horizon, a seafront café appeared, and outside in the shade of an awning was an unoccupied table. Dispensing for once with the formality of consulting Gerald, I sat down heavily on a cool wooden-slatted chair and, after a moment's hesitation, he joined me. Gingerly removing my sandals again, I placed my bare feet on the wonderfully cool grass. Raising them up to the vacant chair would have been better, but one couldn't have everything.

As soon as the last cup of tea was drained Gerald became restive, but my survival instincts were roused, and I insisted on relaxing on the pebble beach rather than wander about satisfying Gerald's need to explore. Surprised, he agreed to go off on his own.

Blissfully detached from Gerald's wishes, Gerald's needs, Gerald's point of view, I lay back on my white cardigan and tuned in to the gentle plap-plopping of the waves.

To my amazement Gerald maintained his stance, refusing to request a change of places for the return journey. But my new-found sense of self-preservation asserted itself, and the couple I spoke to as we were about to board were happy to oblige.

Stony-faced, without a word or look, Gerald took his new seat beside me.

Sixteen

It was not going to be twins. I mourned a little over lost blessings. Two babies, an instant family, would have suited me perfectly.

Just as well that I had not worried Gerald about it.

Now I could think about hunting down the needs of one precious baby in the summer sales. Baby equipment was expensive. I'd have to make do with the second-hand offerings in the village stationer's window, but I found all the baby clothes I needed in Dingle's summer sale; and in the other less expensive new stores, some passable furniture for the sitting-room along with a large carpet square, as well as a cheap bedroom carpet which we were able to fit ourselves. The final purchase was made with the last of our savings, a roll of new red cord carpet for the hall and stairs, inexpensive but pleasing enough. It stood propped in a corner of the hall awaiting Gerald's attention.

Then, two weeks before I was due to leave work, I noticed a slight pain which vanished when I sat down. Probably nothing, I thought; but it was in the vaginal area, a potential embarrassment, and not just to me.

The pain didn't go away but gradually grew worse, until, once home I had to sit down for most of the day. Rising to prepare the evening meal or fetch Gerald's cups of tea became an affliction. I said nothing, still hoping that it was a temporary upset and the pain would soon disappear. But each day it grew worse until the only relief was to stretch out upstairs on the bed. Then the stairs became too much and I found myself lying for hours on the sitting-room floor, a final indignity. The pain was determined to stay; it had staked out its territory. There was no help for it, I would have to see a doctor. But by now I couldn't walk to the surgery, I couldn't walk anywhere. It seemed unwise to summon Roger when Gerald was away at work. I'd have to stick it out till the weekend.

On Friday night I told Gerald he'd have to summon Roger the next morning. He looked up from his book with a curious kind of intensity, and I was aware of the strange sensation of having his full attention.

'Are you sure you need a doctor?' He was worried, but obviously, judging by the conflicting emotions criss-crossing his face, not on my account. Something else was at work here, something peculiar to Gerald, though I couldn't concern myself with his problems just now.

'Yes, I'm afraid so,' I said. 'Don't worry. It's probably nothing much.' Not that I believed that.

By next morning I could hardly move from the bed. I'd be the first on Roger's list when he made his morning rounds.

Wreathed in tension and indecision, Gerald stood at the bedroom door. 'He's here!' he exclaimed urgently.

'Well, send him up,' I snapped, in no mood for his vagaries.

He didn't move. He just stood there, his face mapped with question marks, begging for something.

'What's the matter?' I tried not to sound too sharp.

'I – er – um – shall I –?' His voice tailed off. He hovered uncertainly.

Was every small initiative to be left to me? Would he never say what he meant? He looked so distressed, I made the effort to guess at his predicament.

'Are you wondering whether to stay in here?'

'Er – yes –' He was immensely relieved that I had guessed. 'What do you think?'

It seemed so important to him, I tried not to show scorn.

'It's entirely up to you, darling. Do whatever you want.'

He hesitated before finally moving away. But now was no time to be worrying about Gerald. I needed urgently to know if I would ever be free of this cruel pain; if it would lead to a miscarriage, or to a deformed or stillborn baby; if there was any hope at all that it would prove to be nothing serious.

Brimming with concern, Roger appeared. We had met only as part of a foursome once or twice in the past months and at present he was purely a friend and trusted doctor. I tried to describe the pain coherently, and he listened closely before pulling back the bedclothes.

'I can see nothing at all,' he said presently. 'Let's have a look inside.'

The first touch of the hard probing instrument produced the kind of agony inflicted by pressure on an open wound, and an involuntary scream escaped me. Dimly, through half closed eyes, I realised that Gerald wasn't in the room. I hadn't heard him go downstairs. He must be waiting in the next bedroom or in the bathroom. Strange that my scream hadn't brought him in. Strange, but perhaps not entirely surprising.

Roger replaced the bedclothes and looked at me reflectively. A talented physician, he took great pride in his diagnostic powers.

'I think there's only one thing that can be causing this sort of pain, and that is an abscess. It's most unusual at this stage of pregnancy – in fact I haven't come across it before – but I can't account for this kind of pain in any other way.' He paused, then moved towards his bag. 'I'll give you a penicillin injection and I'll be in to see you again tomorrow.'

I heard Gerald speaking to him on the way downstairs in fair imitation of a solicitous husband. But Roger cared about me. Roger cared.

The next day the pain was even worse. I couldn't bear to stand up; rising to go to the lavatory was agony, lying down little better. Roger came again, exchanged a few words and went away looking grave, promising to return next day with a specialist.

Mr Saunders was a leading gynaecologist; we were very lucky to have him in the district, Roger had said. Small, balding, about fifty, dapper in white shirt, dark tie and dark chalk-striped suit, courteous and competent, Saunders made his own internal examination. Once more my scream pierced the air, and still there was no sign of Gerald, though by now I hardly noticed.

'We'll have to have you in hospital,' Saunders said, glancing at his watch. 'It'll probably be this afternoon.'

A polite nod to me, Roger held the door open and they were gone.

The ambulance provided forty-five minutes of jarring agony leading to a hard hospital bed where the pain was even more unbearable than at home.

A pleasant-faced white-coated young woman doctor directed the curtains to be drawn round the bed in the small ward of four in readiness for yet another internal examination. I tensed myself, and then the first touch of the metal probe sent my piercing scream through the hushed ward. Visibly startled, the doctor protested, 'It's surely not as bad as all that.'

'It is, it is!'

With a glance at my tear-soaked face she left the room, soon to reappear with a nurse carrying a tray covered with a white cloth. I eyed the tray apprehensively.

'It's all right. I'm going to give you a morphine injection to ease the pain. Now turn on your side. Nurse!'

Half an hour later she returned to enquire, in a kindly voice, if the pain had gone.

'It's dulled it a bit,' I said, 'but' – I bit my lower lip – 'it's still there, very much so.'

Disbelief flitted over the doctor's face, and I sensed her thinking I was inventing this odious pain. But scientific caution prevailed.

'I'm having you moved to a ward by yourself,' she said, permitting herself a sympathetic female smile before leaving.

Strong arms presently transferred me to a trolley and wheeled me along corridors. Just like a piece of luggage, I thought, only not so useful.

A few hours later, in the small room containing bed, locker and washbasin, the pain had returned in full and went on steadily worsening throughout the long bleak hours of the night.

At five o'clock in the morning a bowl of warm water, soap and towel were left on the bedside locker by a busy nurse. I cast a reproachful glance at the rising steam. A wash might have been refreshing; but by now I could hardly move. I certainly couldn't sit up and lift the bowl on to my lap and wash. Later, the bowl was removed with no comment other than a scornful tut-tut and a withering glance reserved, I guessed, for malingerers in abject fear of birth pangs.

The breakfast tray arrived. I was longing for tea. Cautiously, lying on my side and hindered by the cumbersome bulge, tight as a drum, moaning at each move, I edged my way towards the side of the bed and managed to prop myself up a few inches on my left elbow. My right arm reached out and grasped the cup and I sipped gratefully, though it was awkward drinking with my head tilted to one side and some of the tea escaped down the side of my mouth, trickling down on to the white pillow-slip.

I returned the empty cup to the tray and slowly lowered myself on to the pillows, wanting a hanky for the tea drying on my face and neck.

With no comment on the untouched breakfast, the nurse picked up the tray. 'The doctor will be along later,' she remarked cheerfully, patronisingly.

'What time do you think that will be?'

'After ten.' A hard bright nod and she was gone.

It was only seven-thirty. How to wait such a long time for the doctor? How to go on enduring this relentless pain? Would it ever stop? I clung to the thought of the doctor. I'd make him see that this was no pretence, that the monster was real and that I must be rescued. Hold on for another few hours, they can't last for ever; they only feel as if they're lasting for ever, grinding you down, reducing you to something less than human.

The sound of the door opening raised me from the deep trough into which you sink when the world is unbearable. From the foot of the bed four pairs of eyes scrutinised their latest enigma.

'Good morning, Mrs Gardner.' Mr Saunders, head man, dark-suited, scientist enough to give me the benefit of the doubt, beside him the white-coated young house-surgeon, he of the twins, pointedly masculine, pointedly healthy, waiting to be led. An impassive ward sister in dark blue and a nurse in light blue completed the entourage.

I was determined not to break down and beg for mercy from this stern tribunal. I had to make my case.

I spoke quietly. 'Good morning, Mr Saunders.'

'And how are you this morning?' He was studying the bed-rail chart handed to him by the sister. Passing it back without a sideways glance, he regarded me speculatively.

My plea was carefully modulated; no use playing into their hands by appearing hysterical.

'Doctor, the pain is worse, much worse. Can't you give me something for it?'

'We have to consider the baby, you know.' The round face was grave, the tone thoughtful. 'Without a definite diagnosis –?' A slow shake of the head, a perplexed shrug.

'But don't you agree with Dr Harris? It must be an abscess. It feels like an abscess. It's that sort of pain.'

'An abscess at this stage of pregnancy is very unlikely. I've never come across one. Abscesses usually come much earlier on,' he added on a kindly note. He glanced at me uncertainly. 'We shall see you tomorrow.' He turned to the door, and the little procession filed out, consigning me once more to the unrelenting tyranny of the pain.

Gerald arrived for the evening visit. In a whispered conversation

132

I masked the worst of the pain, stupidly regretting that both it and I were being inflicted on him. The old gaunt look had returned. He was worrying about me, of course, and feeling inept at being unable to help. After constantly glancing at his watch he rose to go five minutes before the end of visiting time.

'Goodnight, m'dear.' His kiss lightly brushed my cheek.

'Goodnight, darling.'

For two more days and nights the monster prevailed, the nurses directed to washing and feeding me, the doctors coming and going with pursed lips, the tears rolling down my cheeks to disappear into the cool white pillow-slip; the sole distraction the periodic turning, inch by agonising inch, over on to the other side.

On the third grim morning, after the same unproductive doctor's round two bright young nurses arrived with fresh bedlinen and I braced myself for the ordeal of being moved. Practised hands rolled me gently to one side of the bed. Astonishing! No extra thrust of pain. They rolled me to the other side. Still no pain! Back and forth I was rolled, my hands and mouth gradually relaxing as no new onslaught of pain materialised.

'There! That wasn't so bad, was it!'

With cheerful smiles, the bundle of bedlinen was removed. And after a few minutes alone I realised that something very strange had happened. It didn't seem possible; it couldn't be so, it simply could not be so. The pain had gone. Totally, utterly, gone! An illusion, a dream. The monster preying on me for two merciless weeks had suddenly vanished as though it had never been. Obliterated, gone! I kept still, afraid to move lest it return. Minutes passed. Still no pain! Gingerly I straightened one leg. No pain. I straightened the other leg. Still no pain. I moved an arm; raised my head. No sign of it. With extreme care I turned slowly over on to the other side. Still no pain.

It's gone! It's really gone! I sank into a stupor of thankfulness,

133

rousing now and then to test with yet another cautious movement that the enemy had really been routed.

Lunch arrived. 'You'll never believe this, nurse. The pain – it's gone! It's gone! I believe I can sit up.'

Sceptical eyes watched me slowly raise myself to a sitting position. The tray was placed on the locker, the pillows re-arranged.

'It's gone! It doesn't hurt any more; I can't believe it, but it doesn't. Pass the tray over, nurse, I think I can feed myself.'

'Splendid! That is good.' With barely concealed scorn, the nurse moved the tray on to my lap and left me to lunch blissfully on steak and kidney pie and then sleep the afternoon away.

Gerald arrived for the evening visit. Spruced up with hairbrush and lipstick. I held out my arms as he approached doubtfully.

'Darling, look, I'm sitting up. The pain is gone – it's gone!'

'Has it really?'

He drew up a chair. I took both his hands in mine, kissed them, held them to my face. 'It's over, darling! It's really over!'

We talked, the pain now relegated to the files of unsolved mysteries. Yes, of course he had missed me, of course he was glad it was over. Yes, he was feeding himself and his job was going well. But his words lacked conviction, no doubt due to strain and worry, I told myself. Of course he was glad!

Later that evening I was almost asleep when without warning there was an uncontrollable gush of fluid into the freshly made bed.

'My God! I've wet the bed!'

A surge of heat was followed by a curious weakness as the fierce discharge slowed down to a steady trickle. I rang the bell.

'I'm terribly sorry, nurse. Something's happened. The bed – it's all wet.' The bedclothes were swept back to reveal a great blackish stain.

'Lie still. Don't move. I'll be back.'

I heard the nurse running down the corridor and remembered

that running was strictly prohibited except in cases of emergency. But I was far too lethargic to worry about that.

The nurse returned with a new young doctor who proceeded to make a lengthy internal examination. Lying on my back, legs spread, I no longer felt embarrassment; that was now a quite superfluous sentiment. After a thorough scrubbing of his hands at the washbasin the doctor turned to me. 'Well, young lady, I think we've been very lucky.'

'Lucky' was hardly the word that came to mind.

'But what's happened, doctor?'

'Well, it was an abscess, all right, and it's burst.'

That obvious explanation had not occurred to me.

'But I don't understand. Where was it?'

'Well, you see, there's a cavity between the front and back passages, the perineal cavity; that's where it must have been. I think it filled the whole cavity. There must have been a pint of fluid in there.'

'But – but what about infection? The baby?'

'Well, again I think we've been lucky. It shouldn't affect the baby. It has all come out, you see, not gone in. Don't you worry about it. Mr Saunders will be in to see you in the morning. You'll have to have injections, of course, as a precaution, but I think we'll be all right.'

Five days later, I was sitting fully dressed on the edge of my bed, I glanced at my watch. Ten to one. Gerald was to collect me before two and take me home. I hoped he'd be early; it would be wonderful to be home again. It must have been difficult for him, worrying on his own, but now I'd be able to make it up to him.

By two o'clock he still hadn't arrived. I put down my book and went over to the tall window. It seemed a long, long time since I had seen anything but the inside of a hospital and it was strangely reassuring to see the grey slate rooftops gleaming softly in the pale afternoon sun, the outside world still there, unchanged. I sat down with my book. He'd arrive at any moment. He'd have had no difficulty getting away from the office.

Two-thirty. Where could he be?

At three o'clock I heard the trundle of the tea trolley along the corridor and begged a cup of tea. I hadn't expected to wait for Gerald today.

He came at four o'clock, flustered and mumbling something about not being able to borrow a car. 'We shall have to go by bus,' he said irritably, as if I were at fault.

'Never mind, darling. It'll be all right.'

I was weaker than I had thought, and there was also the weight of the baby, due in two weeks, resting on the tender area. Before we had walked halfway to the bus stop I was exhausted.

'Please, Gerald. I'm afraid I can't walk so fast.'

He slowed his pace slightly. 'We shall probably miss the bus,' he said petulantly.

I knew the times of all the buses. There was plenty of time.

We reached the stop with twenty minutes to spare.

'Oh, damn!' We were halfway home. Gerald was fumbling in his inside jacket pocket. 'Ah! I thought so.' In his hand was a letter.

'What is it?'

'My letter; I haven't posted it. I must post it today.'

'What letter?' I was puzzled; writing letters was not something he did.

'Er' – impatiently– 'to my mother. I must post it.'

Useless to ask why the urgency, or why he hadn't posted it on his way to the hospital, or while we were waiting at the bus stop, near to a letter-box; he knew perfectly well that once we were on the bus the opportunity was lost. But his set face left no doubt that, for whatever reason, the letter was going to be, already was, an issue.

I searched for a solution, only slightly resentful at being already saddled with one of Gerald's problems. I was too happy to be upset;

happy to be going home, happy to be rid of the pain, happy that as far as we knew the baby had escaped infection, although worry on that score remained.

I had an idea. 'Excuse me, darling.' I was standing up, giving him no choice but to let me pass.

I made my way to the empty seat near the conductor on his platform.

'Excuse me, do you think –?'

The conductor readily agreed to my request.

Gerald stood up to let me back. 'What – what was that about?'

'It's all right. I've asked the conductor to stop outside the post office in the village. You can nip off and post your letter. You'll get the last post. Isn't it sweet of him?'

Gerald was not effusive in his thanks. But I wasn't going to worry about Gerald or his letter. I was better. And I was going home.

Seventeen

I woke at midnight and dashed to the bathroom. My waters had broken. The phrase echoed back from whispered conversations overheard in childhood. It sounded primeval. But then everything about having a baby was primeval. Best wake Gerald. No, it might be hours yet; let him sleep awhile. Wrapped about in an old towel, I slid back into bed to await my first labour pain.

Ought I to have woken him right away? No, not until the pains were coming regularly. He would only be annoyed. He had been in a constant state of annoyance all the past two weeks I'd been home from hospital.

There wasn't very long to wait, only ten minutes or so. Not a pain exactly, more of a fluttering sensation, a cramp, a feeling of breathlessness as if I'd been running. With no idea how to react I mistakenly tensed myself, holding my breath, and in a few frightening seconds, it was over. The adventure had begun.

Limping now and then into the bathroom to check my watch and change the towel, I held out for three hours before nudging Gerald's shoulder.

'Darling!'

No response.

'Gerald!'

'Yes, what is it?' He sounded annoyed already.

'Sorry, darling, it's started. You'll have to go and phone for the ambulance.'

The click of the bedside lamp pierced the silence like an accusation. Jerking up on one elbow, he said testily, 'Are you sure?'

'Yes, I'm sure. The pains are coming every twenty minutes now.'

'You're quite sure, then?'

'Yes, quite sure. Sorry to have to get you up like this.'

'Well, as long as you're sure.' He flounced out of bed. He didn't want to be made a fool of by a false alarm, I told myself.

The pains were coming every seven minutes when we reached the hospital at nearly five in the morning, the district nurse following in her car in case of an emergency on the way.

I heard Gerald accept her offer of a lift back. Well, he was hardly the type to share ordeals.

Drugged with pethidine, unaware of any pains or contractions and with only a blurred impression of a small ward and footsteps coming and going, I was roused hours later by the sudden brisk drawing back of the bedclothes. A clear decisive man's voice said, 'Now this may feel a little cold.'

Half dragging my eyes open, I blinked muzzily in the unexpected glare of broad daylight. Mr Saunders, unclinical in dark suit and tie, had been conjured up from somewhere and was placing upon my bared shiny mound a small trumpet-shaped metal instrument. The silence crackled with tension as he bent down, inclining his ear. I was vaguely aware of three blurred figures ranged like statues at the foot of the bed. Straightening up, Saunders handed the instrument to the nearest, who now materialised as the handsome young house-surgeon. He in turn bent his ear and listened for a moment or two, then a low hum of voices was lulling me off again when Saunders's raised voice reached me.

'Mrs Gardner! Mrs Gardner! Can you hear me?'

I slowly nodded.

'The baby's heartbeats are getting very weak. We're going to help you to have the baby now. All right?'

How was I supposed to respond to that? Too doped to be more than vaguely disturbed by the note of urgency, I grunted.

'We shall have to move you.'

A nod from the urbane little man and the two others, now blearily

139

identified as sister and nurse, hurriedly left. How long had I been there? I peered at my watch, surprised to find it was nearly midday. I was lifted on to a trolley and wheeled swiftly along smooth corridors and through a door, was lifted off again and deposited on my back. Only when I saw the upper halves of five white masked and gowned figures flitting purposefully about, silently, like apparitions, and then caught the gleam of instruments under strong overhead lights did I realise where I was. I'm going to have some sort of operation, I told myself stupidly; but it's no use being frightened, especially if the baby's life depends on it.

For incomprehensible reasons, two pairs of hands were deftly encasing each of my feet in long woolly socks while two more hands hastily removed my watch and wedding-ring. The overall urgency was impressive, alarmingly so; except, I reminded myself, there's no point in being alarmed.

A constricting rubber mask closed over my face, and a firm masculine voice behind me said, 'Now I want you to breathe normally and count to ten, Mrs Gardner.'

It may be the last thing I shall ever do, I thought, and obediently began to count: one, two, three, four, five, six, seven –

The room was in darkness. To the left, faintly outlined against a darkening grey sky and lit by the creamy glow of street lights, I made out the rectangular panes of a tall window, while high up on the right, a sickly yellowish light filtered through a fanlight over a door. I shut my eyes, trying to think, then memory surged back and I remembered when I had last been conscious. In a panic, my hands flew to my abdomen, where they received a sharp shock of the kind that comes with a fall or in missing one's footing. That great hard bulge which seemed to have become a fixture, a permanent part of me, was no longer there. It was missing! Gone! My hands rested on a flat surface of smooth skin which I slowly realised must belong to me.

My God! My baby! What's happened to my baby?

There could not be a baby. Not an actual living baby, not while I lay here consigned to oblivion. Something dreadful must have happened. Panicky moments passed before my fingers found the will to reach up and search for the bell. I found it at last and pressed the button and waited.

The door opened, admitting anaemic light from the corridor, then a loud click shattered the silence like the crack of a whip as the overhead light came on, abruptly restoring the real world. A young nurse, messenger of mercy, stood in the doorway.

'Oh! Awake, are we?'

'Nurse, my baby! What's happened to my baby?'

'It's all right. You've got a lovely little girl.'

'Is that right? Are you sure?'

'Of course I'm sure.' A sympathetic smile helped to ease my fears.

'Is she – is she – all right?'

'Yes, she's perfect.'

Was this said just to appease me? I couldn't be certain until an hour later when the baby was brought to me in the large ward to which I had been moved. Here everything was very different, normal and real; twenty new mothers sitting up, smiling and chattering, swiftly adapting to nature's wily ways.

The five minutes allowed to contemplate the tiny doll-like face, with kisses and hugs and inept murmurs of hello, gave me the most intense joy and happiness I had ever known. I sank back on the pillows hardly able to believe my good fortune. I had a baby and we were both all right. My watch showed almost visiting time. Gerald would soon be able to share in the joy.

The visitors were well established round the other beds when he arrived an incredible fifteen minutes late, having learnt by telephone of the baby's safe delivery. But for some reason he didn't seem particularly pleased, and when he came closer I saw that his face was haggard. Poor darling, he must be worn out with worrying about me. Thank goodness that was all over now.

But he returned from the nursery looking no happier, no less drawn. Where was the delighted smile of the proud father, the loving embrace of the grateful husband? Searching his face, I was shocked to find that he looked peculiarly ill, much like the night of the cinema, only worse, much worse. A black cloud of fear descended, a dark threat of powerful unseen forces.

I cast about for reassurance. He must be awfully tired; it must be that. We chatted in a constrained unnatural fashion so far removed from normal expectations I thought I must be dreaming. He made a show of listening to the outline of the birth but was obviously disinclined to talk. Disinclined to be here at all, I thought, shying away from terror, from a kind of black death advancing inexorably.

'Would you – would you like to go early and get some sleep?' It was only seven-thirty. Visiting was till eight. I only wanted to shake him out of his gloom, never dreamt he would take me seriously.

'Well, if you don't mind, my dear.' Avoiding my eyes, he quickly stood up and was putting on his coat.

'Of course not, darling. You go home and get an early night.'

'See you tomorrow, then.' A token kiss, a mere brush of the lips, and he was gone, leaving me the only mother minus a visitor. Fighting tears, I pretended to read. He couldn't be in the throes of another of his crises. Not now! He must just be very tired; he'd be better tomorrow.

But the next day he was again late and looked no better, his face grey, ghost-like, far worse than I'd ever seen it before, of a different character from the night of the cinema, almost of another dimension.

'What's the matter, darling?'

'Nothing, nothing at all.' He couldn't quite manage a smile. 'I'm just tired, that's all.'

But over the next two days he looked no less haggard, sticking to the tiredness excuse which I believed in even less when he made no attempt to join the nightly procession to the nursery. On the third grim morning I was ashamed to find myself giving way to tears. I kept my streaming face hidden in the pillows, feigning sleep. What was wrong? How could this be happening now, when we had the beautiful healthy baby daughter he'd wanted, and I was set to recover?

'Hello! What's this, then?' A sensible middle-aged nurse bringing the next streptomycin injection had seen my face and, I guessed, automatically blamed post-natal depression. I wished it had been something so readily accepted.

'There's something wrong with my husband,' I whimpered.

With a doubting glance, the nurse gave the injection and left without another word.

Day four brought the luxury of the first visit to the bathroom and it felt very odd to be standing up. Then it seemed a long way to the end of the ward with footsteps that were strangely short and slow, as if I'd suddenly become old and infirm.

I was standing at the washbasin drying myself when suddenly something revoltingly wet and bulky slid silently out from inside me and dropped with an ominous squelchy plop on to the smooth grey-tiled floor. Trembling, I looked down. Sploshed on the floor was a shiny red bulbous blob roughly the size of a tennis ball. At the sight of blood I was no heroine.

'Nurse!' I called. Nurse!'

I stumbled towards the door and the nurse caught me as I dropped in a dead faint.

'It's nothing.'

I was lying on my back, the blankets were folded back and a nurse stood by as the house-doctor's hands prodded my flattened abdomen.

'Nothing to worry about,' he said, not very convincingly, as the bedclothes were replaced. 'Just get some rest.'

Too exhausted actively to worry, I fell into a doze, to be woken later by the sound of my name. I half opened my eyes. Flanked by house-surgeon, ward sister and nurse, Saunders himself stood by my bed. His presence outside normal consultants' rounds boded ill. The bedclothes were again swept back; experienced hands prodded my abdomen.

'It was a piece of placenta left behind,' Saunders explained after his examination. 'We've probably got it all now, but as a precaution we shall have to give you some ergometrine injections and I want you to sit up all the time.' His voice was exceptionally kind, another bad sign.

I mentioned the pain of sitting up, which had been spoiling the precious feeding times.

'You'll be more comfortable when we can remove your stitches,' he said. (What stitches? I wondered, knowing nothing about forceps deliveries. Due to the imminent danger of the baby being suffocated, mine had been carried out before the cervix was fully dilated, hence the incision under anaesthetic.) 'We'll see if we can do that soon. And we'll get you a rubber ring to sit on; that should make it a little easier …' His voice betrayed concern. He turned aside. 'See to that, Sister, will you.'

I happened to have heard of overlooked lethal pieces of placenta. The same offending placenta, I guessed, had obstructed the baby's exit. I was worried. But it would be something to tell Gerald. Perhaps it would deflect him from his own troubles.

But Gerald remained undeflected, hardly reacting at all, not even enquiring after the baby, just sitting there with the same ashen face, the same denial that anything was wrong, leaving me in utter despair, as if I'd been hurled into a dark dungeon from which there was no escape, no means of communication with the outside world.

Late the next morning I roused from a confused dream to see, of all people, like a knight errant, Roger walking towards me. It was hard to resist falling into his arms. I dared not even take his hand. I could only stare at him in amazement and gratitude. Haunted for weeks by Gerald's problems, Gerald's behaviour, Gerald's point of view, I had forgotten, truly forgotten that someone else might actually care about me. Roger had telephoned Saunders and, though not admitting it, was obviously concerned. Smiling feebly, I reported on the birth, saying nothing about Gerald. Gerald would soon be better.

'Thank you for coming,' I whispered.

Watched by inquisitive eyes, he squeezed my hand and then he was gone, my saviour.

'There you are, darling, you take her.' I thrust the soft white bundle into Gerald's arms and leaned back in the taxi seat. The cushioned upholstery felt very kind to my aching back.

'But I don't – er – don't you think you should –?'

'No, I'd like you to hold her. You don't mind, do you? I'm so tired, what with dressing myself and the baby.'

I was longing to hold the baby myself, previous access having been distressingly brief, limited strictly to feeding times, as if the hospital were the legal guardian and the mother merely a wet-nurse. One almost came to believe that the eventual transfer of guardianship would never really happen, that it was only some kind of hallucination. Now that I had walked out unchallenged with the baby in my arms, half expecting her to be wrested away from me before I reached the end of the long corridor, I could wait. Gerald badly needed the contact with the baby daughter he was supposed to have wanted. Holding her for the first time would surely break down the barrier which seemed to have come from nowhere, like an evil spell.

I pretended to doze, to stress the excuse of tiredness, which as it happened was all too real. It had taken a great effort to dress us both. Merely bending over the bed to coax soft limbs into tiny garments with unpractised fingers had been a surprisingly lengthy back-breaking task.

'All right then, you can go,' Saunders had said with an unusual look of sympathy in response to my tearful plea that something was wrong with my husband, 'but you'll have to get plenty of rest. The district nurse will come in every day to finish your course of injections, and she'll also bath the baby until you're on your feet.'

The taxi was well away from the city, I glanced sideways at Gerald, hoping for a sign that he'd returned to his senses. Perhaps he was smiling down at the baby; perhaps he'd even smile at me or, if not actually smile, then assume an expression recognisably human as opposed to his unbearably doomed look. But he was looking stiffly out of the window, the soft bundle held slightly away on his lap. I saw him snatch a quick glance down at the small face half hidden in the folds of the shawl and then quickly away again as if he were being awkwardly imposed upon. How was this to be borne? It couldn't go on. He'd surely come round soon.

The carpeted taxi was relaying up through my feet a message that hard hospital floors were about to give way to home comforts. I've escaped, I thought, I haven't died, I'm alive, and I've got the baby; I'm going home with my baby. I willed myself into a doze. When I woke, he'd be smiling and life would begin again. The taxi rolled smoothly along; not far to go now. He must be glad I'd recovered, must be delighted with the baby.

We reached Stowbury and slowed down through the village, picking up a little speed for the next mile before slowing down again to turn right off the main road. The sound of traffic receded, the bumpier surface of the lane was beneath us. In a moment we'd be home. I stole another quick sideways look. Gerald was still turned to the window, upright, rigid, the limp white bundle still held at bay.

I looked away. This couldn't last; it would have to stop soon.

The house seemed familiar only in a strange unreal way, as if after a prolonged absence. In the corner of the hall the roll of red stair-carpet stood untouched, like a reproach, where I had left it.

I hung up my coat and Gerald followed me into the sitting-room. I looked round in bewilderment at the new furnishings I had wanted so badly – the light oak dining suite, the wing-back fireside chairs, the carpet square – how could they have mattered so much? How gladly I would have exchanged them all for one kind smile from my husband, standing awkwardly by like a porter waiting to be relieved of his burden. I took the baby from him and went slowly over to my chair, appalled at the amount of effort needed to move.

September had come in damp and cool, and before setting out Gerald had excelled himself by lighting a fire. He had banked it up high and now it was burning through brightly. He bent down close to my chair to remove the wire mesh guard and I waited for his hand to touch my shoulder and banish the nightmare; but he set the guard aside and moved away.

'I'll make tea,' he said.

I hugged the baby close as he left the room. I unwound the shawl and gazed down in wonder at the smooth tiny face still lost in sleep. How could such joy not be shared by a father?

Gerald entered with the tray, and I tucked the baby up in the carrycot I'd left ready. It would soon be time for the next feed. Without a word he handed me the tea and sat down with his own cup, busily turning the pages of the *Radio Times*.

When he rose for a refill I caught him by the hand.

'Darling, please tell me what's wrong.'

'It's nothing,' he snapped, snatching his hand away. 'Nothing – I've told you, I'm just tired.'

I hadn't the energy, or the heart, to pursue it. I stared at the fire, and an old, old question, one that I had thought gone for good, began echoing away at the back of my mind like an ancient whispered curse: how could one feel so broken up inside – as if all one's bones were smashed to pieces – without some physical damage actually having taken place?

Switching on the radio, Gerald kept his head bent over his book

147

while he listened to a long programme about birds, followed by the news and discussions. I dozed for a while, thinking as I roused to feed the baby that he couldn't watch this and remain unmoved. But he didn't watch, his head stayed down throughout, the only sounds the faint sucking, and the intermittent swish and pop of the fire. Too tired, too shocked to protest, I changed the baby, murmuring 'Hello' as she stared up at me with her large dark eyes, thankful that she was ready to succumb when I put her down to sleep. I'd better do something about dinner, I thought, and went to look for tins in the larder.

Fending off all further attempts at conversation, and totally ignoring the eleven o'clock feed, Gerald took the carrycot upstairs for me without a downward glance. I could hardly find the strength to climb the stairs for the four hours' sleep till the next feed.

The next morning he left abruptly for work without a word of goodbye, and I crept about all day in a haze of fatigue, barely able to hope he would come home improved. But the same afflicted face came in the door. No answering kiss, no word of greeting. Even more wounding and incredible, not so much as a glance at the carrycot in the corner.

What was wrong with him? How long would this go on?

It went on for weeks with no change, no sign of improvement, no glance at wife or baby; hiding behind the newspaper during breast feeding; working, eating, reading, listening in, sleeping. And except for brief chilling answers, not a word.

Would he improve with time? He'd probably eaten little in the evenings; hadn't slept, either. And in time, with regular meals and sleep, he did become less gaunt and wan. But he still didn't talk, just ignored me.

I hadn't the energy for tears. It took all my strength to rise, wash and dress, feed and change the baby, wash nappies and other essentials, prepare food. At ten each morning the district nurse came briskly to bath-time on the kitchen table, and between feeds the baby slept well; I must be doing something right. I rested at the window, waiting for the ordeal to end. The weather had brightened, the view over the Erme valley was as lovely and peaceful as ever. Only Gerald had changed, was in the grip of some temporary madness which must soon pass.

Weeks later he at last spoke out.

'I'm afraid I'm impotent,' he said.

I didn't believe this; it was just worry and pressure. And despite a total lack of sexual desire I proved him wrong as soon as the six weeks of post-natal bleeding ended. But it made no difference. The next day the same dead face came in the door, a blank, as if I weren't there at all.

November came in with little change in the mild weather. The autumn colours arrived, and I became stronger and began to wheel the pram out along the lane. Then I remembered how I had looked forward to this simple pleasure and hastily blotted away the tears in case someone came along or the baby woke.

Gerald became very angry when, in desperation, I suggested seeing a doctor. His anger brought a slight relief; it proved that he had some feelings, he was alive and not permanently metamorphosed into some kind of automaton. I threatened to see the doctor myself. 'If you do that I shall leave you,' he said, steely-voiced, grim-faced. My enemy.

How could this have happened? Nothing about it was real.

'You're not impotent,' I told him. 'It must be something else.'

'There is nothing else,' he muttered.

I was living with a dead man.

In an unguarded moment he admitted that the usual tracking down of his forgotten 'points', although continuing, was contained and causing no new problems, and his job was going well.

I ran out of guesses. I could only wait for him to smile again.

I had written telling Helen of the birth, but saying nothing about Gerald. Then I heard that she, too, had given birth to a little girl and both were safe.

There was endless fascination and challenge in caring for Melanie, the name originally chosen by Gerald, though it was impossible to reconcile the prospective proud father summoning an imaginary Melanie along the lane with the man now unable to look at his daughter.

Melanie never relaxed when awake, and she was easily startled by small sounds, always listening intently, trying to ascertain what was going on. I picked up hints about baby rearing from any mother of the slightest acquaintance in the village. I was feeling better and began to enjoy being at home. I even found myself singing again in my old light-hearted fashion, glad to be alive with my baby, as I moved more freely about the house.

Then when Melanie was ten weeks old a curious event occurred.

I was humming while changing her nappy one afternoon when I noticed that she was staring up at me with something more than her usual intensity. She then began to make an odd new kind of moaning sound which could only be interpreted as an attempt to copy my humming. After a minute or two of intense effort, the small body arched, the face rigid with concentration, the moaning sound stopped very abruptly, her body collapsed and she burst into loud frantic crying.

She'd never cried like this before. There was something desperate about it, something frightening. Pacified and tucked up, she fell asleep instantly, almost as if knocked unconscious.

All afternoon I puzzled over this unusual occurrence. A lowering sky was sending down an authentic sample of Devon rainfall, dimming the greens with a fine mist. I stared at the dappled window, wondering what had caused the unprecedented outburst of crying.

Finding Gerald a shade less antagonistic than usual that evening,

I asked him to watch while I changed Melanie's nappy. 'Something odd happened today,' I said. 'I don't know if it will happen again, but we'll see.'

Standing there beside him I felt a sudden curious elation. We were communicating. There was an odd sense of kinship, as if I were sharing a mission with a stranger who also happened to be my husband.

I began to hum as I removed the safety pin and there came the same fixed stare and the same peculiar sound of the afternoon, sustained for a few minutes before being followed by the same collapse into loud hysterical crying. Soothed and petted, Melanie again fell asleep very promptly, like a light going out.

I turned to Gerald. 'Do you see, I suddenly realised this afternoon what was happening. She was trying to copy my humming. Imagine it! I never dreamt a baby could be so responsive at two months.'

Gerald was contemplating his daughter with a grudging touch of tenderness. 'Yes,' he said with a rueful smile, 'there's no doubt about it, she's like me, all right.' His span of co-operation exhausted, he hurriedly left the room, leaving me flabbergasted.

What had made him say the baby was like him? He had shut himself off again, the magic moment of standing over our daughter like normal parents was over, and it was days before I could ask him what he'd meant. Mildly interested, he considered carefully before admitting that he didn't know why the baby was like him. 'I just know that she is,' he insisted.

'But what makes you say that? Don't you wonder? Don't you want to know?'

'Not particularly. After all, we all are as we are, aren't we,' he said, resuming his interrupted reading.

But I wanted to know, I had to know, for here was something I didn't understand about my daughter. The important, the urgent daunting question being, if she did resemble her father, did that – could that – mean that she too might become mentally ill?

And as if that question wasn't enough, another followed:

If she was like her father, could an understanding of her lead to an understanding of what was wrong with him? How had I not realised before that infancy was the one period of Gerald's life I knew nothing about?

But could something so long ago, so unknown, be relevant? The idea that something in infancy could be affecting the behaviour of a grown man seemed to my uninformed mind absurd, irrational, unconnected in any way with real people living ordinary lives. And what I knew of the rest of Gerald's life had so far given no help. There could be no harm in trying to enquire about his infancy. In fact, if only for Melanie's sake, I had to do this.

Are we, I wondered, as Gerald had so often claimed, unalterably as we are? I'd never been able to argue with that, though it had left me vaguely unsatisfied. Were we unalterable? One heard of people changing. Or more to the point, why was Gerald as he was?

New trains of thought provided a kind of escape from the frustration and misery of being married to a robot.

Babies thrive on imitation, so it wasn't necessarily remarkable to try to imitate a mother's humming. But why the unnaturally sudden cessation and tears?

A baby might be aware that she couldn't reproduce the humming accurately, hence the tears of frustration or anger. But would a baby aged only two months be capable of even distinguishing between the two sounds, her own and her mother's, let alone be upset by a discrepancy?

Remembering her peculiarly strained expression as she attempted the copying, another explanation – possibly linked to the first – suggested itself: that the degree of effort needed had been so excessive for her age and capabilities that it quickly led to a collapse in tears of exhaustion.

Of course! That was it! It was not the act of imitation itself that mattered but the *degree of effort* involved. One of Gerald's very harmful tendencies was that he was apt to put far too much effort for ordinary comfort and peace of mind into most of his endeavours. Here, then, was a link, tenuous but still a link, between father and daughter.

The question of excessive effort began to revolve endlessly like a perpetual spinning-top, giving me no peace. Then I remembered that Gerald had not been passed A1 fit at his first army medical because of a condition known as disorderly action of the heart, the medical name for which was Effort Syndrome. This had conveyed nothing to me. I had been content to learn that it was harmless but I asked why it should preclude an A1 pass. Because, Gerald said, they don't know if it will remain harmless under combat conditions so they play for safety.

Now I was even more puzzled and confused. What was the connection, if any, between effort – or Effort Syndrome – and Gerald's mental problems? Could his problems be connected with the heart, which is associated with strain and effort?

What did it all mean?

Eighteen

'Would you like to hold her?'

Mary Gardner backed away from her new granddaughter.

'Oh, no, I can't hold a baby!'

'You can't hold a baby? Is there something wrong with your arm?'

'Oh, no, it's not that.'

'But – I don't understand. What do you mean?'

I hugged three-month-old Melanie a little closer. The death of Gerald's father a year ago had left his mother free to travel, and in the desperate hope that it might do some good, perhaps create a more natural atmosphere, I had suggested inviting her for Christmas, and Gerald had immediately agreed. Was this a good sign? I wondered.

Having brought his mother home from the station on the bus, he was now in the kitchen making tea.

'No,' Mrs Gardner said, looking down at Melanie with a reminiscent half-smile. 'I've never been able to hold a baby.'

'Why ever not?' I hid my astonishment. It might give offence.

'I don't know, I don't, really!' Mrs Gardner gave a careless shrug. 'I just couldn't.'

My astonishment grew. A mother who couldn't hold a baby. And saw this as nothing remarkable.

'But – I don't see how you managed.' I kept a straight face. 'I mean, when you had your own babies.'

'Oh, I never picked them up. I couldn't.' The same offhand manner.

'But how did you manage?'

'Oh, Frank used to help with all that.'

Elaine and Gerald at a friend's farm in Devon.

Elaine, c. 1940.

Gerald in battledress.

The family pub.

Baby Gerald with his mother.

Gerald's father.

Elaine's mother.

Elaine (right) and siblings, on a family day out at Victoria Park.

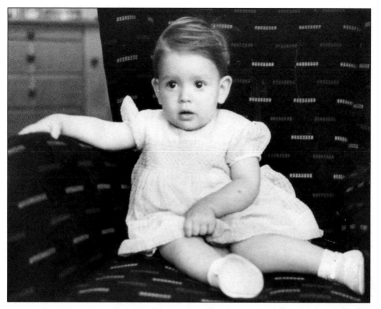

Baby Melanie, aged one year.

Melanie at Paignton beach, aged 2½,
with her bunny.

In Piccadilly Circus, snapped by a street photographer after the wedding.

'Did he – did he hand them to you for feeding, then?'

'Oh, no, I couldn't have them on my lap.' The matter-of-fact tone again. Seeing my puzzlement, with a patient shrug Mrs Gardner repeated, 'I couldn't have them on my lap either.'

'But how did you manage to feed them?'

'Oh, they had their bottle in their cot, of course.'

'Melanie's due for a sleep,' I said. I needed to think about this. 'I'll just tuck her in. Won't you sit down? Gerald won't be long.'

A baby who had never been held by its mother! Two babies, in fact, for there was Gerald's sister, Ethel, who had called in with her two boys and her electrician husband, Dick, during one of my early visits to Beston. They lived nearby in their own modern house and appeared to be an ordinary sensible couple.

When I came back downstairs, Gerald had not yet brought in the tea. No doubt he was wrestling with one of his problems. Sitting down opposite Mrs Gardner, I seized the opportunity to ask what Gerald had been like as a baby.

'Oh, he was all right,' she replied, in the same offhand manner. 'A bit nervy, you know.'

A bit nervy. This was interesting, more interesting than surprising.

'In what way, nervy?'

'Oh, I don't know, really. Always on edge, he was –' Pausing, she added casually, as a mere afterthought, 'Of course, he used to scream a lot at night.'

'Scream –? Do you mean in his sleep?'

'Well, I don't know, really – yes, I daresay it was in his sleep.' Calm and flat, her voice held no sign of emotion. 'Anyway, in the middle of the night it used to be, he'd scream something awful.'

'Poor kid!' I was getting warmer. And angrier, but I kept that hidden. 'What – er – what did you do?'

'Well – well, now –' A dubious pause. I gave an encouraging smile. 'You, er, you won't laugh at me, will you?'

155

'No, of course not!'

'Well, I know you'll think I'm daft – but do you know what I used to do –?'

'No – no, I don't.'

'Well, now …' Another pause. Simpering like a naughty school-girl, Mrs Gardner continued, 'Don't laugh, will you, but I used to go and sit beside his cot and hold his hand. Daft, wasn't it?' She threw me a bashful questioning look and I smiled in feigned sympathy, hiding my amazement as she went on, 'Used to hold it for ages, I did, through the bars, then he used to go to sleep again. Do you – do you think it was daft?'

'No, of course I don't!' At least she had held his hand. That was something. Gerald's entry with the tea brought the session to a close, and it occurred to me later that neither Mrs Gardner nor my own mother in her letters had asked a single question about my confinement. Life's surprises did not seem to err on the side of kindness.

At bedtime I asked Gerald if his parents already had their pub when he was born. Opportunities for delving into his infancy were coming sooner than I had dared hope, his mother's presence having softened him slightly, made him less hostile, and he responded readily, more like the old Gerald.

'Oh, yes,' he said. 'My father had the pub before he married. Probably that's why he married,' he added on a practical note, with no hint of censure, 'to get some free help.'

'Then your mother was pretty busy when you were a baby?'

'She was busy all right, in fact she ran the place single-handed.'

'What did your father do?'

'What he'd always done, he drank. My earliest recollection of my father' – again the note of enthusiasm – 'was of him lying insensible on the floor. He spent quite a lot of time like that,' he added with an indulgent smile.

I pictured the large prone figure on the floor. If only some of this touching devotion could have rubbed off on me.

'And Ethel was two when you were born?'

'Yes, that's right.'

'Your mother certainly had her hands full then. Didn't your father help at all?'

'Oh, he'd do the cellar work and all the heavy lifting. Strong as an ox, he was! He'd sit in the public bar, drinking – whisky, of course – but' – boastfully – 'it would take two or three bottles to lay him out. While that was being soaked up he'd take charge of the bar. It was a pretty rough place in those days. Regular trouble-makers, drunks, you know the sort of thing –'

I knew of no such thing, nor did I want to know.

'I've seen him,' Gerald continued, again with the fond smile that had me squirming, 'pick up a great navvy and hurl him out of the door on to the pavement.' Recalling those hefty shoulders I could well believe it. I was glad I had raised the subject. Not only was some valuable background being filled in, but this was the longest conversation we had had for months.

Keeping up the pretence of normality during this visit was not as difficult as I had feared, especially since Mrs Gardner seemed not to notice that her son never once smiled at his wife or baby and never spoke first to his wife, only answered her in monosyllables. But his face gave nothing away, he appeared outwardly to be his old pleasant courteous self, and I wondered if his show of cheerfulness would continue when we were alone.

No such luck. The cheerfulness vanished abruptly with his mother's departure, like turning off a tap, and I didn't see him smile again until eight months later, when she accepted our invitation for a summer visit.

By now I was gaining strength. Roger had checked my progress with Mr Saunders after each routine post-natal examination and occasionally called with Muriel or the two younger boys to see me and the baby, friendly faces appearing at the door like visitors from another planet, a place where normal people lived, a vision sometimes recalled for a giddy moment when a snatched glance said that nothing had changed between us.

The slow haul back to health had left little energy for rebellion against Gerald. For months after his remark that Melanie was like him I constantly asked myself if I was doing the right thing. Or was I in some obscure way condemning my daughter to a life of misery? Gradually I gained confidence as she made good progress. My fears for her abated and Gerald's coldness, his enmity, rose to the fore. Still no sign of improvement, no explanation, a slow choking existence as if one were trapped inside a thick ball of wool.

By the time his mother arrived for her second visit rebellion had begun to simmer deep down, but I dutifully played hostess while he was away at work, initiating walks, chatting in the garden, trying to smile, only with difficulty resisting the temptation to blurt something out.

Towards the end of the fortnight I had worked myself up to a pitch of desperation for some sign of a reprieve. I brooded about it. Gerald should long ago have told me what was wrong. I couldn't wait any longer, I had to know. Wheeling the pram up the lane with his mother on a warm August afternoon, idly discussing the Devon weather, I decided that something would have to be done. No more delay.

I waylaid Gerald after dinner that evening as he came down from the bathroom.

'Would you come into the kitchen a minute? I'd like a word.'

Carefully checking that the sitting-room door was closed, he stepped into the kitchen and I followed him in, quietly closing the door and turning to face him. He regarded me warily.

'Look, Gerald, I've been thinking. Perhaps – perhaps your mother could help.'

He stiffened. Probably, as I had feared, this was a poor idea; but what else was there?

'What do you mean, help?' His voice was steely.

'I wondered – couldn't we tell her you've not been well? Perhaps – I don't know – perhaps she could help.'

His voice rose in anger. 'I forbid you to say a word.'

'But we've got to do something. We can't go on like this.'

'There's nothing we can do.'

'But there must be something.'

'There's nothing.'

My pent-up frustration began to surface. I didn't want to check it; I was ready to explode.

'Well, are you going to tell me what's wrong?' I shouted.

I'd never raised my voice to him before, but now I was past caring. Little good had it done me, avoiding scenes, endlessly kowtowing.

'I've told you, I can't.'

'Well, let's talk to your mother, then. It might do some good.'

'No, I won't have that.' His voice was razor-sharp. It roused me to fury. I'd been tormented long enough. Subservience and caution were cast aside. I lost all grip on myself.

'Well, if you won't tell her, I will!' I shrieked.

Boiling with anger, Gerald took two fast strides towards me, and the next moment had struck me hard in the face.

'Oh!' I reeled backwards, a hand clutching my face. Sobbing uncontrollably, I ran out of the room and out of the house and on up the lane to the main road until breathlessness slowed me down. I was beside myself with hurt and rage. Didn't he know I would never actually have said anything to his mother? Didn't he know?

In the few frantic seconds before leaving the house I had known what I was going to do. I had even summoned up the presence of mind to snatch up my coin purse from the kitchen table. I was going to phone Roger and ask for help. Why care any longer that Gerald had forbidden it? What if he did leave me? I had done all I could. It was time for someone else to take over.

Between sobs, I gasped into the phone, 'You've got to help Gerald.

I think – I think he's mad. He hasn't spoken to me for nearly a year – ever since the baby was born. He won't see you about it and he won't go to a specialist either. What can I do?'

Roger's voice, his professional one, calm and soothing, came over the wire. I sensed the presence of a patient. He must be taking evening surgery.

'Now try not to worry, I'm sure we can help you. When will you be free? I'll come and see you.'

He meant when would I be alone. Today was Friday. Gerald's mother was leaving on Sunday. 'Monday morning,' I said.

'Right-ho, I'll come and see you then. Now try not to worry too much.'

Rounding the last bend in the lane, I became fearful. My home had become enemy territory. Tucking my sodden handkerchief into the sleeve of my cardigan, I opened the front door and stepped inside.

An unnatural hush hung in the air, broken by a furtive murmur of voices from behind the sitting-room door. Thank goodness Melanie was asleep upstairs. The voices ceased abruptly as I entered the room, and my drawn blotchy face drew uneasy glances.

Something happened then. Perhaps those hastily hushed voices had suggested a conspiracy which I must now fight. What had Gerald told his mother? No doubt some plausible fabrication making light of our raised voices. Without a glance at my adversaries I walked over to Gerald's radio and switched on the Third Programme, then I crossed to the chair by the window and sat gazing out at a serene summer world.

Music filled the room. Beethoven's Eroica.

To Gerald's ears, and to his mother's, classical music was as jarring as jazz was to mine. Through half-closed eyes I saw uncertainty cross their faces, then without a word they rose and together left the room. The door closed behind them.

I leaned back, closing my eyes as the music rose above my head like healing waters. At the end of the symphony I looked out across the sloping fields towards the distant skyline. And it dawned on me then, for the first time in that long year of estrangement, that somewhere out there another kind of life existed. It was out there, somewhere.

Hold on to that, I said to myself, gazing into the distance. Hold on to that.

Nineteen

I had given up going with Gerald to the front door in the mornings. The hope of some last-minute sign of farewell, a mere flash of recognition, had all but gone. But today change was in the air, and on an impulse I went and held the door open for him with a murmured, 'Bye'. But I might have known he would just stride past without a look.

I watched the back of his fawn raincoat descend the stone steps. No parting twist of the head, no little nod, just the set shoulders disappearing down the lane.

I stood still for a moment, contemplating the damp greens of the garden. Soon leaves would begin to fall and a second winter of despondency would be upon us. But perhaps I'd now be spared.

What if Gerald had known not only that a week ago, here in our own house, he had not only been discussed with Roger but that this morning some of his innermost secrets were going to be shared with a psychiatrist? Would he attack me? Leave me?

I closed the front door and went upstairs for Melanie. She'd be fed and bathed and ready for her morning sleep by the time the new doctor, Roger's psychiatrist friend, head of the local mental hospital, came at eleven. Probably there would be no choice but to tell this man all he wanted to know. 'Don't worry about it,' Roger had said. 'He's a very decent chap. You won't find it at all awkward.'

I knew better. I would find it extremely awkward, parading naked – so to speak – before a stranger.

Finding myself alone with Roger had been like coming home after a long, tiring journey. All my fine resolve melted away in an instant and I collapsed on his shoulder as he walked in the door.

'Roger, darling, darling.' I kissed him frantically, and the next moment we were lying on the carpet, my dress was up, and a storm of passion stripped away the long bleak separation.

It was quickly over. We lay there in silence, lost, gone. I came to slowly, as from a deep faint, and sat up. Sitting up beside me, Roger laid an arm round my shoulders, kissed me.

'Sweetheart,' he said, 'I want us to go away. When I heard you on the phone the other day – I can't stand any more of this.'

I kissed him, then drew back, gazing into his frank blue eyes.

'Darling, I'm sorry. I shouldn't have done this. I don't know what possessed me, but I couldn't –'

His fingers touched my lips. 'Don't ever say sorry to me. There's no need, you know that.'

'Yes, I know, darling.'

'So what about it? Haven't you had enough punishment? I know I have. Are we going to be together? Isn't it about time?'

'Roger, darling, you know we can't; if only we could. The children –'

He was quiet.

'Come here.' He pulled me on to his lap. Clasping me round the waist, he began rocking me to and fro, kissing my hair. 'Yes, I know you're right,' he murmured. 'I wish you weren't.' He kissed my cheeks, my eyes, my lips. His face rested against mine for a few moments.

'Now,' he said, drawing back and looking into my eyes, 'tell me what's been going on …'

I settled Melanie down in her cot and came downstairs ready to commit myself to the coming inquisition, but with one important stipulation: I was not going to talk about my sex life. If all the stories one heard were to be believed, it seemed that little else counted. I had often wondered if sexual information was sought by psychiatrists purely in the interests of the patient. Was there a need to fill in gaps in their own experience? Or were they, perhaps subconsciously, feeding a salacious curiosity?

The expected knock came promptly at eleven.

About forty-five, tallish, broad-shouldered, good-looking with plentiful dark wavy hair and a well-fed unlined face, Mr Richardson looked very solid and reliable in his dark blue double-breasted suit. My kind of man, I thought, the kind I should have married.

'Mrs Gardner?'

I held out my hand. 'Mr Richardson? It's so good of you to come.'

His quick searching glance flicked down the front of my plain white blouse, and I felt his eyes travel down the back of my straight navy skirt as he followed me into the sitting-room. I sensed his swift appraisal of the room and pictured the comfortable home of this man of substance and his lucky wife.

He declined coffee. We sat down in the two facing armchairs, and I braced myself for a string of embarrassing questions as he leaned back, hitched up a trouser leg to reveal a neat dark blue sock, crossed his legs and flung me a disarming smile.

'Now tell me about your husband.'

It was like one of those ensnaring exam questions: 'Discuss the novels of H. G. Wells'. Where to begin? What to include? What to omit? There was nothing for it but to plunge into a lengthy recital of all that seemed relevant, which appeared to be what was wanted, judging by the understanding nods and the lack of interruption. Until I blundered by mentioning Gerald's fear of impotence.

The dreaded question was put in an offhand manner: 'And how is your sex life?'

I felt myself blushing. 'It's perfectly all right,' I said firmly and, I hoped, dismissively.

There was no further probing. I needn't have worried.

Mr Richardson was turning the pages of a pocket diary.

'From what you say' – his manner was crisp and professional but not unfriendly – 'your husband definitely needs treatment. Now can we make an appointment for him to come and see me at the hospital?'

After all my explanations, how could this expert imagine that that would be quite so easy? 'I've tried that,' I said. 'I'm afraid that's one of the difficulties. He won't go.'

'Well, then, I shall have to come and see him.'

How simple he made this sound. Had he not heard me? He turned a page of his diary. 'What about tomorrow evening?'

'Well …' I bit my lip. 'It's very good of you. He'll be here, but – I don't know how to tell him.'

'Well, no need to tell him. I could just turn up.'

I shuddered, envisaging untold violent consequences. Was the man a simpleton?

'I don't think that would be a good idea.'

'Well, I shall have to leave that to you,' he said briskly, rising to go. 'Shall we say eight o'clock tomorrow evening?'

'All right, doctor. And thanks again for coming.'

I had only a vague idea of how to inform Gerald of my treachery. First give him his dinner to promote relaxation. Later, when I saw him looking through the *Radio Times*, I knew the moment had come.

'I've something to tell you.'

He looked up. For more than a week, ever since the angry slap, we had hardly exchanged a word.

'Now please – please don't be angry with me. The other day' – he obviously knew to which day I referred – 'I was very upset. I had to do something. We can't go on like this.' I was watching his face; he didn't look angry, not yet. 'I phoned Roger.'

His expression changed to something more like embarrassment than anger. 'You did?' His voice was icy.

'Yes, I had to. You mustn't mind.'

He minded. Very much. His face said so.

'And what did you tell him?'

'Don't worry. I didn't tell him much, just that you're over-wrought.'

'And what did he say to that?'

'Well, he thinks you ought to see a specialist.'

'I'm not going. You know that.'

'Yes, I know. But – look, you won't get angry, will you. He's coming here.'

'Who's coming here?'

'The specialist. At eight o'clock this evening.'

Now he looked angry, but not explosively so. In a quiet controlled voice, he said, 'You had no right to do that.' A trapped expression came over his face. His eyes darted about uncertainly. Then, hurriedly thrusting his newspaper down on the table, he sprang up and strode out of the room. I heard him go upstairs, where Melanie was asleep in her cot.

A void of silence descended on the house like a death knell.

At seven-thirty I heard him come down. Had he been packing his bags? Was he going to attack me? Would he merely refuse to see the doctor?

He came into the room looking peculiarly stern and more severely withdrawn than I could ever have thought possible.

'All right.' More than curt, his voice was corrosive. 'I'll see him,' he said, 'but it won't do any good.'

I rose and went to the door. 'I'll make some more tea,' I said.

Promptly at eight o'clock I heard Mr Richardson's knock at the front door. Not daring to look at Gerald, I went to let him in. With a nervous smile, I took his coat and showed him into the sitting-room. Would Gerald be aggressive? Nasty? Violent?

To my great relief and, once more, to my surprise, he rose from his chair and held out his hand, the picture of courtesy. It struck me, not for the first time, how he could always contrive, in his worn old blue

166

sports jacket and baggy grey flannels, to look the picture of a confident young country gentleman who need never bother about making an impression with smart clothes.

'Good evening, old man.' Gerald indicated my vacant fireside chair. 'Do sit down.'

Much as I longed to be able to listen in, I couldn't leave the door open, Gerald would only get up and rectify the omission, and he would not forget it. Closing the door quietly behind me, I retreated upstairs.

Chin in hand, I crouched on the edge of the bed near the wide open door, straining forward to listen but catching only a faint drift of voices from below. Twenty unbearably long minutes passed as I sat out this longed-for interview that could save our lives. The tone of the voices seemed pleasantly conversational, civilised. At least there was no angry scene, not yet. What were they saying? Was Gerald admitting to his problems? Was he agreeing to treatment? If so, did that mean he would be cured? That he should ever be cured seemed far too much to hope for, an almost forgotten dream. Prisoners can be drained to a point beyond hope, beyond dreams.

The sitting-room door opened and a soft murmur of voices filtered up from the hall. I slipped out on to the landing and, without shame, leaned over the banister to listen.

'Well, goodbye, old man.' (Gerald's voice, very cordial.)

'Goodbye, Mr Gardner. Now you will phone and make that appointment, won't you.'

'Leave it to me, old man.' (Gerald's hearty human voice, the one reserved for social occasions.)

The front door closed. I subsided on to the bed. Face in hands, I rocked slowly back and forth like an abandoned infant in an orphanage.

Of course! Of course! How obvious his plan was! And how simple! I might have known. I should have known that Gerald would never be so easily caught. All he had needed was a neat way to avoid being trapped into an appointment, for naturally he had no intention of keeping that glib promise to telephone.

I stared numbly down at my new pink carpet. Beaten! Defeated! Was there any other way of dealing with the situation? No, the patient himself had to volunteer for treatment. The whole painful exercise had been for nothing.

Twenty

'All right, then, since you must know, I'm going to tell you what's wrong.'

Gerald's voice did not sound friendly. But not only was he breaking a long silence, he evidently meant to say something important.

In the few days since the consultant's visit there had been no eruption of anger, as I had feared. Instead, he had wrapped himself up in a thick blanket of silence, his lean face shrunken away to a point where in no way, on no level, could he be reached. We had been enduring another hostile evening when he had suddenly lowered his newspaper.

I looked up from my book. He was no less gaunt or disturbed. His eyes were blazing with a suppressed fury as he regarded me with a decisive no-nonsense air which I then countered with a convincing show of steadiness. So contact, of a kind, had been made, though the etched lines of his face put me in mind of duels at dawn. Swords or pistols? Melodramatic nonsense, I told myself.

Folding his newspaper, he slapped it down on his lap. No more delay now, no awkward pause. Gerald had made up his mind.

'You remember when you were ill and Roger came to see you here?'

'Yes.'

'Well, do you remember what happened?'

'Of course I do.'

'You remember everything?'

'Yes, of course!'

'You remember, then, that I – that I – ?' He paused, looked away.

'That you what?' I spoke quietly. Was he going to prevaricate now? Stop altogether?

He turned slowly back. 'That I wasn't in the room?'

'Yes – I remember.'

'I mean, that I wasn't in the room when you were examined?'

'Yes, I do remember that.'

'Well, that was it!' he exclaimed dramatically, lowering his eyes again as if this were more than sufficient explanation, the concluding statement for the prosecution.

'But – I don't understand …'

There came a breath of suspicion that perhaps I did begin to understand, that here was a glimpse into Gerald's bizarre point of view which, however unlikely, must represent the cause of his breakdown. But the only sane response was to reject this explanation as too trifling to be worthy of recognition, beyond reason.

He raised his head. His face wore the look of a hanging judge passing sentence.

'That sort of thing is very important to me,' he said curtly.

'Well, I thought it was, that's why I left it to you.'

'Precisely!' The clipped tone again, the foreman of the jury pronouncing me guilty. But guilty of what?

'What do you mean?'

'You must know what I mean.'

'I don't.'

His face registered disbelief.

'I really don't.'

He looked away, and I wondered if that would be the end of it. But he turned back belligerently. 'You didn't want me in the room with you.'

'But I did!' I felt a certain relief. The long drawn-out battle over nothing – just one of his trifles – must be ending. But I was forgetting the importance of 'trifles' to Gerald.

'Then why didn't you ask me to stay?'

'I was thinking of you. I thought you might be embarrassed. That's why I left it to you.' (This nonsense must be nearly over.)

'You didn't want me.'

There was an appeal here that I couldn't resist. Entirely forgiving him the angry slap, I moved on to his knees and began kissing his set face. 'Darling, I always want you, I always need you. You know that.'

No reply. He didn't budge. But I could still win him over. Tilting his face back, I kissed him on the lips for the first time in months.

No response whatever, like kissing the lips of someone asleep – or someone dead, I thought in dismay.

'Darling, kiss me and let's forget all about it. Let's be happy. I love you, you know that.' He must know it. Not in the way I loved Roger, of course, but in the older, purely romantic way that clung to me like a second skin.

Not a move. His eyes stayed averted.

'Please kiss me.'

'I can't.'

I resumed my chair. I must be dreaming. Could this feeble explanation by any ordinary known reckoning, by any reach of the imagination, account for such drastic consequences? There must be something else. He was staring blankly ahead, wreathed in tension, looking horribly drawn and ill.

What was the right thing to say, the right line to take? Slumped on my elbows, I kneaded my temples with my fingertips, thinking, thinking – I raised my head.

'Look, Gerald, you must see that you've got it all wrong. I can understand that you were upset at the time but don't forget I was in agony and I was very worried about the baby. It was really up to you, wasn't it, to decide whether you wanted to stay in the room or not.'

'You decided for me.'

'But I didn't. I left it to you.'

'It was obvious,' he said coldly, 'that you didn't want me there.'

'But don't you see, that's where you're wrong! I did want you! I always want you with me!'

171

'Well, there's no point in arguing about it. It's done now.'

In the deathly silence that followed I burrowed deep for clues, for escape from a dead end.

'Tell me,' I said, 'what is it that's really bothering you? That you think I didn't want you with me? – because we both know that isn't so, don't we – or was it, is it, something else?' A glimmer of a possible truth had flashed up only to vanish like a half-remembered dream.

Gerald was not answering, and the thin suspicion gained ground.

'Look, I've got to ask you this. It doesn't make sense but I'll ask you anyway. Is it that – is it because you weren't actually in the room, the fact that you weren't actually present, that's upsetting you? I mean, regardless of why you weren't there, regardless of how that came about?' Now I was sure I had guessed the truth. Not that I understood it.

He met my gaze. 'Yes, I suppose that was it.'

'Did it – does it – really mean so much to you?'

'Yes, it does.'

'But it's over now! It's all finished! And there's the baby; we've got the baby now. We can forget all about it.'

'I can't forget.'

He sounded inexorable, final, immovable. But it was preposterous, incredible! He must soften eventually.

'I'll go and make some tea,' I said, thinking, give it time, give it time.

Had I had any idea how long the battle between optimism and despair would last, my despair would have been the greater, but we are spared such knowledge. At one moment the explanation seemed far too flimsy to last, it would evaporate away to nothing; at another was the near certainty that to Gerald himself the reason was all-important, compelling, ineradicable. Why had he not simply stayed in the room if it meant so much to him? To this I could not begin to find an answer. Why did it mean so much to him? An altogether different question, this, to which I suspected I already had the answer, but it lay beyond recall, like a face clearly seen in a crowd for a moment before vanishing from view.

This exchange in some way eased the atmosphere. Gerald was no less cold or distant but the tension between us was a notch easier, allowing an occasional brief release from Coventry, though the distance between us remained fixed, unbreachable – Gerald never the one to speak first, never glancing at the baby, keeping us locked in our padded cell to which there was no key.

Twenty-one

Baby, pushchair and suitcase had been dragged and shoved and lifted on and off two buses and on to a fairly crowded train, and a struggle along the narrow corridor had eventually led to a window seat opposite an elderly couple, who apologised for not being able to help with the luggage. The biggest obstacle to this long-awaited trip had been the train fare, scraped together a shilling at a time from the housekeeping, but Helen wouldn't be told about that.

Sitting back, I began to savour the extraordinary freedom of being away from Gerald. He'd be all right on his own. I'd left him well provided with his favourite Victoria sponge cake and packets of biscuits, and his main daily meal would be taken in the café at lunchtime.

The low hills of Wiltshire seemed to go on for ever with little sign of life, green and pleasant enough but lacking Devon's colourful charm.

How would I feel about London now? But London meant Helen; and the question would not go away: what, precisely, should be said about Gerald? How to explain the dreadful breakdown which I myself could not understand?

Aged nearly two, Melanie sits bolt upright on my lap, absorbed in the passing scene, but I am not yet relaxed. The question of what to say or what not to say about Gerald seems to have acquired diabolical powers to spoil these reunions. It seemed wiser in my phone calls and letters to say nothing about his breakdown; it could do no good and might have created a rift. Best to keep to the safe ground of child rearing or health. Or should I have spoken out and face being told to leave him?

Helen never writes letters. Poor schooling, she maintains, has left her unequal to the written word, and now there is young Harriet to care for, not to mention numerous other calls on her time. It seems that the spending of money alone, when you have it, demands much time, especially when there are choices to be made among the welter of new goods now flowing into the shops like so many rivers in spate – elegant Danish furniture, carpets, kitchen gadgets, electrical equipment.

But we can talk. Helen insists that I make use of reverse-charge calls 'at any time', but ingrained abstinence keeps me strictly to the cheap-rate periods, on non-tearful days when I can enjoy our extended talks to the full and not give myself away.

I like to think that the red telephone box still stands on the grassy knoll up on the right-hand corner where the lane meets the main road. The little huddle of crooked stone cottages on the left-hand corner has probably long ago been 'updated', but, fortunately for their occupants in these pre-motorway pre-supermarket days, the main road, the old A38, is comparatively quiet, the relentless grind of holidaymakers' cars and jumbo food lorries still years away.

Opposite the telephone box was the bus stop for Buckfastleigh and Exeter, eastwards gateway to modern civilisation. And towering black and forbidding and rounded like a hunchback a thousand feet behind it was the gateway to an ancient civilisation, the Western Beacon on the southern edge of Dartmoor. In happier days we'd been directed up to it by Charlie, who had heard about it from a farmer friend but never ventured up there himself. He and his wife Valerie regarded us with the usual suspicion afforded to Londoners who for inexplicable reasons invaded their native territory and made strange expeditions, a suspicion softened slightly by our interest in birds, which gave added status to their patch and thence to them.

The route up to the beacon was via a mile or so of overgrown steep track at the end of an isolated country lane near the bus stop. Halfway up you felt the air change from humid South Hams to bracing Dartmoor. And the view from the top was heart-stopping, the hunchback no longer black but quilted in pinky-brown bracken, the borders of a fairyland; to the north and west, mile upon mile of undulating moorland, lit up in spring sunshine with patches of brilliant yellow gorse but more often than not shrouded in mist: a world of itself, silent, brooding, timeless.

No other person was ever seen up here. We stood in awe at the edge of this apparently uninhabited wilderness until the blue flash of a wheatear or a golden circling buzzard, or one or two frizzy white lambs, or a little band of burnished brown ponies announced that life was not as extinct as it first seemed.

Eastwards, the picture changed dramatically as your eyes were drawn downward across twenty miles of quaint multicoloured hills and meadows to the sea at Dawlish and Torbay. In good visibility, especially after rain, you could follow the glinting blue sea band southwards along fifty miles of coast to Start Point, then to the right another thirty miles or so westwards along the southern coast to Plymouth Sound. A ship might pass in the distance as we stood there, washed away on the ocean of time.

Halfway down to the main road, the warmer air settled about our shoulders like a noose, trapping us in the muggy uncertainties below. We had taken Helen up there and she was impressed. But Devon was for holidays; home was in London.

There was one chief daily train to and from the West Country in those days, usually on time and arriving at Paddington mid-afternoon.

Seeing Helen on the platform, hugging her, landed me on the verge of tears.

'Lovely to see you!' I said as we held each other at arm's length.

'And you!'

'Where's Harriet?' I was trying to be practical.

'Oh, she's finishing her morning sleep. She's running a bit late today. I left her with Olive.'

'Who's Olive?'

'My daily help. She's marvellous, a lovely woman. I'm so lucky to have her.'

This new evidence of affluence was absorbed in silence. Good for Helen.

'Come on,' she said, with an approving smile down at Melanie, 'I've got the car outside.'

Exhausted by Harriet's cornucopia of toys, much to my relief on her first night away from home Melanie had taken to her new cot without a murmur, and both infants were safely asleep. Earlier, I'd seen Helen's quick glance of concern at my drawn face and knew that questions would follow the fillet steak and wines and liqueurs.

I sank back in the soft beige cushions. Alan, a genial but disinterested host who recognised problems only in concrete terms, had taken to his study with no reason to revise his estimation of me as a misguided fool. Helen and I were alone.

'Come on, now, what's been happening?'

'I think I will have that other coffee.' I held out the white bone china cup and saucer. Tearfully blurting out my troubles would only increase antagonism towards Gerald.

I watched Helen pouring coffee from one of the latest stainless steel percolators. Motherhood suited her. She shone with a new confidence, smooth olive skin and hair like polished slate vying with my fair flat open Anglo-Saxon looks.

I replaced my coffee cup on the handsome small round onyx table. The subtle clink of two expensive surfaces meeting struck a different note from the hollow clunk of my Formica kitchen table. Yet here I was, undivided from my friend by the treacherous trappings of wealth. It suddenly seemed quite easy to talk.

'To be quite honest,' I confessed, 'I'm afraid Gerald's been rather ill since Melanie was born.'

'Ill? In what way? You didn't tell me. I thought you were the one who was ill.'

'Yes I was, but, er, Gerald has been, well, it's hard to explain. He's been, not himself at all.' My head dipped down for a moment, then I looked up with a frown. 'It's so difficult to explain –' Helen listened gravely as I stumbled on. 'Ever since – ever since the day the baby was born he's hardly been able to speak to me. Something has upset him terribly and he won't tell me what it is – well, he's told me something but I don't think that's it, not all of it.'

'You poor darling. Isn't he seeing a specialist?'

'No, he won't. He wouldn't go.'

'It must be awful for you. What does he say it is?'

'He says – he says it's something to do with the fact that he wasn't present when I was examined by the doctor at home – when I was ill before Melanie was born.

Helen nodded. 'Yes, you'll have to tell me all about it. Now this so-called illness of Gerald's, it all sounds like a lot of rubbish to me. You don't believe him, do you?'

'Well of course I do! Only – only I think there's far more to it than that.'

'Now look, love. You can't go on like this. Look at what it's doing to you. You're worn out.' Helen had always envied me my youthful looks and good complexion but now I looked pale and drawn, my cheeks were less plump, lines were beginning to appear.

'But you don't understand,' I protested. 'It's poor Gerald that's ill.'

'All I understand is that you've stood enough and it's time you stopped.'

'But what can I do?'

'There's only one thing to do, you'll have to leave him.'

'Oh, no! I could never do that!'

'Well, promise me you'll think about it.'

'All right, I'll think, but it's crazy. I wouldn't dream of it.'

'Don't dream. Just think for a change. Think of yourself. You've a life to lead. You can't spend the rest of it worrying about Gerald.'

'I'm afraid that as long as he needs me I can't help it.'

Helen sighed. 'Well anyway, love, try to forget him for a while. You're going to enjoy yourself. I've got tickets for two concerts and the opera – *The Walküre*; it's Hans Hotter again.'

'Oh, how lovely! You're an angel. But what about the babies?'

'Babysitters all arranged. Don't worry, my sweet. Your little treasure – she is a pet, isn't she – will be well taken care of. Now I expect you want to get to bed. It's been a long day for you.'

For six blissful days I was absorbed into the rhythm of London: music, laughter, impromptu chatter, sumptuous meals with sauces rich in cream and wine. My favourite was the fresh salmon, which I'd never had before, lightly baked in butter and herbs and served with a gleaming Hollandaise sauce. I was staggered at the extravagance of freshly squeezed orange juice and freshly ground coffee with cream, Alan presiding with casual expertise over amazing hissing juicers and buzzing grinders. Catching myself frivolously discussing cooking recipes and babies' food, I felt a little guilty at straying so far from Gerald and enjoying it.

'You know you can stay here,' Helen said tentatively. 'Alan could fix you up with a secretarial job and he could probably find you a flat as well. He's a gem. He's so generous. You'd be surprised the people he's helped. And he'd do it gladly. In fact you'd be doing him a favour; it's very hard to get good secretaries.'

'It's very kind of you both but I couldn't.' (At least I was valued for my secretarial skills.) I didn't bother to add how much I treasured my first real home, however inadequate by Helen's standards, or that even if baby care were available and affordable, I found the idea of working mothers abhorrent. Entrust my daughter to someone else? And why bother to mention to Helen, a confirmed city dweller, how much I loved living in the country. London was fine for occasional visits but not, I'd decided, as a place to live. The sheer weight of buildings, the unremitting tides of traffic, the press of people, were no longer an unnoticed backcloth, they had outstayed their welcome in my mind.

Just the same, were it not for Melanie I knew that I would immediately accept Helen's offer, that I needed to escape from Gerald and start again. I blinked away an image of myself dressed in a business suit leaving my bedsitter for work as though Gerald had never existed. And the step would not be all that difficult or painful. As a warm living person, Gerald didn't really exist. Beneath the appealing exterior he was without real substance, a mere shadow, a butterfly flitting across my path. Helen had been partly right in her original assessment of him. 'There's nothing in him,' she had declared, to my annoyance and disbelief. I knew now that, in the sense that there was nothing to be gained from him, there was nothing in him, nothing for me to leave.

But Melanie did exist, and as a mother I was not a free agent. If only in his capacity as a father, even a token father, Gerald, along with all his problems, could not yet be written off. Helen shook her head in amazement when I bought him an expensive leather wallet in Regent Street as a returning present. I'd never be able to make her understand why I needed to stay with him, neither did it seem opportune to tell her about certain problems with Melanie.

The peaceful greens soothed my eyes away from strident London streets. It was wonderfully good to be going back, though returning to Gerald's fixed detachment was quite another matter. Viewed from this distance, his behaviour seemed unreal, a bad dream; I could easily believe that when I got back his arms would reach out for Melanie, his eyes would welcome me back. Staring at the placid unfolding scene, I began to think I'd imagined the whole dismal story.

Melanie had dozed off in my arms. I closed my eyes, and the rhythm of the train lulled me back to 1949, the Christmas before our wedding, my first stay at Gerald's home. Wartime restrictions were fading, there was the carefree feeling that celebrations were once more in order. I had Gerald's room; he was on the living-room settee. His mother was welcoming and smiling but left no opportunity for lovemaking, though for my part snatched kisses were all the sweeter for being an end in themselves; I was loved for myself, not just my body.

Gerald strode about humming, full of loving smiles and approving glances at the new pale blue soft wool dress I had made myself. I knew he'd like the emphasis of plump breasts and small waist under the close-fitting bodice. The long flowing skirt, the New Look, fashion's answer to wartime austerity, had overnight outdated all knee-lengths and sent us scurrying to the nearest fashion shop like starved prisoners released to a banquet.

A poignant sound rose above the train wheels: Richard Tauber, a voice we both loved. Gerald's old portable wind-up gramophone, ceremoniously placed on the living-room table on Christmas Eve, had treated us to a recital of his records: 'You are my heart's delight, And where you are, I long to be –'

I opened my eyes and stared out at the rolling grandeur of Salisbury Plain. 'You are my heart's delight.' So much love, so much tenderness, so much caring: all gone, vanished as though they had never been.

The green sweep of Somerset hills gave way to Devon's smaller curves and ripe colours. It was useless hoping for miracles, yet I went on hoping.

The train pulled into the station. Carrying a sleepy Melanie, I saw Gerald's lanky figure a little way off on the platform and my heart bounded, but not with joy as it used to, because in that instant I wished I was anywhere but returning to this dark enigma; and was appalled that such a thought should have entered my head. It was strange and sad and felt like a betrayal not to be glad to see him again; but it was a homecoming, of sorts. This was where I belonged, to this place and to this man.

I wasn't going to think that I was also near to Roger.

'Hello, darling.'

'Hello.'

Gerald's lips were hard and cold, his eyes weren't soft, he wasn't smiling; his arms hung limp at his sides, they weren't reaching out for his small daughter.

The next day he made a show of listening as I chatted about my visit. I handed him the small package. 'Here you are, darling. A present for you.'

In silence he unwrapped the pigskin wallet, his favourite leather. I'd had his initials stamped in gold across the bottom right-hand corner.

He looked up with a wry smile. 'You shouldn't have done it, should you. You're far too good to me.'

'Darling, I love you. Didn't you miss us at all?'

'Yes, I missed you,' he said flatly, adding thoughtfully, impersonally, as if to a stranger, 'You'd be far better off without me.'

I was shocked. 'Darling, don't ever say such a thing!'

'You really should think about it. I've nothing for you.'

Cupping his face in my hands, I kissed him on the lips. 'Darling, there's nothing to think about. I love you. Things will get better, you'll see.'

'You don't understand. They can't get better.'

'They will, darling. They've got to.'

He was unconvinced, unmoved.

He made nothing of Melanie's second birthday: no sentimental card, no present, no smile, no 'Happy Birthday'. I told her she was two, gave her presents from two loving parents. Reared in a silent house by a mother who (perhaps too well) understood her needs and anticipated her wishes, Melanie was largely silent, observing all with her father's round enquiring eyes.

Mrs Gardner's second Christmas with us passed without note. Then periodically in the new year Gerald remarked, almost casually, that there was no other way than for us to part.

Unable to take this entirely seriously, in the lighter spring evenings I walked the pushchair up the lane to meet his bus and we strolled home together, a family of three, the hedges bright with primroses and forget-me-nots and violets and pink campion. There was some comfort in this semblance of normality, and I began to believe that if only for the sake of the child we'd survive together.

Then one Friday he stepped off the bus carrying under his arm a small brown paper parcel, and my spirits dropped like a lead weight. Gerald never carried anything to or from work.

We walked down the lane, and I was afraid to ask what the parcel was until we were nearly home, when I halted.

'What – what's in the parcel?'

'Just a few things from my desk. I've left.'

I stared at him. 'What – what do you mean?'

'It's quite simple,' he said, clipping his words. 'I've left. I shall be returning to London.' For one scary moment his eyes met mine squarely, very coolly, then he looked away, over the top of my head.

I stood staring blindly ahead, unable to move, then after a moment I moved slowly on down the lane. All my old pleading arguments were squashed, silenced. Gerald had given up his job. He had given up his job. The end of us, nothing more worth saying. No use mentioning the predicament I'd find myself in after he'd gone, no use pointing out that I was penniless. He was going, leaving me, deserting me, deserting us.

I walked on, my mind in pieces.

The ritual of the evening meal and getting Melanie to bed exacted a show of normality. Later, Gerald switched on the radio and calmly listened to a play, an hour-long murder mystery. The words droned unintelligibly in the background. When the play ended it was nearly bedtime, and I asked him when he would be going.

'Monday morning – I shall have to pack.'

'I see.'

He brought in his parcel from the hall and opened it out on the table. A few pens and pencils and notebooks; then a heavy bulky book. He removed the stout cardboard covering.

'Look, they gave me this as a leaving present.'

With a terrible twist of anguish I realised that in more than two years this was one of the few remarks he had voluntarily addressed to me. And with that thought I was overcome by a tremendous lassitude and didn't want to move from my chair, just wanted to stay there and give up entirely, resign from all spheres of effort. But something drove me and I got up and went to the table.

The book was the handsome new single volume of the *Shorter Oxford Dictionary* he had wanted. I imagined the generous staff contributions and instructions from Gerald that had made this possible. Departing staff were never given presents, it was not something that was done; there was no staff camaraderie at the factory, just an impersonal busy working atmosphere. I myself hadn't expected or received a leaving present from the staff, though Mr West had given me a handsome watch, but for Gerald this unusual effort had been made. No one there was likely to have heard of the *Shorter Oxford Dictionary*. I shrivelled at the thought of him graciously expounding the precise details of the gift he wanted whereas to me he was unable to speak. Little could they have guessed why he was leaving. No doubt he had given a vague impression of other more fruitful avenues to be pursued. Vague impressions were a speciality of Gerald's.

The curious experience of standing beside him jointly admiring the book gave an odd sensation of friendliness and normality, and I suddenly longed to feel his arm on my shoulder as though nothing was wrong. To him, of course, there was nothing wrong in standing together admiring the gift, mindless of its provenance.

A new kind of silence, the silence of the graveyard, hung over the weekend like a curse. He had packed his solitary suitcase but not his books, though I could read nothing into that.

On the Monday I was as ready as I could be for the parting. Half-way through the morning he had made no move towards going, and I offered coffee.

'Yes, all right. Thank you.' He didn't look at me.

I sensed a possible change. 'Aren't you going, then?'

'No, I shan't go today.'

He wasn't going – not yet. Was I glad? Sorry? Annoyed?

'What will you do, then?'

'I don't know. I may go tomorrow. Don't cross-examine me.'

'All right.'

The depth of silence in which the next few days passed rendered the preceding years almost light-hearted. Each day I expected him to go, each day he was still there, sitting about, reading, poring over his notes, listening to the radio. On the Friday he gave me the usual six pounds housekeeping money.

'What are you going to do?'

'I'm not sure. I may look for another job.'

He wasn't going, yet he had given up that coveted job, had contemplated life without me, without us. Why had he not gone? This I could not begin to answer. With only a few pounds between us, economic considerations were paramount, and for once Gerald seemed aware of this. Before a second week was over he returned from a bus trip to Plymouth and placed three pound notes on the table.

'I've found a job. I start next Monday. I'm afraid you'll have to manage with that till next week. It's all I have.'

'I'll manage somehow. What – what's the job?'

'Oh, it's with a television firm; they want someone to keep records of the rentals, act as cashier and so on.'

Television was the new beckoning miracle, the luxury of the few, a mysterious new kind of Pandora's box regarded with mingled desire and suspicion.

'What – what's the pay?'

'Oh, quite good; the same as before, in fact.'

The post-war economy seemed to be picking up. At least there would be no cash crisis, although the future prospects of this job did not look good. Neither did the prospects of our marriage.

Gerald now appeared to be slightly less cold and distant, but if I was enticed into complacency by an occasional wan smile I was quickly disillusioned. 'Don't forget this job is only a stopgap. I have nothing for you, my dear. You'll be far better off without me.'

A chill ran over me. An existence outside marriage was unthinkable. What was really wrong with him? – that was the question. What lay behind his rejection of me? And his other difficulties?

I pleaded with him. 'Look, darling, I know you can't ever love me the way I love you, but that's no different than it was before the baby was born. You wanted her. You wanted us to be together. What's made the difference now? Why don't you want me any more? Don't you need me at all?' (I meant beyond the usual sexual activity, which hadn't changed and was now a source of humiliation.)

'I've explained all that. There's nothing more to say. Why can't you accept it? You'll be better off without me.'

'But I can't accept it. I've done nothing.'

'You know what you've done.'

'I can't believe you mean it. You know how much I've always needed you, wanted you in every way.'

'It's too late now. The damage is done.'

'But I've done no damage. I've done nothing.'

'As far as I'm concerned, you have.'

'But if that's so, if it was so important to be in the room with me when I was examined here, why didn't you want to be with me when I had the baby?'

'That was different.'

'In what way? How was it different?'

'If you don't know then I can't explain.'

'But I don't know. I can't understand it. Please explain it to me.'

'I can't.'

'As far as I can see, that means there's nothing to explain. You just want to be rid of me. If that's it, why not say so? At least I could understand that.'

'You know it's not that.'

'I don't know. I don't know anything.'

'You don't have to know. Why don't you take my word for it? You'll be better off without me.'

'I still love you, you know.'

It was true. I was not yet ready to desert him. But what if he could never change?

Random thoughts about his illness, and its possible causes, had for years been hopping in and out of my mind, playing a puckish hide-and-seek, and I had to try to make sense of them. Until I knew the underlying cause of his illness, how could I tamely accept that he was incurable?

Twenty-two

But how to find the underlying cause? Nothing that Gerald had told me about himself had been of any real help, even though it seemed that nothing of importance had been left out. So the solution must lie hidden in his infancy. No harm, anyway, in trying to explore this. But how to begin? I had tried books. But after struggling through those famous works on the mind I had been left more baffled than ever, bamboozled with enigmatic phrases:

> 'Fluid Electric Current' (Freud)
> 'Man is a freak of the universe'
> 'Existential dichotomies' } (Fromm)
> 'Historical dichotomies'

Equally confusing, equally baffling:

> We may now take the view that the ego is the real locus of anxiety, and reject the earlier conception that the cathectic energy of the repressed impulse automatically becomes converted into anxiety.
> (Freud, *Inhibition, Symptom and Anxiety*, 1927)

I gave up. If I could not discover anything about Gerald's infancy, or about his mind, from books, I wondered – dared I think of it like this? There was another infancy going on right now before my eyes, Melanie's. Melanie wasn't Gerald, of course, but was she, could she, as Gerald had said, be like him in some essential respect? But in what respect? Was my beloved child, in spite of all my precautions, all my attempts to do 'the right thing', still liable to become mentally ill? Was there nothing I could do about that? I had to know.

So: in what ways, precisely, did Melanie resemble Gerald?

Back to the 'humming' incident. And there was something else, something slight (if anything ever is slight in these matters), the comment Gerald had once made on Melanie's intent way of staring – the same comment he had made about the 'humming' – 'Yes, there's no doubt about it; she's definitely like me.' Gerald never readily committed himself, never made rash observations. This one had the ring of truth.

I thought to myself, if her stare was merely reminiscent of his set of face, his trick of expression, then of course it was of no particular significance. But was there, as Gerald's remark seemed to imply, more to it than that? On the other hand, were these thoughts merely the distraught musings of an inexperienced mother? Nurture your baby, feed it, warm it, protect it, give it security and love, and all is bound to be well. What else is there? Think … think.

Meanwhile there was Melanie herself to deal with, now aged two and a half, small, pale, diffident, only just beginning to speak. Since her father still only spoke to her when addressed, I was reduced to suggesting something for her to say to him in the hope of initiating a dialogue between them.

'Go and ask Daddy the time, darling.'

In a minute Melanie returned. 'Daddy says it's twelve o'clock.'

'Thank you, darling. Now go and ask Daddy if he'd like to take you for a walk before lunch. You'd like to go, wouldn't you?'

'Yes, Mummy.'

'Ask Daddy to help you with your coat and shoes.'

'Yes, Mummy.'

I longed to know if he ever ventured a remark to her when they were alone together. He held her hand, that was something, though nothing else seemed to change, there was no sign of a dialogue. So on with the farce.

'Go and tell Daddy dinner will be ready in ten minutes.'

I said nothing of this to Helen, of course, especially about Gerald's attempt to leave us or his change of job. 'I'm not forgetting your advice about leaving Gerald,' I wrote, positive that I could never contemplate such a move, 'but feel I have to give it a little longer. Melanie badly needs contact with other children of her own age and I get her to friends in the village when I can, but I'd like her to go to the Dartington nursery school when she's three and a half; that's when they start. It's the only nursery school down here but it's fifteen miles away and one needs a car because there's no bus service. I'm going to look for a part-time secretarial job in that area and perhaps that way I'll be able to manage the car and the fees. What do you think?'

To Comfort Always: A new BBC programme about the mentally ill. Books and doctors had failed me; here was new hope. I told Gerald I was going to listen, and grudgingly, surprised to hear me express a preference of my own, he agreed to join me. 'It may help,' I said.

The talk was about the constant needs of the mentally ill for support, for forbearance and comfort, and I waited expectantly for mention of various mental states and difficulties, for causes and cures, for a saving ray of light. I waited for reference to people in my plight (there must be others, hundreds, thousands of them). But I waited in vain; we were not mentioned: we could stay in Siberia, enslaved in the Gulag.

If Gerald, too, had been hoping for enlightenment he gave no sign of it, merely listening attentively but like a long-term prisoner expecting no reprieve. Then without a word he rose and went up to bed.

I switched off the radio. My head slumped on my hands. 'Who's going to comfort me?' I said aloud.

There was no one to hear.

There was to be no help, either, from Helen, who was due to visit us in the summer with Harriet. 'I'm sorry,' she said on the phone, 'Alan doesn't want me to come.'

'Why not?'

'Well, after what you've said about Gerald –'

'What do you mean?'

'Well, come on, Elaine, he is mentally ill, isn't he.'

'Yes, of course, but – I don't understand.'

'Alan doesn't think it's safe.'

'But that's nonsense. You know what he's like; you've been with him.'

'Not since you had Melanie.'

I was silenced.

'Look, sweetie, I'm sorry, but you do understand, don't you.'

'Yes, of course.'

I didn't really understand. And what of my own danger, imaginary, of course, but in Helen's view, real?

'Can't you come to London soon?'

'I don't think so. Perhaps next year –'

If only I could have believed in God! If only divine guidance could have been sought, some nourishing crumbs of comfort caught as they dropped indiscriminately from heaven! When I was about eight it dawned on me that our parents professed their religious beliefs purely for the benefit of our grandparents, and from that time on there was no divine guidance for me. Later attempts to stake my claim in the Great Healer all ended with the admission that if I was honest I was unable to believe.

Back to Melanie: in what way, if any, did I think she differed from other babies? She was a very alert, nervous baby, very tense, easily upset, oversensitive. As I see it, she was born with what I call a Nervous Temperament. Consequently her feelings were necessarily more pronounced, more intense, than is normal. Monopolised as she was by fierce, urgent feelings she was then at the mercy of a pull towards extremes – in everything she felt, everything she wanted, everything she feared. In other words, like Gerald, she was born with an innate tendency towards emotional extremes.

Gerald is certainly going to extremes now: in not speaking to me, and in keeping it up for so long. And he goes to extremes with his note-taking; he can't let anything drop – any everyday lapse of memory. He *has* to remember, is under compulsion to do so. He *has* to go to extremes, he can't help himself.

Go on thinking about Gerald. Think – think –

I looked down at the plain dark blue cover of the book on my lap: Gerald's *Concise Oxford Dictionary* – his number one bible. I smiled to myself. Typical of him that it showed so little mark for years of heavy usage – not a trace of a creased or marked page, only faint signs of wear at the edges of the covers. It was casually referred to by him as the *COD*, as if the term were universally recognisable, like USA or HM, as if everybody had a copy constantly at hand as he did. It felt wrong even to touch it, let alone actually open it and read from it, almost like intruding into a private diary.

But in a final desperate search for answers, and for want of a better idea, it seemed worth reverting to the terms Gerald had applied to himself, generally when referring to his breakdown after the war. Could those terms provide any clues? The one most often used was 'nervous', and it seemed silly to look up such an ordinary word: it surely only meant timid. Nevertheless, I looked it up, turning the flimsy pages with no idea of what was to come.

Twenty-three

I badly needed confirmation of my tentative ideas, and now there was a new weekly half-hour on the Third Programme – *Parents and Children* – sympathetic insight into family problems. One never knew. Perhaps if I wrote to them I'd be able to find out if I was on the right track. I typed up the notes I had made, designing them as two fifteen-minute talks, ready to send off to the Editor.

The only sounding board for my conclusions, strangely enough, was Gerald himself. I'd caught him one night in a half-amenable mood. Dinner was over and we'd just reached the end of a fascinating talk by Ludwig Koch on recording birdsong. Anything to do with birds always lifted Gerald out of himself, lightened his mood.

'Do you see, darling, I've been trying to work it all out.'

'Work what out?'

'Well – please hear me out. If, as you say, Melanie's like you, and I'm sure you're right, I need to know in what way she's like you, what it all means.'

'Why do you need to know that? Why should it mean anything?'

'Well, don't you see, you're probably right to say we are all as we are and there's nothing much we can do about it. Perhaps there isn't once we're grown up. But what if the way we are now is determined in some way or to some extent while we're babies? And what if we can alter what happens to us as babies?'

'I don't follow.' He became suspicious. 'You're not dragging my mother into this, are you?'

'No, of course not.' I smiled reassuringly. 'Nothing like that. What I mean is, as an adult you've been mentally ill and we don't really know the cause of that, do we.' He listened warily. 'What if the cause is mostly to do with what one is like as a baby, the kind of person one is when born?

'I don't see what you're getting at.'

'Well, look, darling. Please hear me out. Suppose we're trying to find out what sort of person you were when you were born – and this is where the dictionary comes in.' The word 'dictionary' lit a spark. He was really listening now. 'Start with a word you yourself were given by the doctors – neurasthenia. Let's look it up. Do you mind if I borrow your dictionary?'

He hesitated a moment before handing it over, watching in silence as I turned the pages with care, knowing that he'd be more concerned about them getting creased than about anything to do with his so-called illness. He didn't think he had an illness. He was just as he was and that was all there was to it.

'Here we are – it's under "neur"; "neurasthenia". All it says is, "nervous debility". When I first saw this I thought why not look up "nervous", though it seemed a bit silly to look up such an ordinary word; I thought it only meant "timid", but I looked it up anyway.'

I still had his attention. I turned the pages again. 'Here we are – "nervous"; this is the bit that caught my eye:

> Having disordered or delicate nerves, excitable, highly strung, easily agitated, timid.

'All those definitions seemed fairly straightforward to me,' I said, 'except for "highly strung". I've never been quite sure what this means. I could find nothing relevant under "high" or "highly", so I looked up "strung"; I know it seems a bit daft, but you'll see what I mean in a minute. "See *string*", it says, and under "string", right at the bottom there is "highly strung", and the definition of this is:

> Nerves or person neurotic, susceptible, oversensitive.

194

'When I saw this I thought perhaps this wasn't a waste of time; I was getting warmer. So where next? Do you see, I thought, all those words deriving from or connected with "nervous" can be applied to you – you'll agree with that, won't you?'

Again he nodded warily. 'May I see?' He held out his hand and I passed the book over.

'So then I thought, what of it? What does that really amount to? That you're susceptible and oversensitive?' I carefully omitted the word 'neurotic'. 'We knew that already, so I was no further forward.'

'I thought so,' Gerald said. 'How could you expect to find out anything that way?'

'That's exactly what I thought, but –' This was by far the longest conversation we'd had since the birth. And astonishingly, he wasn't annoyed, wasn't dismissing me – not yet. I went on, 'But in spite of this, in spite of thinking I wasn't getting anywhere, that word "nervous" simply gave me no rest. I couldn't stop thinking about it. It went round and round in my head, along with all those other definitions. Those words were trying to tell me something.'

Gerald turned a few pages in silence while I recalled how for days those few words had to be digested, assimilated, allowed to rotate endlessly like the jagged little bits in a kaleidoscope before falling into place.

'Are you still with me, darling?'

He looked up with an even stare. 'Yes.'

'It must have been some days later,' I went on, 'that a question suddenly popped into my mind. Could I perhaps be thinking of something like a nervous disposition? What exactly did "disposition" mean? Surely I knew that already. But I looked it up, anyway.' I held out my hand. 'Would you like me to find it?'

'I'll find it.' His patience was wearing thin.

As he turned the pages I recalled the relevant bit of the definition of disposition:

Bent, temperament, natural tendency; inclination to.

and recalled also the excitement of realising that I seemed to be going in the right direction.

'Have you got the place, at the end I mean, those four words: "Bent, temperament, natural tendency, and inclination to"?'

He looked up with an impatient nod. Just let his attention hold out a little longer.

'Of those four words, "temperament" was the one I wasn't quite sure of, so again – if you don't mind – I looked it up. I promise you, I've nearly finished.'

Gerald again turned the pages and I remembered my back going damp as I read and re-read the definition of 'temperament':

Individual character of one's physical organisation permanently affecting the manner of acting, feeling and thinking.

One word in that sentence seemed to leap out at me: the word 'permanently'. Gerald looked up. His impatience was edging up, but for the moment he was thoughtful.

'Do you see, darling –' I spoke quietly; any hint of excitement would only put him off. 'If this definition of temperament is true – and we're not going to argue with the COD, are we – then it means that from the moment of birth, even, perhaps, before birth, the manner of one's acting and feeling and thinking is already – if only to some extent – decided. Or, in other words, the manner of one's reacting to external circumstances and events and influences is already – again if only to an extent – prescribed at birth. You do see that, don't you?'

'Yes, I see it – but –' His impatience was now very near the surface.

'Don't you think that's astonishing and significant?'

'Perhaps. But I don't see that it's of much help.'

'But I have to know if that's what Melanie has, don't you see – a nervous temperament, I mean. Does it mean that she, too, might become mentally ill? Have I done everything right to try and avoid that? It's all guesswork, you know.'

'I'm sure your guesswork is as good as anybody else's.'

I didn't like the way he said this. The antagonism was surfacing. 'Anyway, I just thought I'd mention it all because – I hope you won't mind – you know that programme, *Parents and Children*?'

He nodded vaguely. It was something he ignored while I listened.

'I'm going to send all the notes I've made to them. See what they say. You don't mind, do you?'

'Do as you please.' He had switched off, his mind already on more important matters.

Twenty-four

'Well, come on, then, tell me what's happened.'

I leaned back in the cushions of Helen's large, comfortable arm-chair. The children were in bed and Alan was safely in his study. We could talk. I slipped off my one good pair of high-heeled black leather court shoes, once daily office wear and now reserved for special occasions. The destination to which those thin leather soles had borne me this morning was still tinged with unreality. Seated in an enclosed space rather like a box at the opera only smaller, I'd heard my voice speaking into a microphone while in another soundproof box a BBC producer, a small thoughtful-looking elderly woman, listened through earphones. Beside her sat Melanie, whose presence had been requested. Afterwards we were taken to lunch at the nearby Quality Inn, and we sat on for a while chatting about Gerald, about Melanie and my plans for her. We shook hands on the pavement outside. She'd let me know, she said, and I walked away elated; perhaps I wasn't such a fool, after all.

Gerald had supplied the train fare to London from his savings without comment, disinterested in the exciting summons from the BBC, his mind elsewhere. But Helen was impressed, and I had gained confidence in my hard-won conclusions about Melanie. Even Alan's usual veiled scorn was less marked after Helen had read my script last night. She'd handed it back to me this morning. 'Looks fascinating, love. We'll talk about it later.'

'Let's hope they go on with it,' Helen said, when I had reported the morning's events. 'But there's a lot I don't understand. For a start, I can't see anything wrong with Melanie – anything to worry about.

She's such a little pet. She's healthy, she eats well, sleeps well, loves playing. Where's the problem?'

'Ah,' I said. 'That's all true, and I can't tell you what a relief it is. But it hasn't just happened automatically. There's always been that thin line between trying to hit on the right thing and mucking it all up by doing the wrong thing, hitting the wrong note, whatever ...'

'But we all have to do that, don't we.'

'Yes, of course. But there's more to it than that. I haven't been able to get everything into this stuff I sent to the BBC – that was only, really, a summary; it's far too lengthy and involved to put it all in. I think I see the connection between Gerald and Melanie as far as it affects her and what I ought to do about that. I only hope I'm right. But I've still got to work out exactly what's behind his attitude to me. I've had plenty of time to think, because he still doesn't speak to me.'

'You don't mean, never speaks to you at all? All this time? More than two years?'

'Yes, I'm afraid so.'

Helen was shocked. 'It – it doesn't seem possible.'

'Yes, he just ignores me, and Melanie. Comes and goes, never even says hello or goodbye. I've tried everything. Nothing makes any difference. Oh, he replies, when he has to, just mutters the odd word or two.'

'But that's dreadful! You'll have to leave him.'

'I can't. No yet, anyway. For one thing, there's the question of where to go.' I smiled. 'I haven't any money, you know. Besides, I don't feel it's right to break up the family unless I have to. I must do what's best for Melanie. He may yet come round, and I'm still hoping to get her to nursery school. I keep looking in the paper. Something may turn up, a part-time job, I mean. I'm only telling you all this to explain why I was so concerned about Melanie. Lots of points arose in her first year, especially after Gerald had said that she was like him – you read about that in my notes.' Helen nodded. 'So naturally I was alarmed, wondering if she was going to grow up to be mentally ill. Not if I could help it, I thought. But what could I do? So I watched her, trying to find out what was going on in her mind, as far as one can with a baby. I can tell you, I had to dismiss all my preconceived notions about dealing with babies; I soon found I was responding to her differently from what I'd always imagined.'

'In what way differently?'

'Well, for a start, when I first got her home, she was startled by various noises.'

'What sort of noises?'

'Oh, that was the ridiculous thing; I mean very ordinary sounds; while she was having her evening feed, if Gerald just put his hand in his pocket, or turned the page of a book, she'd jerk off the nipple as if a spring had been released, very tense, so disturbed she wouldn't resume feeding till she'd heard me say, "It's all right, only Daddy" – when she knew from my tone that it was safe. I thought it a bit odd that she should be so tense, so on the alert, especially during a breastfeed, when I rather expected a baby to be soporific. As a matter of fact, that was the first thing the doctor remarked on when he examined her on her first day. 'She's an alert little thing,' he said. And I looked down at this sturdy naked little body in the cot, my own personal little miracle, arms and legs waving about like feelers, and I could only take the doctor's remark as some kind of obscure compliment. It was only later, after I got her home, that I realised how uncomfortably on the alert she was, and then I recalled that first sight of her – not the arms and legs waving about, that seemed natural enough, baby trying to get its bearings in a strange new world – but her body so rigid, arched, the ribs outlined, and her little face screwed up with intense effort. She wasn't just idly wondering what was going on; she was straining, trying very very hard, unnaturally hard, you might say, to get some answers.'

Helen looked slightly sceptical, half humouring a first-time mother but half interested in spite of herself.

'I know it may sound a bit far-fetched to you,' I said. 'A bit of a fuss about nothing.'

'No, no, do go on,' Helen said, mindful perhaps of the interest shown by the BBC.

'Well, it wasn't just during her feeds that she was so obviously edgy, wanting to know what was going on and needing reassurance. It was all the time she was awake. I'd bring her down when she woke up in the morning and straight away her eyes were darting about and she was listening intently. Don't forget it's a very quiet house, so any sound from outside is heard loud and clear. "That's a rook," I'd say, not knowing what else to do when she was obviously so anxious about it, or "That's a plane", or "That's a car", and that seemed to do the trick; it seemed to satisfy her. I'd never thought of it before, but I suppose when the baby's in the womb she does hear the mother's voice, so that's something familiar and reassuring in a strange world, though I'm certain she soon recognised the words, too.'

'But surely we just cuddle and hug babies to soothe them.'

'That's another strange thing,' I said. 'Not only strange but very upsetting, at first. You see, she seemed to get no satisfaction at all from being picked up or petted. She'd be all tensed up, listening to some sound or other, her face screwed up, her body absolutely rigid; and cuddling, rocking, none of that made any impact at all. I expect that's where I first began to depart from preconceived notions about babies, because speaking seemed to be the only way of making contact. And I kept asking myself, am I merely being over-anxious, overprotective? But every time I doubted my good sense, Melanie's face seemed to leave no room for doubt; her face was asking questions and I had to answer them. Mind you, she never accepted the answer automatically, even during her breastfeed. She'd jerk off the nipple and after I'd spoken there'd be a long pause for due consideration, you could see her weighing things up, before she'd relax and resume feeding.'

'Well,' Helen said, 'if speaking like that did the trick it sounds simple enough to me.'

'Well, there were lots of other things.'

'What sort of things?'

'She wasn't only anxious to know what was going on, there were some sounds that absolutely terrified her, usually in the evenings, because during the day, there'd be nothing much happening to break the silence. And when I say terrified, I mean crying loudly with terror, and inconsolable.'

'Really! What sort of sounds?'

'Well, any kind of rasping sound: curtains being drawn; the fire being made up; paper tearing; even a cough or a sneeze. So what should one do? Let her scream? Say we've got to live, too? She'll get used to it?'

'What did you do, then?'

'Well, fortunately, Gerald and I both agreed here. I know it sounds stupid, but he'd go out of the room to blow his nose; so would I. And we'd take her out of the room if we needed to make up the fire, or draw the curtains.'

'Did you really?'

'Yes, we did.'

'And was it worth it?'

'Well, yes, I'm sure it was. All my reason tells me it was. But, of course, we can never prove it, can we. But if she hadn't reacted quite so violently, if she'd just perhaps been a little bit frightened, then it would probably have passed by more or less unnoticed. She might have just cried out, say, then been quickly reassured with a sympathetic word or a hug. But her reaction was so extreme, I was forced to take notice.'

'All the same,' Helen said, 'it does seem to be going a bit to extremes yourself to go to all that trouble.'

'Well, I so often thought that myself. But I'd started to try and see things from the baby's point of view. I asked myself, why is she so frightened? And then I realised: this was a young baby unable to move very much or to see much beyond the side of her cot or the

sheet, and the ceiling, and the light, suddenly hearing this uniden-
tifiable harsh sound. I reasoned that once she could sit up and see
the origin of the sound and see that it was harmless, she wouldn't be
frightened any more.'

'And did that happen?'

'Yes, it did, gradually. But early on the same thing happened when
I walked the pram to the village for shopping. She was terrified by the
noise of the traffic, so until she could sit up and see for herself where
the noise was coming from I only went to the village on Saturdays,
when I could leave her at home with Gerald. But the biggest fright
of all was the vacuum cleaner; that took longest for her to get used
to. I only used it when I could put the pram outside.'

'Well, you've certainly had your work cut out. I hope it was worth
it. But I still don't see the connection with Gerald.'

'Well, neither did I, in those first months. I was just taking precautions, trying to play for safety, in case any of it did matter, otherwise
I wouldn't have bothered. Then I began to wonder what Gerald was
like as a baby, and it suddenly dawned on me that that was the one
period of his life I knew nothing about. And of course, it seemed
ridiculous to think there could be any connection between what he
was like as a baby and his behaviour as a grown man, but I had
to know why he was rejecting me, what really lay behind it; and I
thought there's no harm in trying to find out what I can, so when his
mother visited us I questioned her.'

'And did you find anything out?'

'Well, a certain amount. He certainly didn't get anything like the
care I was giving to Melanie. He was mostly left in his cot while his
mother worked, and I suppose if he cried she'd have thought that's
what babies do, he just had to get over it. And I began to think, what
if, as seemed likely, he was a very sensitive, alert little baby like Melanie? How would this lack of attention – the right kind of attention,
though he was well cared for physically – affect him?'

Helen shifted a little in her chair. 'So what next?'

'Well, once she could sit up and look around, the kind of suppressed curiosity behind the waving arms and legs, and then later the head twisting and turning, became open driving curiosity about everything in sight; she needed to touch everything – needed to explore density and texture. Natural enough, I thought, except that there was a desperation behind her curiosity that gave it a peculiar urgency, very marked, as if her life depended on it. So I'd take her up to anything that seemed to have attracted her attention – she'd have been reaching out, straining towards a bowl or a picture on the sideboard, or the clock on the mantelpiece – and when she touched it, when she got her prize, she'd be quivering with excitement, shaking all over. She'd also go from one object to another and from one surface to another – the back of a chair, the table, the wall, the doorknob – with a mounting hysterical kind of excitement, her whole being vibrating with the effort to make the most of her opportunity. I was very surprised, I can tell you, and very concerned, and I felt very strongly this had to be curbed. I dared not let it go on: it was too fraught, too dangerous, somehow. But how to stop it? After about ten minutes I experimented by saying, "That's enough now; time to go to sleep," and I was very relieved when she immediately accepted this, perhaps even welcomed it; perhaps she'd had enough excitement for the moment; and she knew the word "sleep", you see.'

'How did she know that?'

'Well, it may sound silly, but as well as naming noises for her, like "car", I'd got into the habit of saying key words to her to explain what was going on. I thought, we pick a baby up, put it down, bundle it about in various ways; just in case it helped make her feel more secure I'd say "Daddy", or "bath", or "sleep".'

Helen's eyebrows lifted. 'It sounds a bit far-fetched to me. Do you think it achieved anything?'

'Well, at the time I thought it couldn't do any harm; and now I think it did do a lot of good, especially with sleeping.'

'And how did she sleep?'

'Remarkably well; much to my relief, I can tell you, because it helped me to think I must be doing the right things.'

'But you don't know she wouldn't have slept well anyway.'

'Well, I'm fairly certain she wouldn't. If you'd seen her in those first months, her little face continually mapped out with question marks, I think you'd agree. She was always so tense, so on edge, and later, so excitable when she wanted to touch things. And then when she started crawling, well, she was so incredibly excitable all the time, like an automatic engine in top gear that goes on running and running.'

'But lots of babies are like that, aren't they?'

'Yes, I know. But rightly or wrongly, I always felt it wouldn't be good for her to get too worn out with her own excitement, so over-tired that she couldn't sleep. I kept to regular mealtimes and rest times, and she did seem to thrive on that, though when it came to solid foods, that was another problem.'

'In what way?'

'Well, it wasn't that she disliked the new food but rather that she recognised nothing but milk as food. I'd coax the spoon in between closed lips, and sometimes the food disappeared but often she'd resist swallowing at the last moment and out it poured. "She doesn't want it," I was told. "Let her go without and she'll eat the next time round." But although mealtimes took ages I felt I had to persevere, and then the magical day came when the little mouth opened at the approach of the spoon. You can't imagine how pleased I was to see that mouth open.

'And then I could sometimes take her with the pushchair on the bus to Plymouth and wheel her round shops and streets and in to a little lunch at Dingle's self-service restaurant. The world without tears, and she loved it. Everything seemed to slot into place then; it had all been leading up to this moment after all that uneasiness, that inability to relax and take things as they came. And all the time, the strange unawareness that I was there to help her –'

205

'What do you mean by that?'

'Well, it was odd, but all that first year, no matter what I did, no matter how much I hugged and cuddled her, there was never any response. It would have been frightening if it wasn't so puzzling. She never snuggled up to me, never showed the faintest sign that she enjoyed being cuddled and she never hugged her soft toys, either. She hated dolls, wouldn't have them anywhere near her. Then, when she was nearly a year old, there'd be a faint smirk of satisfaction when I held her close, and, very slowly, it seemed to dawn on her that I was on her side and she began to show some affection but in a stilted, self-conscious way which she then gradually extended to her bunny. It wasn't till she was nearly two that things improved and she began to fling her arms round my neck and actually kiss me. I'll never forget the first time I felt those little arms tighten round my neck.'

'It must have been very disappointing, very frustrating for you, going to all that trouble and getting nothing back from her.'

'Yes, it was. I sometimes wonder now what other mothers make of babies like that.'

'Give up. Concentrate on more rewarding children, or other interests.'

'I expect you're right, but quite honestly, I didn't think too much about that at the time. I was so intent on trying to fathom out what was going on.'

Helen was silent for a moment. Then she said gently, 'Do you think your anxieties might have communicated themselves to the baby and affected her?'

I smiled. 'Well, I think what saved me from that was that in spite of everything I did so love having a baby, and I did so love her. That was my first instinct; it was much stronger than all the enquiries going on underneath. I'd think about those when she was asleep.'

'What about the second year, how did that go?'

'Well, so much happened. There was lots more wanting to touch and handle everything in sight, the same driving curiosity, the same desperation, but once she could move around, of course, on a much bigger scale.'

'What did you do?'

'Well, lots of things I'd never have dreamt of if it hadn't been for the connection with Gerald, I can tell you. She'd be sitting up in her pram in the sitting-room in the afternoons – she still slept in the mornings – reaching out, wanting to touch everything, so I'd give her all sorts of things to handle. I was amazed what an enormous variety of objects could pass unscathed through a baby's hands – hats and scarves, old handbags and diaries, cotton reels, all kinds of kitchen items like wooden egg-cups or baking tins. She would end up dwarfed by this huge pile on top of the pram cover, and eventually she was sated, she'd had enough, she didn't mind when I came to put everything away.

'Then later on, the same sort of thing on the floor. There would be this enormous pile, only the awkward thing was, she didn't want her little kingdom moved if we were going out, or if one of the village mums was calling with her baby; and then she didn't want this other child to touch anything, which was even more awkward. Sometimes I'd end up in the kitchen wading ankle-deep in a litter of torn-up newspapers, saucepans, everything imaginable. And she'd follow me round the house, upstairs and down, wanting to know what was in every cupboard, every drawer. I thought the mess would never end, that I should never have allowed it.

'And then, at last, when she was about eighteen months old she'd watch me putting things away at the end of the day and she'd want to help me put them away, hand them to me, and so on. Then she wanted to do it herself: and when I say *wanted*, I mean wanted so desperately, so passionately, she didn't just *want* to do it, she *had* to do it. She was incredibly upset, practically in hysterics if I ever tried to stop her, hurry her up, or, God forbid, do it myself. You see, she doesn't, she didn't, just *want* things, she *had to have them, had to*. There was always this awful compulsion, right from the start. She

207

even wanted to put other children's things away when we were leaving their house.'

Helen smiled. 'I suppose that might have been welcomed. But I must admit, it does seem a bit unnatural. What did you think was going on?'

'Well, I thought about it, of course, like I thought about everything else. It was all part of the picture I was forming of her, this compulsion, this drive, this absolute necessity to act in one way and no other.'

'Wasn't she just being wilful, trying to get her own way?'

'Well, I wondered about that, but I didn't think so, and now she's walking she does things that show I was right about her; she does behave strangely, even though she seems so docile to you.'

'What sort of things?'

'Well, for example, only last week we were going for a walk up the lane. She was wearing a summer dress, the first one on this year, and I had put her cardigan on. The cuffs are just the right length for her and they don't turn up. She looked at them, then she started tugging away at one, trying to turn it up. It was useless saying it doesn't matter, it's all right like that. She just wouldn't have it; she pulled back, wouldn't go out the door, and she does love her walks. And I'm thinking, what the devil is she playing at? What's going on here? Is she just trying to be awkward? And then I realise that all last winter she's been wearing jumpers which do turn up at the cuffs, so she thought this one should turn up, too. And could I deflect her from this? I could not. And I did try, because it seemed ridiculous to let her think it was so important. But you see, to her it is important. Terribly important. So I gave in and turned the cuffs up. And what do you think she did then? She placed her two wrists together and scrutinised the two cuffs for ages, very carefully – and I realised she was making sure they were both turned up the same length.'

Helen showed astonishment.

'That's not all. A few days later it was much cooler and rainy, so she had her mac on over the cardigan. But she started peering underneath each mac sleeve, trying to make sure the cuffs hadn't been disturbed when she put it on. Now why would she bother about all that? It's not because of anything she's ever seen me do.'

'A bit weird,' Helen agreed. 'But kids are weird, aren't they. We can't explain everything they do.'

'No. But I have to take it all in context, add up everything she does to see what it may amount to.'

'What else, then?'

'Well, the same sort of thing, really. She has this set of picture blocks. You know, the kind that makes six different pictures, with their own little wooden box. This was ages ago. She suddenly objects to the way I'm putting them away, and when I say objects, I mean she starts pulling at the box, trying to get it away from me, crying, so distressed. And I'm racking my brains, trying to work out what she's after. Then I think back to the last time we played with them, and it so happens I can remember the last picture we did. God knows what would have happened if I hadn't remembered. Anyway, I tip the blocks out again, I can see that's what she wants, and I start to make that last picture. "Yes, you remember, darling," I say. "Is that right?"

'She nods and smiles – well smirks, really – with satisfaction. "Now shall we put them away?" I say, and she looks on, so tense, again you'd think her life depends on it, while I place the blocks, with that picture uppermost, back in the box. But it wasn't quite the end of it. You see, the blocks don't fit tightly in the box, there's a margin of space left over along two sides, and as I shut the lid she peers away at the inside of the box so intently, you'd never believe it; then when the lid is shut she's still not satisfied, she opens the lid, not once but several times, to make sure the bricks haven't moved. And then when the lid is finally shut again she's bending her head about very anxiously, trying to peer underneath the lid again to make sure the blocks haven't been disturbed. So, of course, I assure her that it's all right, they won't move, and we carefully place the box back in her toy cupboard. After that, the same ritual every time; the same picture, the same anxiety and peering. And, I might tell you, the box has to go back in the same place, the exact spot where it was originally. She has these two shelves underneath my kitchen cabinet, and I suppose I've always put her things away fairly neatly just so as to get them all in, and I didn't realise how she'd been watching me.'

'I begin to see,' Helen said. 'And what about now? How is she now? I mean, she seems so well-behaved, so content. A bit timid, I agree, perhaps a bit lacking in confidence.'

'Well, you're right there. That's why I feel it's so important to try to get her to nursery school, get her with other children, build up her confidence. I still keep strictly to her routines, but I know, I *know*, that if I disturb the routine or let her get overtired or overwrought, then it could be bad. That's why, you see, I can't begin to think about leaving Gerald, not yet – if ever.'

'Well, if you must wait I can see that might be good for Melanie, though I'm not so sure about having a father that never speaks to her.'

'I hope he may as time goes on and she can speak to him more of her own accord. She might even be a bridge between us. I mean, surely he can't keep this up for ever.'

'Well, we shall have to see. But I don't like it. And I don't really see the connection with Gerald. I've read your notes, but I still don't see it.' Helen looked at her watch. 'It's getting late. Let's leave it till the morning.'

After Alan had gone to work the next morning we sat on at the kitchen table, listening through the open door to the two youngsters playing happily in Harriet's bedroom.

'Do you still want to talk about the connection with Gerald?'

Helen nodded. 'Yes, of course I do.'

'Well, I discussed this only the other day with Gerald himself.' And I repeated the dictionary-led conclusions about the word Temperament. 'Note the word "permanently", I said. What that means, to me, is that at birth, right from birth, mark you, the brain and the nervous system, or whatever else is involved, are physically organised in a way that will permanently affect the manner of acting, feeling and thinking.'

'Is that what you meant when you wrote about the nerves in babies like Melanie being wound up too tightly, like violin strings, and every impression on them going deep?'

'That's right.'

'So, are you saying that we can do permanent damage to our children by what we do or don't do with them as babies?'

'Well, with babies like Melanie, yes.'

'You're getting me worried now,' Helen said. 'You've got me wondering about all the things I've done wrong. There must be dozens of them. Hundreds. I mean, there's so much guesswork, isn't there.'

'Isn't there just. But I'm sure you've no need to worry. Harriet doesn't seem in the least bit highly strung, does she.'

'Well, maybe not. But how does one know? She has her moments, you know. She's not all sweetness and light. She has a will of iron, and quite a temper. She likes to get her own way.'

'Don't they all. But in her case, from what I've seen of her and from what I know of you and Alan, I put that down to character, or personality, which of course, isn't what I think of as temperament.'

'I must say,' Helen observed, 'for a first-time mother you seem awfully sure of yourself.'

'Well, I may be sure of some things, but there's far more that I'm not sure of. Anyway, when I say I'm sure about this temperament question, I feel sure of it at the moment because all the facts seem to fit so perfectly. But, of course, I'm wide open to correction. If someone can come along and prove me wrong, then I'll be the first to be convinced. But where's that someone going to come from? As far as I can see, there isn't any consensus of opinion about any of this; if there is, then why aren't we mothers hearing about it? We're

211

the ones who need to know. That's why I wrote to the BBC. I didn't know what else to do.'

'Well, I'm sure you've done splendidly. And you've certainly made me think –' Helen's expression became anxious. 'Now before we go any further, are you sure about Harriet? I mean, she can be a little devil at times.'

I smiled. 'Yes, I'm sure.'

'But what makes you so sure?'

'Well, she's so positive, so self-possessed, so relaxed compared to Melanie. She wants things, yes, naturally, but I've looked at her face; they show everything in their faces, don't they. And there's no sign of the tension, the desperate eagerness, the terrible compulsion that Melanie's always had, though it's toned down a lot now. So whatever you've done, right or wrong, it's all working out all right. Perhaps you've shouted at her unjustly, or she's been frightened by something, but she can adjust, she can be reassured, she's normal. That's what I'm getting at, you see. With the normal baby, if we make minor mistakes, then there's probably no lasting harm done because the baby understands at some point that she was frightened for nothing and the shock wears off. But if the Geralds of this world get shocks, I think they don't wear off; they're sort of bruised inwardly and the bruises can't heal. They fester away in there and show themselves in some other form later on.'

'Well, thanks for the reassurance, my love, but I've still got some niggles. I still don't quite see. What happened to Gerald, for example. Do you know? What's his mother like?'

'His mother was another one. As far as I can see she has the same temperament as Gerald. You should meet her. Rigid as a flagpole. Can't show affection. And she's the type that "has to do her work", babies or no babies. So he's missing out on a sense of security for a start. He's pulled by his temperament towards extreme feelings with nothing to counteract them; so he grows up his own worst enemy, the victim, if you like, of his own extreme tendencies.'

212

'All right, then. Perhaps we can talk about that some other time. But what I want to know is, what on earth has all that got to do with his not talking to you, for heaven's sake? And Melanie, too.' Helen shook her head in bewilderment. 'I can hardly believe it – his own baby. It doesn't seem possible. I don't think I could bear that – when I think how Alan dotes on Harriet. I'm even a bit jealous sometimes, I can tell you.'

'It was hard for me to believe, too. And I still keep thinking it's bound to stop, it can't go on. I have to try to understand it, if only to keep sane.'

Leaning forward, Helen took both my hands in hers. 'My love, what have you got yourself into? Whoever could have dreamt of anything like this?'

'I know – I've had to revise my ideas about living happily ever after. What about you and Alan?'

'Well, we have our differences. But on the whole, yes, I suppose I'm very lucky. But – just what does Gerald want?'

'I'm still trying to work that out.'

'I'm afraid to me it sounds as if he just wants to get rid of you.'

'Well, most of the time I think that, too. But why? Exactly why? He insists it's because I've "let him down", as he sees it. I've got to think about it all. I'll let you know if I come up with anything.'

Twenty-five

The BBC regretted that they could not make use of my material. It was controversial and I was unqualified. They could not take the risk, but sent their best wishes.

It's not as upsetting as it might have been [I wrote to Helen], because I've just got myself the most perfect part-time job. Of course, I'm disappointed. I suppose if I'd had a degree in psychology – and what does that prove? – they might have thought it worth sticking their necks out. I may try writing to other people later on. The office is only a few miles from the nursery school, and the hours are nine to one, which fits in perfectly, an absolute godsend. The pay is quite good for down here, local authority rates, so I'm saving everything I earn for a deposit on a Mini. Then I've got to learn to drive and can start Melanie at the school. There's a local village mum with a girl Melanie's age who will look after her in the mornings for now, and later on in the school holidays. Melanie gets on very well with this little girl, and it's an adventure for her to spend time in someone else's house, so I think it will be all right.

I'm afraid Gerald takes no interest whatever in any of this, any more than he was interested in the BBC. He just shrugged and said nothing. But he doesn't seem to object to the job, or the school or car. I'm sure this is right for Melanie.

Eighteen months later, I wrote:

I've saved enough for a deposit on the new car Gerald has

insisted on. He can't abide anything second-hand. In the afternoons he teaches me to drive along some of the wider country roads before going into town traffic. He stays calm so I don't get flustered. Melanie sits in the back not making a sound, and there Gerald and I are, close together but separate, never a smile exchanged, strictly business; he won't allow his obvious pleasure at having the car to stretch to actual enthusiasm.

And three months later:

Have just passed the test. Melanie has started at the school, which seems wonderful and she's thriving on it. My seven-hour day by bus is now reduced to about five and a half by car.

Later still:

Gerald is just as cold and distant and seems more or less unaffected by all the new activity. It hurts so much that he takes no interest whatever in Melanie's school life, never enquires about her progress or even asks her about her day. She's in her second term and I've begun to settle for this dull semi-existence, trying to keep things cheerful and practical.

Twenty-six

'Gerald, we haven't seen Jill and Robert for ages. Shall we ask them to dinner next week?'

Barely glancing up from his newspaper, Gerald said quietly, 'I shan't be here then.'

His matter-of-fact tone broke the Friday evening calm all the more effectively for carrying no particular emphasis, no note of drama.

Please let me be wrong, I said to myself.

Aloud I said, 'Oh?' – 'What?' – 'Where?'

No response. His head stayed down.

I tried again: 'What's happening, then?' I knew perfectly well what was happening but only in the limited way, in the state of incomprehension, in which one learns of a dreadful accident.

Half glancing up, he said coolly, 'I shan't be here, that's all.'

'What do you mean?'

He raised his head. His determined, unruffled expression left me even more shaken. Open antagonism would somehow have been preferable; it would have betrayed some sort of feeling rather than this impersonal air of a business administrator inured to handing out redundancies to long-serving staff.

'I'm going back to London,' he said curtly, quickly returning to his newspaper.

'Oh, no!'

I began to take it in. 'But – but your job,' I gasped.

He looked up impatiently. 'I've left,' he said testily.

'You mean – you've actually left?'

'Yes.'

'Today?'

'Yes.'

'You mean –'

He looked up. 'Yes, I mean it this time.' His face was cold, set. 'I'm going back to London.'

'Oh!'

For some minutes I could find nothing to say.

'When?' I heard myself whisper.

'Sunday.'

I believed him. He was going. Was this happening to me or to someone else? I stared at the dark top of his head. He was going, really going, a fact which had to be accepted; but not immediately, not right away.

A sleepless night brought a Saturday locked into misery which somehow had to be kept hidden from Melanie. Helen's glib 'good riddance' rang in my ears but found no sort of echo in my heart. All along I had thought that he was resigned, if not reconciled, to our marriage, and all the while this was afoot. Or had he done it on a sudden whim? Not that it mattered now.

He packed two bags. He was to get the midday train on Sunday.

'I'll drive you to Plymouth,' I volunteered. (Stay with him a bit longer – perhaps he won't go – not really.)

'There's no need. I can get the bus.'

'I'd like to.'

'All right. Thank you.'

I didn't think he would change his mind, not this time, but there was a vague feeling that seeing him off on the train, being physically present, might introduce a note of normality into an otherwise monstrous situation. Beyond that, nothing; nothing but a kind of oblivion.

'We're going to take Daddy to Plymouth, darling. You'll be able to see the trains.' At least Melanie was going to get something out of it.

'Where's Daddy going?'

'To see Grandma, darling.'

'Is Grandma coming to see us?'

'Not yet, darling.'

When the train came in, Gerald bent down and gave his daughter a quick kiss on the cheek. 'Goodbye, Melanie.'

I blanched. It was the first time I'd known him of his own volition address or kiss his daughter.

'Goodbye, Daddy.' The thin little arms encircled his neck. I couldn't bear to look. To me he nodded awkwardly, a stranger relieved to be going. I looked dumbly into the granite face of the man I had loved and cared for for more than ten years. Why wasn't I flinging my arms round his neck and begging him to stay? His set face gave back his answer.

'Goodbye.'

'Goodbye.'

I watched the shadowy figure, a ghost from the past, disappear into the train without a backward glance. I returned to the car, the walking wounded, my senses clogged by a battle-weary sense of disbelief. Was this really happening? Had he really left his job? If so, then he must have given in his notice, so he had known about this for at least a week, yet he had given nothing away.

The sense of unreality persisted throughout the drive home: deserted Sunday streets, an uncontested route out of the city, empty country roads – all hallucinations; a bad dream from which I would soon wake.

Once home, it was real enough that he wasn't there. Every corner of the house shrieked its emptiness. I went slowly upstairs, looking for ghosts. It was real enough that his part of the wardrobe was bare, that his drawers were empty. I stumbled downstairs and looked across the sitting-room. The little table beside his chair was bare, his dictionaries and reference books gone. He was gone, wiped out without a trace as if by a deadly ray-gun. We weren't going to see him again.

My mind was a blank, unable to focus, unable even to dwell on how to survive financially. I had only about five pounds in my possession, enough to last another week or so, my small salary being reserved for child-minding and school and car expenses.

Most of the night was spent tossing about like flotsam in the bleak spaces of the bed. The next day an automaton pretending to be me drove Melanie the fifteen miles to her school, then on to my office in Totnes.

The office was housed, improbably, in an irregular terrace of varied old low brick and stone buildings at the lower end of the narrow main street, one-time cottage homes that were now small shops with rooms over. We were above a hairdresser's, with a separate side entrance to which I had the key. A brass plate beside the door was inscribed 'Devon County Council. School Psychological Service'.

Today, likeable young Gordon Adams was not due in for his periodic dictation of reports. He occasionally paused for a chat, and once or twice I'd been tempted to confide in him about Gerald, perhaps ask for his advice. But his reply, though sure to be sympathetic, was all too predictable: consult a psychiatrist.

And once I'd uttered the words 'mental illness' a barrier would be set up. I'd be treated differently: with untoward care, with caution or condescension; I'd be a marked woman, singled out for pity, for sudden halts in conversations, for avoidance of potentially delicate ground. Whereas my own well-being, my very sanity, depended on ordinary personal contacts with friends and relations, with neighbours and local traders. The best way, the only way, was to keep information about Gerald to a minimum; mention only where he worked, or perhaps his interest in birds or in English.

Just as well that today I was working alone, otherwise I might have lapsed into tears and confessions to an understanding Gordon. I applied myself to the clacking typewriter, then collected Melanie and drove home, and spoke and cooked and ate and put the child to bed, and then sat for hours staring down like a bereaved person

219

at the geometric pattern in the red-grounded carpet; and at last, very late, drifted up to bed and in the small hours slept the sleep of exhaustion.

The next day the automaton again took over. And the next.

The morning post always came early. On Thursday I came down in my old blue wool dressing-gown to see lying on the mat a postcard addressed to me in Gerald's distinctive, tiny pointed handwriting. I gaped at it. Would there never be an end to his twists and turns? I picked up the card and turned it over. It read:

London
Weds. Arriving Plymouth 4 p.m. Friday. Can you meet me?

I gazed at the card in bewilderment, then took it into the kitchen, placed it on the table and turned away, waiting for the kettle to boil. When the tea was made I picked the card up and took it with the tea tray into the living-room. I set the tray down and picked up the card and read the message again – Gerald was coming back. I laid the card on the table and poured out the tea. HE WAS COMING BACK. We would go and meet him. There was a sort of blockage then, like coming to the end of a cul-de-sac.

It was time to wake Melanie and give her the news.

Gerald gave no reason for his speedy return and was far too unapproachable to be questioned. But finding a new job similar to the last one turned out to be amazingly easy. New television retailers were springing up and it was merely a matter of making a few personal calls, so there was the relief of knowing where the next week's wages were coming from. But why, and where, had he gone? To his mother's? And why had he come back? Perhaps his mother had refused to condone the desertion of wife and child, in her view something not only strictly prohibited but practically unheard of.

Twenty-seven

'I've thought of something that might be the answer for you,' Helen said.

'Oh yes? What's that?'

'First, I take it that Gerald's no better?'

I shook my head. In the two years since I'd last been in London Gerald hadn't changed, hadn't relented one jot, and Helen had seen the hopelessness eating into my face, etching out the sad story. But the story wasn't all sad. My job was going well, and two years in the nursery school had turned Melanie into a fairly confident, happy five-year-old. So it seemed that on that score alone I'd been right to persevere and keep her there.

Alan had retreated to his study after playing his nightly role as washing-up partner with Helen and their new Bendix dishwasher. I'd watched their performance in fascination, Alan dapper in his dark Simpson suit standing beside Helen in her chic black dress and high-heeled court shoes in front of their twin gleaming stainless steel sinks: Helen holding each used item in turn under a jet of steaming water and then passing it on to Alan, poised like a runner in a relay race, ready to lodge it deftly into the slatted depths of the machine. A novel kind of modern assembly-line. It occurred to me that our meal of veal escalope and the heating of those torrents of hot water must have cost more than my own housekeeping for a week. Money doesn't mean a thing to us, Helen once assured me. Probably she considered their basic natures and values unchanged, which seemed largely true. Largely, but not altogether.

'Well,' Helen went on, 'I've only recently heard of this but I've a friend, Esme. She's my physiotherapist – you remember you met her here once when she was doing my back.' I nodded, recalling the self-assured professional in a white coat I had once seen kneading and pummelling Helen's slightly strained back.

'She's been telling me all about herself. She's older than you, about forty, divorced. Of course she's pretty well off; lovely home in Hampstead, two kids at boarding-school, a good income from her ex-husband, and of course there's her practice. There's just one snag. She wants to get married again but she can't seem to meet anyone and she's fed up with waiting. Anyway, someone told her about this magazine, *The Lady*. Now don't turn your nose up. I know it isn't our sort of thing. The point is, there's a small-ad section where men with children to bring up but no wife look for a woman to run the home. Sometimes they just want a housekeeper, but often they're really looking for someone who fits in that they can marry. You get me?'

'You mean – you mean there are really all those men out there? Decent sorts?'

'As far as I can see there are all sorts. But it's worth thinking about, don't you agree?'

'Well, it sounds too good to be true though; I must say, I don't like the idea of telling my life story to strangers.' Until that moment I hadn't known that I might be ready to desert Gerald. 'What happened to your friend,' I asked. 'To Esme?'

'It's an absolute scream, really. She's been ringing me up for months – what do I think of this one? Do I like the sound of that one? Bringing me round letters.'

'Has she met anyone?'

'Well, initially she met lots of people, all sorts, careered all over the country, day-trips, weekends, but there was no one she actually fancied. Then she did meet one she liked, same age as herself, a dentist, quite well off, good-looking. Anyway, it seems that they fell for each other pretty heavily, and before long she was going to stay with him at Highgate all the time, midweek, weekends. According to her,

222

she'd never had a sex life like it before and they got on well in other ways too, lots in common. She was ready to get married.

'Then I had a phone call from her. She was crying. I thought he must have changed his mind. Not a bit of it. She'd let herself into his house one evening ready to stay the night, went up to the bedroom, and there, lying on the bed was a black leather rig-out – jacket, short skirt, high boots, and, can you imagine it, my dear, a riding whip.'

I was finding all this very hard to believe. 'What did she do?'

'What do you think? She ran like hell down the stairs and then she met him coming up.'

'"Hello, darling," he said, cool as a cucumber. Esme managed to say, hoping for a moment it wasn't what she thought, "What are those things on the bed?" And he said, very calmly, mind you, "You'll put them on for me, won't you darling?" His face, Esme said, looked odd then, for the first time, sort of twisted. Well, she ran and she never looked back. What she couldn't get over was the wonderful time they'd had for weeks up till then – not a hint there was anything peculiar going on. It was a shock, I can tell you.'

'I'm sure it was! I'm afraid it's a bit of a shock to me, too. Don't laugh, but I didn't know that things like that really happened. I mean, I've heard vague references to sadism, masochism, things like that, but I never really understood what happens.'

'My love, where have you been all your life? I don't see how you could not know.' Helen gave a knowing half-smile. 'On the other hand, perhaps I do see.'

'What, er, what happened to your friend after that?'

'Well, something good at last, I hope. Of course at first she was terribly upset. Apart from the shock, she'd been really in love with him and to lose him like that – it took her months to get over it, and she swore she wouldn't answer any more adverts. Then eventually she did, and a few weeks ago she rang me to say she'd met someone else. He's a bit older, some sort of financier. Practically the first thing she said to him was, "I don't suppose you'll want anything to do with me, I've been married and divorced three times. And he said, "Well, don't worry about that, I've been married and divorced five times!" So they had a good laugh and then they got on famously; she's already thinking of chucking up her practice and taking up residence as wife of the country squire. She showed me some pictures of the house and grounds in Gloucestershire. Lovely place! I suggested she give it a bit more time and she agrees, but already she's spending most of her time down there; then he travels back and stays with her here. Apparently he's made a fortune in business and now he just dabbles in stocks and shares. Esme says he's a dear. So there you are, it looks as though she's all set up. I hope so. I'll let you know how it goes.'

'Will you? Good. I'd like to know.' Not that I could quite believe in all these weird practices and multiple marriages. My own continuing sex life with Gerald was quite weird enough for me, short and purposive, with the same old superficial satisfactions which now made me feel ashamed. But I daren't object. You never knew what might set Gerald off.

Good fortune such as Esme's was far removed from my expectations. But all those decent men with good homes and children needing love offered the first practical solution to my problems.

My rejection by the BBC appeared to have lowered my stock with Helen. She seemed offhand when I said I had received replies to letters I had written to Professor Eysenck, Arthur Koestler and Anna Freud.

'Oh, yes, and what did they have to say?'

'Well, Eysenck was the least encouraging.'

'Well, I warned you, didn't I.'

'Yes, I know you did, but I had to try everything. He's in the limelight at the moment and what he says is interesting, in a way, a little sidelight on trying to boil down everything that's happening to Gerald to a science.'

'What did he say, then?'

'I have it here. I'll read it to you. He says, "A good deal is known about the genetic factors in obsessional and other neurotic disorders and there are several fairly extensive studies of groups suffering from these disorders. A single case could never be used to prove very much as it's impossible to sort out the tangled skein of heredity and environment in this way. While, therefore, the material you mention might be of considerable interest to a psychiatrist working in this specific field and having access to other similar cases, I am afraid it wouldn't be of much help to me as I am not and have no other cases to use as controls.'"

'H'm. Not much joy there.'

'No, I was very disappointed. If, as he says, a good deal is known about these problems, how is it that our own GPs can't tell us anything about them or give us some practical advice?'

'Because the only people who know about them are the ones working in that special field.'

'Well, that doesn't help people like me. I wonder what the disorders being studied are. I mean, we've all heard about obsessions with washing hands, checking doors, that kind of thing, but I've never heard of obsessions like Gerald's, or what's to be done about them. I know a single case doesn't prove anything, but do these lengthy studies of groups with controls prove anything either? Or do they just get grants to go on working in their own "specific field", as he puts it? What help is any of that to people like me who have to live with neurotics? Why can't they tell us how to behave and react? How to try to make life bearable? Give us some dos and don'ts.'

'Perhaps that's just what a specialist would do,' Helen said.

'I wonder. I get the feeling they would just give him some drug or other to "calm him down", as they say, slow down his thought processes. But that doesn't bring us any nearer to the cause, does it? How to deal with babies, that sort of thing.'

'From the sound of this letter, and from what the BBC says, I think I begin to see how these professionals would view it: someone trying to muscle in on their territory.'

'I suppose you're right, more's the pity. I thought it was terribly callous of Eysenck just to say that my notes might be of interest to other psychiatrists but not to him. Why didn't he at least put me in touch with someone who might be interested? Don't you think that every psychiatrist has some sort of duty to help people with mental problems?'

'Well, if they have, then there's nothing in Holy Orders about it, is there? It seems from what he says that they're not obliged to do anything other than carry on with their own little bit of research into their own little bit of the mind.'

'As if you can divide the mind up into specialities, like Heart, or E.N.T.'

We were silent for a moment.

'What did the others have to say?' Helen asked.

'Well, Anna Freud was mildly encouraging. She said she agreed with everything I wrote to her and would be glad to see my notes. Said they all believed that children were born "with different possibilities" – whatever that means – and that "the earliest experiences are extremely important for the formation of their personalities". Then she said she'd be away for a month but when she came back she'd be "very ready to read my observations and perhaps to send me similar ones made by other people" – which rather suggests, doesn't it, that there's nothing new to learn about signs of obsessionalism in babies.'

'Yes, it does rather. Still, you'll follow it up, won't you?'

'I suppose so, though somehow I'm not very hopeful about any of it.'

'What did Koestler have to say?'

'Well, he was the most encouraging of all, in a way, though I don't really think anything will come of that either. He did say my letter was "interesting", and I suppose it's a compliment of sorts that he suggested I send a short summary of my observations to the Editor of the *British Journal of Psychology*, with a copy to Professor Cyril Burt, who's on the Board. He said that I could mention that I was sending it at his suggestion.'

Helen uttered a sceptical 'Hm … I suppose it can do no harm.' Her tone suggested that my time might be better employed. Theories or explanations didn't really count with Helen, only facts. Her next remark confirmed this.

'I don't really see why you want to bother with all that; you're not getting anything from Gerald, are you, that's the point.'

Perhaps she was right. Perhaps it was not our business to delve, but to live. But 'living' revived the question of babies. I tried one more tack.

'I still think we've got to get to a stage where we all know some elementary facts about the way our minds work, just as we do our bodies. There must be lots of people like me desperate to understand what's going on, and there's no way we can find out.'

'I think, my sweet, you're getting into very deep water if you start to think like that.'

'But surely, in time, we can at least get to know how to stop things going wrong.'

'Do you realise what you're saying? Do you really imagine we can ever get a world full of sane, well-balanced people who know how to be happy?'

I smiled. 'Well, I suppose that's a bit of a tall order, but we've got to try. We've got to start somewhere.'

'And you think that "somewhere" is with our babies?'

'I don't know. But we all begin as babies, and an awful lot seems to happen just in those first couple of years, doesn't it.'

'I agree with you there. It is quite astounding.'

'Yes, astounding. What bothers me is the thought of all those tyrants out there, murderers, terrorists, extremists of all sorts, they were all babies once.'

'My dear girl, don't you think you've enough to cope with without going into all that?'

'I can't help it. I do worry about it.'

'Worry about what?'

'Well, for one thing, evil. Do you think people are born evil?'

'Well, it's a bit difficult to see a newborn baby as being evil.'

'But if a baby had a propensity towards extremes, he could be pulled towards extremes of evil, couldn't he?'

'Perhaps. I really don't know – now come along, my sweet, stop frowning and start to think about yourself for a change.'

Twenty-eight

This is right. I know it is. At last I'm nearing the answer that has been eluding me all this time. Even though I've had this inkling of what it is, I couldn't quite get hold of it, like trying to get hold of a slippery fish; every time you try to grasp it, it slips away.

Gerald and I were sitting reading on a warm June evening; not yet quite dark, the curtains open to a still blue sky. When I say reading, I was reading. Gerald as usual was poring over his notebook.

I let my book slip down on to my lap – *Dangling Man*, by Saul Bellow, very new-looking in its bright yellow cover. I'd found it, priced two-and-sixpence, on the little shelf of books outside the village stationer, and the first lines had attracted me, a reference to the habit of addressing oneself inwardly, which gave a kind of legitimacy to my own silent sleuthing. The brain has its own intricate devices for threading back to previous lines of thought. A remark in the book about the undesirability of advertising one's business to the entire house by untoward shouting had put me in mind of Gerald's mother and her antipathy to this kind of behaviour, thence to Gerald and his infernal problems, or rather my infernal problems with him.

I found myself facing the unpalatable thought, the knowledge which for some reason had not previously registered with sufficient force, that Gerald must have what amounted to an unhealthy interest in, let's say an obsessive fixation on, the sight of a woman's private parts. A little clue about this morbid interest came when I suddenly remembered a childhood incident of my own. It took place at the birthday party of twin cousins of mine, boys aged eleven, when I was about eight. At the height of the games and play they beckoned me out of the living-room, and honoured, if mystified, at being singled out, I followed them upstairs to their bedroom.

When they told me to lie down on the bed I feared something was wrong. Then the order came, 'Take off your knickers,' and I dared not disobey. I wriggled out of my knickers, and with the soft cotton garment crushed in my fist I sat facing my tormentors, lips pursed, awaiting further orders.

'Lie down again.'

I felt very far removed from the innocent gaiety of musical chairs downstairs. Fearful of what might follow, I lay down. Side by side the two boys faced me from the foot of the bed.

'Pull up your dress.'

Not daring to look at them, I obeyed.

One of the boys leaned over the footboard of the bed, grasped my two feet and drew them wide apart. There was a sharp intake of breath. I glanced up. With intense concentration, very serious, both were staring down at the mysterious area high up between my legs. There was a long silence.

'There, you see.'

A slight grunt. Another long concentrated silence.

'All right?' The second boy nodded.

'You can put your knickers on and go back downstairs, and mind, don't you dare say a word to anyone.'

Shaking my head in promise of my unswerving silence, I hastily pulled on my knickers and made my escape. And until this moment, more than twenty years later, I had not consciously thought of it.

Whilst it was true that the penis of a naked little boy was ostentatiously there to be seen at bath or dressing times, a naked little girl standing up, as well as posing the intriguing enigma of being different from the corresponding area of a boy, revealed only a sly secretive little slit which might well hide untold unimaginable secrets; and those secrets must present an object of intense interest to any normal little boy, especially a boy with a lively enquiring mind. But Gerald's curiosity was not normal. As with all his feelings, all his emotions, it went to extremes. And so, inevitably, this secret area, the female hidden territory, assumed an exaggerated importance in his mind and later came to be identified as his own inviolable property as constituted by his wife.

That Gerald had satisfied his own curiosity on this score long before we met was certain. He had had a number of affairs with other women and undoubtedly, as well as carefully scrutinising their naked bodies, especially in the relevant area, would also have verified all pertinent physiological details by consulting reference books, including his comprehensive *Encyclopaedia of Sex*. I had once or twice glanced at this tome and found it to be copiously illustrated in colour with all aspects of human anatomy, including genitals, leaving nothing to the imagination, and as could only be expected from a properly brought up prude I'd found it rather distasteful and avoided dwelling on it.

I had also passively succumbed to Gerald's periodic, brief but no doubt thorough inspections of my hidden territory, regarding his intent silent scrutiny as of little real significance, something to be tolerated along with his other peculiar but ostensibly harmless habits.

With a frightful new awareness I now recalled the very first time Gerald made love to me, in his room at the camp. It was far from the passionate encounter I had expected from this dark prince of my dreams. I lay on the bed with only my skirt – nothing else – demurely removed, naturally leaving every other initiative to him. My briefs were deftly removed. So far so good. But then instead of the expected kissing and caressing there was a long silence during which I risked a surreptitious glance at my suitor, who to my astonishment was crouched purposefully at the foot of the bed, directing a searching gaze at the apex of the gap created by his gentle but firm parting of my legs.

I didn't know what to make of this unexpected development, but being a novice in such matters could only regard it as yet another proof of my profound ignorance, wondering if it were customary for a sensible worldly man to search thus for signs of unmentionable diseases. If so, who could blame him? A few minutes later he was lying beside me and matters proceeded along more predictable lines, which were then rather disappointing: no passion, no endearments, just a businesslike means to an end. Probably, I thought, I had been misled in my vague expectations.

That, of course, was what worried me when I first found I was pregnant, the vague fear that some hidden danger lurked in the undue importance placed on this visual fixation of Gerald's. Only a slight worry, much like his preference for a baby girl, something I mistakenly thought amenable to common sense and therefore probably of no great importance. I now realised that common sense did not enter into it; it couldn't. There's no way that common sense can be injected into the impermeable wall of obsessionalism.

Then with a shock of recognition I remembered something he had told me years before, something which somehow, to my cost, I had completely forgotten. It is hard now, very hard, to understand how I could have contrived to forget this, how I could have failed to attach to it the importance it deserved, probably dismissing as merely another kind of quirk something occupying such a vital place in his obsessive mind. But I was no connoisseur of obsessive minds, any more than I was a connoisseur of fine wines. Neither had entered the limited orbit of my experience.

Gerald had told me, in a rare confessional moment before we were married, that before the war when he was nineteen he had met and married a local girl, living with her at her mother's home till the outbreak of war and call-up. Apparently sexual intercourse was 'unsatisfactory' because she had what he called an 'elastic hymen' which had never been broken and formed a partial barrier. They planned to consult a doctor, but while he was away doing his basic training, the girl, probably with his interests in mind, went to see her GP and was examined in his absence. 'Well, that was it,' he said, with that air of implying that the import was obvious.

But it was far from obvious to me. I was probably content to hear that for him, the marriage was over, leaving the field clear for me. He went to court (the High Court, in those days) for an annulment, conducting his own case and closely examined by the judge in minute detail as to intercourse, which he maintained with conviction had never taken place because of the girl's condition. He got his annulment.

The whole pathetic picture now began to unwind. The original boyish curiosity (because it was repressed? because of Gerald's nature?) had been turned by his own complicated internal mechanism into an obsession which dictated that his wife and the precious property – namely the vagina – constituted by that wife, were his alone, sacrosanct, not to be violated by exposure to the eyes of another man. Perhaps this was even more important to him than betrayal with another man. (Would he have been able to forgive that? I thought not. But would unfaithfulness in his eyes have constituted the lesser sin?)

There is another reason why that medical examination by Roger might have been so important to him. Most of us assume that, in some given situations, other people's emotional reactions will closely resemble our own; it doesn't occur to us that they won't. Gerald couldn't help unconsciously assuming that the sight of a woman's vagina was just as important to any other man, even to a doctor, as it was to him. Perhaps, who knows?, in some cases he was right. In the case of Roger I knew him to be wrong, but Gerald did not equate private examination by one doctor working alone with the unavoidable exposure during childbirth under clinical conditions and in the presence of more than one person. The fact that husbands were excluded at birth times perhaps helped to make the birth scene acceptable, whereas the private examination registered on his nervous system as a shock of betrayal from which no reprieve was possible, a knee-jerk type of reaction which could not subsequently be moderated.

Why had he chosen not to be present at the fateful examination?

Did he, perhaps subconsciously, need to escape from family responsibilities and the daily work routine to be free to indulge his memory obsession, still the dominating factor in his life?

Did he have suspicions about Roger? Was the disowning of me a punishment? I did not think so, although it seemed amazing that he did not have suspicions. If he had, I think he would have voiced them without hesitation. No, he probably knew that we liked each other but also thought we weren't the types to do anything about it. Perhaps, for once, possibly for the only time in his life, he had trusted someone, namely me, and in so doing had erred in thinking me entirely incapable of deceit. Perhaps his notion of a passionate nature was clouded by his own limited potential in that direction.

One thing was now quite certain; for whatever reason, Gerald was not going to forget his 'betrayal'. It was as fixed in his mind, as unalterable, as final, as death, something to which he was grimly reconciled since it suited his own perverse needs. If he had once smiled at me in all the terrible five years since Melanie's birth, I might have been – probably would have been – stupidly buoyed up with new hope. Perhaps he genuinely thought he was doing me a service by consistently showing that there was no future with him to such a blatant extent that even I had to give in and accept the inevitable? But no: he was not capable of being really concerned with my interests, or even with Melanie's – a sad truth which I conceded with no malice whatever. It was far too tragic a truth to be belittled with malice, this lameness of soul allowing no humane consideration, an enclosed icy mode of being, a sunless satellite revolving perpetually upon its own axis: 'an onlooker at the rich feast of life' – I must have read this phrase somewhere; how apt it was for him.

It didn't occur to Gerald that I had no money and nowhere to go. He seemed to have a childlike confidence in my ability to 'manage', even to 'manage' this impossible task. (One blessing: the Mini was paid for.)

It seemed that I had little choice. But could I face a break-up?

234

Was it right to deprive Melanie of her natural father, however inadequate? Had he shown the slightest sign of personal attachment to her, I could never have considered parting them.

I'd have to wait as long as possible before making any definite move. The idea of all those lonely fathers and children needing the right woman to look after them was very appealing, but as long as Gerald was working I could give Melanie more time at the school, which was so good for her.

Twenty-nine

'Wait here, Mummy.'

'What for, darling?'

'Just a minute, Mummy, wait here.'

Melanie ran a dozen yards or so up the lane, turned about, and with an expression of joyful abandon ran very fast towards me, leapt up and flung her arms round my neck. Holding her tight, I looked down in surprise at the ecstatic face.

'When I do that, Mummy,' Melanie said, very intense and eager, 'it means I'm happy.'

I hugged her closer. 'That's lovely, darling.'

It was a moment to resolve any lingering doubts about the rearing of a difficult child.

'By the way,' Gerald said. I looked up from Saturday's breakfast dishes in the washing-up bowl. Gerald was standing by the open kitchen door. 'Jack Day and his wife will be calling in this afternoon.'

Another Gerald surprise, on two counts: he was addressing me voluntarily, and, for the first time, he had invited someone to call. Although his tone had been forced and polite rather than friendly, was this perhaps a sign that he was changing, improving?

'Who's Jack Day?' I asked in a light even voice.

'He works in the office. He's an ex-policeman. He chases default-ers on hire payments.' With which he turned and walked away.

Jack Day and his wife – 'Call us Jack and Mavis,' they insisted – were a practical, pleasant, warm-hearted couple who seemed to have nothing whatever in common with Gerald.

Jack, large and florid, walked over to the window with his teacup.

'Nice view you've got here,' he said, 'but you're pretty cut off, aren't you. How do you stick it?'

'We like it,' I said with a friendly smile. 'Do you live in the country?'

'No fear. We're townies. We're in Plymouth, up at Mannamead' – this was a quiet residential district. He looked round the room. 'Where's the TV?'

'We haven't one,' I confessed.

Concerned glances passed between him and Mavis. 'What, no TV! And Gerald in the trade! What do you do with yourselves?' He looked over at Melanie sitting at the table with a jigsaw puzzle, then over to Gerald and back at me. 'Tell you what,' he said. 'I'll get you one.'

'Yes,' Mavis chimed in, 'Jack'll get you a set. Easy. They're coming back all the time, aren't they, Jack.'

'That's for sure,' Jack agreed. 'I'll let you know when the next good one comes in.'

'We can't really afford it,' I said, avoiding mention of long-standing reservations about this questionable form of entertainment.

'Don't you worry about that,' Jack said. 'Shouldn't cost you more than a tenner.'

The set – a ten-inch black and white screen in a varnished wooden console standing three feet high – came in Jack's small van two weeks later. 'There,' he said, switching it on and standing back to admire the picture of an elegant lady news announcer. 'Not bad, is it. It's a new one, nothing wrong with it; chap had it six months, never paid a penny.' He held out his hand. 'Eight pounds to you, Gerald. Not bad, eh?'

Gerald never carried any money other than loose change. Every Friday his wage-packet was handed to me unopened, leaving me to allocate the cash needed for his fares and lunches, which he pocketed without a downward glance, his mind occupied with far more important matters than money.

237

Seeing him fumble uncertainly in his trouser pocket, Jack smiled reassuringly. 'That's all right, Gerald. Give it to the office next week if you like.'

'Er, are you sure?'

'Course I am. You're not the first, you know.'

I imagined the magic boxes wafting the outside world into the living-rooms of Jack's numerous friends and acquaintances. Perhaps we had been cut off for too long. Now doors were about to open: we would make exciting discoveries, we'd see the world, we'd join the human race. But what of the effect on children? I thought of the remarks made by mothers at the school doors: 'Oh yes, we let them watch the BBC but' – with a shudder – 'not the ITV, of course, not those horrid advertisements.'

I found the children's programmes, both the BBC's and (surreptitiously) also ITV's, surprisingly good, a great boon for an isolated only child; and incidentally providing unexpected memory aids for Melanie as she danced about the house singing the rather wordy introductory verses to the Robin Hood series, which she soon had off by heart. Gerald and I welcomed the news and travel programmes – to this day I remember a wonderful introduction to the grandeur of New Zealand lakes and mountains.

Melanie was watching television one Sunday morning while Gerald sat reading, and in the kitchen I was preparing lunch. I was about to check the shoulder of lamb in the oven when suddenly the door burst open and in stormed a very wild-looking Gerald. As I looked up with a start, two fast strides had already brought him to where I stood by the small blue plastic-topped table where the carving-knife lay ready for tackling the joint. In one swift ongoing movement he had seized the knife, and before I could begin to guess what was happening my hair was gripped from behind, my head was tilted sharply back, and his other hand was holding to my exposed throat the gleaming tip of the knife.

I discovered what it was to be truly struck dumb with fear. I could only stare up imploringly at the two large protruding brown eyes blazing into mine. There was a shuddering as the whole of Gerald's frame shook. The hand holding the knife, which I could feel touching, almost pricking my skin, was quivering with malevolent anger and intent, and I did my share of quivering – inwardly. Mercifully, the thrust towards my throat went no further. With a huge effort, his face horribly contorted, his hand still shaking, Gerald managed to stop short, glaring down at me in enraged indecision.

Like an entombed person desperately seeking a saving chink of light, I had to decide urgently whether or not to seek salvation either by speaking, if only I dared, if only I could think of the right thing to say, or by remaining silent and praying for sanity to prevail. Although silence seemed by far the wiser option, I was close to giving way to hysteria and shrieking out the first thing that came to mind. But whatever came out that way was almost bound to be disastrous. If I did say something, the choice of words was crucial, a split-second decision between life and death.

'Come on, darling.'

It was my own voice. In some extraordinary way the decision to speak, along with the choice of words, seemed to have been made for me. It was alarming to hear words uttered which could so easily be the wrong words, which could in fact be my death sentence. I gave silent thanks that by some lucky fluke my voice had sounded even and controlled, which might have a calming effect. A hysterical outburst, a show of fear, might well have incensed him further.

Gerald's eyes were still burning into mine, laser points of fury.

Tense moments trembled between us, wings of the angel of death. The vicious dagger-point of the knife was still quivering against my arched throat, about to cut into the soft white skin. And then, as if by divine intervention, the hand clutching my hair suddenly slackened, and my head immediately recoiled an inch or so back, away from the sharp point of the knife. With a sharp crack like a rifle shot the knife crashed down on the table, and without another glance Gerald broke away and as suddenly as he had entered the room, turned and staggered out. I heard him clump upstairs.

Shaking and shivering, I collapsed on to the chair and slumped forward, head in hands, waiting for the worst of the shock to dissipate. After a while, still stupefied, leaden-limbed, I stirred into a kind of half-life and rose to make some tea. Sitting down, I slowly drank a cupful. I was still shaking. The teacup rattled on the saucer as I put it down. My head hurt a good deal; I was surprised how much it could hurt from the sustained rough pull on my hair.

Slowly the ability to think was restored.

What should be done now? Third-party intervention, the first option to suggest itself, did not seem a good idea. I could run the two hundred yards down the lane to Charlie and Valerie but couldn't risk leaving Melanie behind, and she would unavoidably be frightened if I grabbed her and took her along. Once there I could either telephone the police or embarrass Charlie by begging him to come and intercede for us. But involving Charlie would only make Gerald even more furious.

I could seize Melanie and drive to the main road to phone the police or Roger, but Gerald might chase and catch us before we reached the car; our parking space was a hundred yards or so up the lane in the wide grassy entrance to Charlie's apple orchard. Whether or not Gerald gave chase, Melanie would be terrified. And the idea of confronting him with the police was not only repugnant, I didn't really feel it would do any good. It became clear that involving anyone else would be a mistake. I would have to deal with it myself.

Would Gerald have calmed down? Would he attack me again? Why had he done it? One possible answer had suggested itself, and if this was right, then carrying out my next step would work; and perhaps, scary though it was, the sooner I faced him the better; to delay seemed not only unwise but dangerous, allowing him time to get worked up and come at me again.

Dare I take him a cup of tea? Melanie, fortunately, was still engrossed in the Robin Hood film she was watching.

With shaky hands, I poured two cups of tea and was about to add Gerald's two spoonfuls of sugar and stir it as usual when I hesitated. Fool that I had been, pandering to his every little need! Stupid, stupid fool! But on further reflection, now was not the time to risk provocation. With a wry smile I added the sugar and stirred, then slowly carried the cups upstairs, one in each hand, terrified of what I might find.

The cups clattered on their saucers all the way up the stairs, warning of my approach. I clung to the thought of possible salvation. If I had guessed correctly, then Gerald had inadvertently resolved my greatest problem for me.

From the landing outside the open bedroom door I saw him sitting hunched on the edge of the bed. I waited a moment, undecided. He must have heard the clatter up the stairs but he hadn't looked up. At least he wasn't immediately pouncing on me. I stepped into the room, into the lion's den. He didn't move. I went over and put his cup down on the bedside table.

'Gerald, here's a cup of tea.'

With a slow sullen upward glance he picked up the cup and began to sip, his eyes staying fixed down on the pink carpet.

Taking his acceptance of the tea as a sign of a truce, if only a partial or a temporary one, I stood by the window, drinking my tea, mustering courage. Replacing my cup on its saucer, I spoke quietly.

'I've been thinking about what you've said about our parting. Well, you're right.'

He looked up. His face wore a furtive suggestion of relief.

In a mild tone, I went on, 'It's what you want, isn't it?' A cursory nod. His head drooped again.

'It's a question of where to go.'

'You'll think of something,' he muttered.

I ignored the injustice of this remark.

'Well I have, actually.'

The voice didn't sound like mine. Nor did the words. They sounded more like something read aloud from fiction or from a play, nothing to do with me. But in a roundabout way the actual utterance of these words seemed to have made a decision for me, they had brought a half-digested idea into the realms of action.

'But the only thing is' – my voice seemed to be continuing of its own volition – 'it may take time.'

His head stayed down. 'How long?' he murmured.

'Well, I don't know, and I don't know if it will work at all. You see –' And in a strangely detached way, as if I were not personally involved, I heard myself explaining briefly Helen's idea of answering advertisements.

The moments of waiting for a response helped to restore a certain sense of reality. We were communicating, we were transacting, something was happening at last. Looking down at the top of his sleek dark head, I recalled with a wrench of pain the feel of the taut scalp yielding beneath my fingertips. Now it was turned away from me in enmity. The pain tightened as I realised that I no longer wanted, was no longer impelled, to touch or comfort this stranger; the close unit of two had been split wide open, had changed into two separate entities set on diverging paths.

If I had half expected Gerald to be averse to the idea of another man taking over his wife and daughter, I was mistaken.

'I see,' he said, glancing up with a cool nod as if satisfied with the clarification of some impersonal point.

'Of course, I shall have to start writing letters. I can't give up my job or notify the school until I've something definite. Would you – would you want to stay on here if we'd gone?'

'No.'

The safe anchor of my home was slipping away. How could I let this happen? My voice went on: 'Would you be willing to stay on here until I've somewhere to go? I can't manage without your wages.'

'All right. I'll stay – for the present.'

My anchor was not quite gone, not yet. I picked up his cup. 'I'll get you some more tea. Will you come down for lunch soon?'

He nodded. It hurt that I was never going to call him darling again. I stumbled downstairs, still trembling.

Now came the task of hiding the horror from Melanie.

Up to a point the tension was eased by my promise to leave, though anger and violence still lay dangerously near the surface ready to be revived by an untoward word, a look, an ill-timed rise of the eyebrows. But self-preservation had at last gained a place, if a shaky one, on my agenda. I had to learn to regard Gerald as an enemy.

Forget about the house. Forget about possessions. Forget about love. A new future had to be organised.

How was a small child best told that she might soon have a change of father? With a studied air of casualness I broached the subject as we walked home along the lane.

'How would you like us to get you another daddy, darling?'

Melanie nodded eagerly, 'Yes … yes!'

'Well, darling, we'll have to see.'

With a faint wave of repugnance, I hastily thrust the magazine into my shopping bag. What was I doing? How did I come to be seeking a market-place for my services? It was all wrong. It bore no resemblance to life as I had once envisaged it. But of course, Helen was right. Realism about the future was long overdue.

Walking towards the car parked in a side street near the office, I glanced down at my bag with a rise of spirits. Adventure lay in that bag. But I'd have to be careful. Snares and disappointments probably lay there too. Yet whether or not anything came of it, something was happening. The door of the punishment cell was creaking open. I wanted to dance down the street. Through the smooth pages of this

243

magazine real life was becoming mapped and accessible. By the time I reached the car I was longing to get home and open it.

'Well, good for you!' was Helen's response to my decision. 'And about time, too! Let me know what happens. And you know you can stay here any time, don't you.'

The knife episode had not been mentioned. Helen would only panic and urge immediate flight at all costs, without knowing, or too closely enquiring, what the costs were.

It was time to give the required term's notice to the school, to avoid complications saying simply that we were moving away. Ending this educational dream proved to be nearly as shattering as leaving Gerald and our home, but it had to be done. To test Gerald's patience any further would be far too dangerous. If by the end of term nothing had happened, the situation would have to be reviewed. A knife held to the throat was a very effective way of imposing a time limit.

Thirty

Replying to advertisements that can change not just a career but an entire life – tricky: what to include? what to omit?

BASIC INFORMATION: simple enough: age; age and sex of child; car-driver/owner.

INTERESTS: open to misinterpretation. Omit them altogether and be taken for a moron? Admit to reading? to music? to walking? – too ambiguous. What about "wide interests"? Yes, that's safe.

STATUS (married, widow, etc.): Difficult one. Say as little as possible.

Was this the right thing to do? Was it foolish? Answer debatable. From the purely practical point of view, given a cool head and common sense, it was right. Foolish only if it turned out badly. Answer: carry on and see what happens.

Was it degrading? It certainly felt degrading – a new, modern way of selling oneself to the almighty male but with the saving grace that, unlike the marriage contract, there would now be a small but important element of choice in that this was, ostensibly, more a business transaction than an emotional commitment. For that essential roof and crust, services only would initially be for sale; if the body should become involved, that would be another matter. Or so I thought, little knowing how ill-equipped I was to put this admirable theory into practice.

The hardest part of replying to advertisements was my explanation for leaving, eventually summed up as, 'My husband is mentally ill and needs to pursue his life alone.'

When it finally came to interviews I was pleasantly surprised at how readily this simple explanation was accepted. 'As far as he's capable of loving anyone,' I found myself saying without a blush, 'he does love me, but he's not really capable of loving anyone. He has to be alone.'

Amazing to find understanding nods greeting this hard-won declaration. But how true was it? I wished I knew.

Weekend interviews all over southern England involved thousands of miles of travelling. Fears about meeting with questionable characters proved groundless, but the time and expense were far greater than I had expected; it helped that money need no longer be reserved for school fees, and a week's stay with Helen at half-term allowed for more interviews in and near London.

An astonishing variety of people seemed to be in desperate need of a woman, in one capacity or another, to take over their household. The advertisements were numerous, the requirements varied. I became proficient at targeting replies, skimming over those that were too distant, or banned children, or required someone younger or older, or stipulated specific interests like riding or animals.

Melanie was usually required to be present at interviews, which unfortunately meant dragging the child along on lengthy tiring journeys.

'I was divorced two years ago,' said Jim at my first interview. He was a busy writer of technical literature, working at home and looking after his three children. Burly, dark-haired, rather older than myself, brisk but kindly, he immediately put me at my ease over coffee in the hotel lounge in Bristol where we met at the end of a five-hour drive; he was from Cambridge, so this was a halfway point for both of us.

Once I had settled Melanie down with a glass of milk and a book at the further side of the table, he listened with sympathy and understanding to my brief halting account of Gerald. Strange, to be sitting here in an expensive hotel in my best blue suit, being listened to and looked at, admitted once more to the human race.

'Unfortunately,' Jim said, 'my wife – my ex-wife – lives not very far away from us. She's manic, quite mad, really, has these terrific brainstorms, shouts and raves, hates everybody, including the children – and me, of course!' He smiled amiably. 'I had ten years of it, much like you, and then I had to get a divorce, if only for the sake of the children. I have full custody. The trouble is, she, Peggy, my wife, won't give up. She won't leave us alone. She's liable to come storming up to the house at any time, day or night, and make a great scene. Knocks and bangs on the door for hours and won't go away. She really is a tigress.

'Now you, my dear, you'd be wonderful for the children. I'd love you to come. But I don't think –' He smiled warmly.

My heart sank. Already I had seen myself enjoying a close relationship with this man and providing a kindly buffer-zone for his children. The thought of the closeness was rather disturbing: he was a bit like Roger, sturdy, reliable.

(Was I really contemplating a transference of affections from Roger so soon after our parting? Was that what my love amounted to? Was I just fickle? No, I was more ready to move on than I had known.)

'I don't think,' Jim went on, 'that would be fair to you.' A kind glance partially softened my disappointment. 'You've had more than enough of that sort of thing, from the sound of it. You need someone, something, different, a chance to forget all about trouble and have a happy life. You deserve it. I'm sure you've earned it.' Another sympathetic smile. I watched his large, rather beefy hand pick up his coffee cup and fought a desire to grab it and feel it close comfortingly over mine. 'I'm sure you'll get it,' he said.

I wanted to protest that I didn't in the least mind sharing trouble with someone like him, but obviously he knew far more about it than I. His judgement had to be accepted. Wresting my glance away from his hand, I stood up. We shook hands, and in a much subdued mood I drove on to Bath.

The next man was disconcertingly young, smiling courteously as he pulled out a chair for me in the hotel lounge. A solicitor, but with none of Alan's slightly bombastic manner, gentle and quietly spoken, wearing a well-cut suit. He was only twenty-five and had been married three years when his wife died of asthma at the age of twenty-one, a year after giving birth to their baby daughter. 'My wife's parents are very wealthy,' he said. 'They're heartbroken. My wife was an only child. They did everything they could for her, saw specialists all over the world, spent the last year with her and the baby in Switzerland. Nothing could be done. Now they want to take the baby over, take her to live with them so that she's properly looked after; and, of course, I want to keep her. Up to now I've managed with a daily woman but if I get someone living in then they won't really be able to object. What do you think?'

My heart ached for him in his tragic plight. And ached at the tantalising thought of a comfortable home free of mental strife and financial problems. But – I smiled in commiseration.

'I'd love to come to you, I really would. But I'm afraid the problem for me would be that, for my daughter's sake, I must try to find somewhere permanent if I can. I don't want to have to move her again. And you see, you're young – and much as I'm sure you can't think of it now' – his air of loss confirmed this – 'you're practically bound to marry again one day; and then, you see, we shouldn't be needed. So I'm afraid it just isn't possible. I'm really sorry. But I'm sure you'll find someone.'

In the coming weeks the hard-working Mini took us on a tour which left lasting impressions. Mr Frobisher, a dynamic London financier, wanted someone for his large country house in Gloucestershire. Short, good-looking, with sleek short oily dark hair and a boyish jolly fat face, stockily built and wearing an expensive dark grey double-breasted suit, he seemed possessed of superabundant energy. We had been shown into a large reception room by the temporary house-keeper, a local woman. He bounded into the room like a football landing in goal and briskly shook my hand. Standing a few yards from my leather tub chair, for there seemed to be no time for him to sit, he declared in the commanding businesslike manner of the chairman of a board meeting that he and his wife had recently parted. 'We simply found,' he said, in a loud voice startlingly lacking in feeling, 'that after fifteen years we had nothing left to say to each other.'

Was that all there was to it? I wondered. His two boys, he added, came to the house for part of their boarding-school holidays, and there was the occasional weekend entertaining of friends and business colleagues.

He was interrupted by a telephone call from an adjoining room. Innocently surprised by a business call on a Sunday, I overheard loud forthright remarks about the pros and cons of 'buying' or 'selling'. Only later, driving home, did I wonder why I had been conducted through the grounds and shown over a very attractive modernised three-bedroomed centrally heated stone-built cottage, the quarters of the new incumbent, if I was disqualified from the post since I could not offer the required cordon bleu standards of cooking for weekend dinner parties. That this service might have been obtained by other means, had I interpreted his veiled appraising glances differently, had not occurred to me.

Mr Bates was unprepossessing, inoffensive-looking, about my own age and desperate for a housekeeper to look after his London home and his six-year-old son. We met in Helen's house. Very ill at ease, he explained that his wife had left him. 'The funny thing is,' he said earnestly, 'if my printing business hadn't been doing so well, it wouldn't have happened. I'd thought for twelve years we were happily married, though we had some hard times while the business was struggling. Then when things improved my wife got the au-pair girl she'd wanted.' His voice faltered; he hung his head. He looked up with a confessional air.

'I'm sure you'll find it hard to believe this. I still find it hard to believe myself, but what happened was – my wife – well, my wife and this au-pair girl, she's Spanish – my wife got very fond of her. Of course, at first I didn't think too much of it, how could I? I'd no idea about such things. Gradually, though, I realised something was going on. Once I knew what it was, I told my wife the girl would have to go. She said no, she wouldn't have that on any account. Do you know what she wanted to do? She wanted to share a room with the girl, actually wanted to sleep with her in the same house. Said she loved her and couldn't give her up. Can you believe that? I argued with her for weeks, of course, months. She didn't even seem to care about Michael, our son, any more; well, she said she did care about him, that's why she wanted to stay, but this – this girl – was more important to her. If I didn't agree, then she'd have to leave.

'I never thought it could go that far but it did, although it meant supporting herself again, going to work, finding a home; none of that seemed to matter to her; she was besotted by this girl. So they left. That was months ago. I have a daily woman now, but I do need something more than that.' He looked at me pleadingly.

Never doubting his sincerity, but finding him rather seedy and repellent, I promised to let him know, but had inwardly already said no.

Mr Roberts was very different – extremely attractive, a very young middle-age, well-dressed, prosperous-looking, self-assured, with a tanned open-air look derived from his boating activities at Southampton. He had three children, and a second house on the Isle of Wight. 'Of course,' he said in a breezy confident manner, 'we have daily helps, all that sort of thing.' His eyes were busily removing the smart dress I'd bought for interviews – knee-length, slim-fitting, navy polka-dots on a white background. I was puzzled by the frequent references to swimming activities, as if the only qualification needed for this housekeeping post was a love of swimming.

I had been carefully directed to our unusual meeting place in a prominent town-centre car park, and initial discomfiture on finding my Mini parked alongside his gleaming light blue Jaguar had quickly been dispelled by his easy manner. 'No need to decide now,' he said, producing a card. 'Just give a ring any time and come down for the weekend and you can meet everyone.'

On deciding a week or two later, despite vague doubts, to satisfy my curiosity and arrange a weekend, I was answered on the telephone by a very positive-sounding lady who insisted that although Mr Roberts was not present she could take a message. 'I'm Mrs Roberts,' she said pleasantly, her tone conveying that she knew perfectly well who I was.

'Do you mean – do you mean Mr Roberts is married?'

'Yes.' The nonchalant tone implied that nothing was amiss.

'Oh!' (I had naturally assumed Roberts to be a widower.) Flabbergasted, not knowing what else to say, I speedily ended the call by promising to ring back later. Precisely what services would have been required I never discovered, the frequent allusions to midnight bathing parties in the two private swimming pools where bikinis were de rigueur having left me in a state of puzzlement which I can now look back on with high amusement.

There was often the difficulty of having to make an immediate assessment of a whole new life package, home, children and prospective husband. I learnt to look first for negative deciding factors: when in doubt, don't, became the guiding motto. There were many choices; it seemed that someone like me was much in demand.

I rejected a schoolteacher – a serious, scholarly, not unattractive man in his forties with two small sons whose fit young wife had recently dropped dead of a heart attack during a game of tennis. The poor man was still shaking with shock. 'She'd never had a day's illness … I just want someone to take over,' he said, scarcely looking at me. But though I thought his lack of interest in me might in future be remedied, he was deeply religious, an active member of the local church. It would never do.

Resisting a very personable doctor, a GP whose wife had been recently killed in a car crash, was more difficult. He, too, was still in a state of shock, but as soon as he opened the door there was a powerful physical attraction between us. An hour later, over two large sherries I had listened to a detailed account of a comfortable if rather hectic lifestyle including golf and a busy social round. Dr Jones needed someone to take over the hostess/housekeeper functions of his wife, a very accomplished woman, a wonderful cook and organiser. Very beautiful, too, I saw from a portrait painted by an artist friend hanging over the fireplace, a veritable film star. Regretfully, I was sure I would not fit in, on no level could I compete with the dead woman.

There was a shaky moment standing on the Persian rug in the hall saying goodbye to Dr Jones. I had only to give the correct eye signal or place a comforting hand on his shoulder and he would have gravitated naturally towards me. We had only to touch and a pact would have been made; we might even have kissed – he was ready for it even though his face showed deep mourning for his wife – and then we'd have been committed further. I turned away with the feeling that he was grateful for my good sense; he knew he was in danger of making a mistake.

There were others. The term was nearing its end. We travelled more than three hundred miles to North Wales to meet a wealthy semi-retired elderly businessman who was looking, not for a housekeeper, since he was well served with daily helps, but for someone to live in and drive his large Rover car, failing sight now preventing him from driving. The duties were light; it was a sinecure. Also, the man obviously liked me. Best keep his offer in abeyance should nothing better turn up. The idea of a peaceful secure retreat was attractive. A granddaughter of Melanie's age lived near the man's substantial country house and Melanie could attend the same excellent village school. She would have a ready-made friend.

I was incapable at this time of actively seeking a man. I was far too worn down for that, far too exhausted physically and mentally. The idea of a husband and family belonged to some vague future. For the present I was content with the freedom from Gerald and his everlasting problems, with no longer being chained to them like a prisoner to a wall.

Not yet absolute, the freedom gave tantalising glimpses into possible futures, tasty nibbles at their edges. Each week's new magazine was a mystery parcel hiding untold gifts. Just opening it was exciting, receiving letters even more so. Something was happening. Hope had stolen on to the scene. My step was lighter, weekends away the happiest release of all. The moment the house was out of sight the road ahead beckoned with a welcoming light.

Certain penalties were exacted for these pleasures. After the scare of the knife, whether I should continue to sleep with Gerald or take to the spare room was a question demanding a speedy answer; and I chose to stay with him. His violence ensured that I wanted never to sleep with him again, but what alternative was there? Taking to the spare bed might rouse further demons, I dared not risk it. Although his occasional sexual demands continued as before, I could only hope they would be short-lived.

These sacrifices had little effect in easing the tension between us. Gerald remained hostile, never speaking, ignoring Melanie, never enquiring about our progress. We departed for the weekend leaving him provided with prepared meals, with no mention of our destination, since he obviously did not wish to know, only saying when we'd be back. For a day or so after our return he'd be slightly less aggressive, then as the week wore on, irked perhaps by my presence, his impatience increased as though a fuse had been lit and was burning inexorably towards the detonator, entailing great care with words and actions, and avoiding any hint of new-found lightheartedness.

It was perhaps carelessness on this score which provoked Gerald again to fury. Not that I had any idea what sin I might have perpetrated except, perhaps, the sin of looking cheerful.

I was alone in the kitchen preparing supper when he burst into the room and at the same moment, it seemed, was gripping my throat with both hands. I looked up to see a madman's face glaring down into mine, a man driven to the edge.

The mania lasted only a few seconds. With a huge effort he recovered himself and with a parting look of intolerable hatred, flounced out of the room. Nursing my bruised throat, I decided that if nothing else had turned up by the end of term I would have to accept the Wales offer. I had to get away.

Preparations for departure had included spending some scarce pounds on having the house redecorated to fulfil our tenancy obligations. Nothing had been touched in our years there. The attractive new wallpaper I had hankered after, bought in the July sales and hung by a very efficient and reasonable local decorator, was a sad reminder of lost hopes.

The strain of trying to avoid provoking Gerald while awaiting our fate at last made me forget myself. Bringing in the evening meal, I found Melanie quietly bent over a jigsaw puzzle while Gerald was scanning the *Radio Times* with both the radio and television pouring forth a confusing babble of sound.

'Do you have to have them both on at once?' I flared.

Too late, I realised that he had been trying to listen to the end of a programme on the radio whilst at the same time, in those days

254

before the blessed invention of the silencer button, not missing the beginning of another on television.

Retribution was swift. Like a tensed tiger, Gerald leapt from his chair and in one bound had hurled himself forward and swiped at the underside of my tray. Three platefuls of hot shepherd's pie and vegetables and a gravy-boat of thick brown gravy, made specially for him, flew with great force high in the air. Some of the food hit the ceiling, most of it, amid a tremendous crash of breaking crockery, landing near the top of the newly papered wall, moist lumps sticking to the wall, thick brown liquid trickling down.

Silence occupied the room with a dull deadening force.

Torn between distress over the damage and concern for Melanie, having tried for years to shield her from such a scene, I stared help-lessly at the brown sludge. Hurling the *Radio Times* down on the floor, Gerald stormed out of the room, crashing the door to behind him.

'Don't worry, darling, Daddy will soon be better. Go on with your puzzle while I clear up this mess, then I'll make you something to eat.'

Brazening out my own fears helped, for the moment, to withstand them myself. As long as this doesn't last much longer, I thought, bat-tling with the brown grease, hoping the ugly stain would go, trying stupidly to ignore the misfortune of Gerald going without his dinner. Probably he'd come round later and fill up with tea and biscuits.

At least the decision to deprive Melanie of her natural father need no longer be questioned.

I handed in my month's notice at work, then passed the news on to the various mothers I had befriended at the school and in the village.

'I've something to tell you,' I said. 'I'm afraid Gerald is mentally ill. I have to leave him.'

Amazed disbelief and veiled looks of condemnation greeted this announcement.

From sensible, rational Gillian, my best friend among the school parents, a gifted Cambridge maths graduate, I had expected nothing but sympathy and understanding.

'Oh dear!' Gillian exclaimed, turning white, her face assuming a wary look as if she had been made privy to some shameful sin.

Near to tears, I drove away from her lovely old village house near the school where many a happy hour had been spent discussing music, the theatre, education. Gillian's shocked face had joined in the general condemnation: not only was I callously deserting the sick and needy, I was also depriving a defenceless child of her father.

Dabbing at my eyes, I concentrated on driving. No one wanted any details. Not one of these kind, compassionate, educated people, not even Gillian, had asked a single question. I was written off like a bad debt. The genial invitations to tea at Gillian's house would not be repeated; we would not keep in touch. Where Melanie and I would go, our financial situation, none of that mattered. We were outcasts of decent society.

Only my boss, Gordon, ventured to ask, 'Are you sure you're doing the right thing?'

'Yes,' I said, grateful for his concern and wishing I could make him understand. 'This has been going on a long time. It's the only way.'

Gordon questioned me no further. Was this, I wondered, because of the natural British aversion to prying? Or did he, too, the professional psychologist, secretly also condemn me?

It was during the last week of term – and the last in my job – that I received Derek Parker's telephone call at the office. I had answered his advertisement for a housekeeper weeks ago and was no longer expecting a reply.

'We've been in Spain, camping, for the last month,' he explained, his voice warm, but urgent and businesslike. 'We go every year. I've only just had your letter. Are you still free?'

'Yes, I'm still free.'

'Look, I'm very keen to meet you. I've a daughter aged six, like yours, and a grown-up son. My wife died a year ago. I'd like to get this settled as soon as possible. I'll explain everything later.'

As soon as we met in a private room in a London hotel we each knew in our different ways that a bargain had probably been struck. Tall, medium-built, forty-two, pleasant-looking, with curly brown hair and a frank face, Derek had a straightforward sincere manner. His wife had died tragically after several years of suffering from an incurable skin disease. 'The skin continually peels away,' he explained with sadness; an absolutely horrible illness.

'I have my own business, a ladies' dress factory. My son works with me. He's nineteen. Up to now I've managed with a very good daily housekeeper, friends help out, and so on, but there are things, stupid little things, like taking my daughter for a haircut. Well, of course, what's needed is someone to be there. I'd keep on Mrs Taylor, my housekeeper, subject to your approval, of course. I wouldn't want you to do housework, there's no need for that, although some cooking would be nice.' He smiled. 'That would be up to you. Do you like cooking?'

I nodded, pleased to note the lack of emphasis on the demands of a man's stomach.

'I've a large house, and I haven't yet heard of any modern aid I haven't got.'

I liked the way this was said, unpretentiously, as a matter of fact, with no hint of a boast. This was a man I could talk to; we would understand each other, we would get on well, even though it appeared that certain interests such as music would not be shared. And there was nothing of the romantic about him either, nor anything speculative about his glances. After more than twenty years of marriage his wife was obviously still very much alive for him.

His home was in a country village near Solihull. 'Shakespeare country,' he said. 'If you'd like to come for a weekend soon, you'll be able to see for yourself.' He glanced at Melanie sitting at a table

257

at the end of the room colouring a picture-book. 'Your daughter would be treated exactly the same as mine.' Patting his knee, he added with a smile, 'I have two knees. If you agree, she could go to the same private school as Sarah. I think it's quite a good one. I'd pay all expenses, of course. And there would be a car for you. Would you be willing to drive them to school? We have to have a taxi at present.'

The weekend at Solihull was a success, both Melanie and I got on well with all concerned, and to my relief young Sarah, a very pleasant appealing child, welcomed her new playmate with enthusiasm and me with an encouraging warmth.

Told that we had somewhere to go and would soon be leaving, Gerald asked for no details, not even about where we were going. Then, as we were undressing at bedtime he said hesitantly, 'Do you mind if I look at it, just once more?'

There was no doubt about what he meant. 'No!' I said, indignant, angry and disgusted, but relieved when my rebuff was accepted without demur. We got into bed in silence. I drew the bedclothes round me: I had learnt to sleep well to one side of the bed without the aid of human contact. I fell asleep thinking about possible future contact with Derek Parker.

Hearing myself say 'No' to Gerald was very strange. I could hardly remember ever having refused him anything before. Was I right, I wondered, in finding his sickening request a vindication of my theory about his illness?

Gerald agreed, icily, to stay on at the house for as long as necessary to give us a trial period in our new home. Later he intended to take up the offer by Jack and Mavis Day of a room in their large Plymouth house, a plan I found incomprehensible since he shared no interests with them. This, he hinted, was one of the advantages. He hoped to be left largely to his own devices, inviolate in his room but with meals conveniently provided at low cost.

So this was the reason for cultivating their acquaintance. He had planned it all along.

Saying goodbye to Roger and Muriel posed an unexpected difficulty. Roger insisted that I was making a dreadful mistake, taking far too much on trust; I should reconsider. Muriel was inclined to agree with him. 'Roger's right,' she said. 'You don't really know anything about this man, do you. Do sit down and I'll go and make some coffee.'

The moment she was out of sight Roger drew me close and kissed me passionately. 'I can't let you go, darling. Kiss me! Kiss me! I love you, you know that. We've got to be together. I've thought it all out. Let's take the two young ones and go away. I'll get a new practice. The older boys can stay with Muriel and finish school. Please, darling, say you'll do it.'

I wanted his arms to stay round me for ever; but I was pushing hard at the soft wool of his pullover.

He held me tighter, kissed me again.

'Roger, darling, please darling, you must let go. Muriel will be here in a minute.' Hearing myself utter the almost forgotten endearment came very near to breaking my resolve.

'I'm ready to tell Muriel. I think she guesses, anyway. You do still feel the same, don't you?'

'Yes, darling. You know I do. I always will. But we can't do it. You know we can't. Apart from the boys, there's Muriel. You'd never forgive yourself.'

Hearing Muriel returning, I somehow found the strength to push him away. I could not rob another woman of her husband, and Roger, too, would find that Muriel could not so easily be dismissed from his mind, or his heart or his conscience. He seemed, as Muriel came back, to accept my decision but continued openly to look at me so reproachfully, I was sure she must notice.

She must have sensed our tension, and noticed my smudged lipstick. Hiding behind the coffee-cup, I tried to maintain small talk.

259

'I'll write,' I said in the doorway, leaving them both gazing after me, with what different feelings I could well imagine.

Early on a warm misty August morning we were ready to leave. No kisses or hugs, not even for Melanie, who fortunately was pre-occupied with the excitement of the journey. Gerald's calm quiet 'Goodbye' outside the front door, one dispassionate civil little word of farewell of the kind reserved for casual friends, was a final knife-thrust. And at same time its very formality seemed to set an official seal on the whole proceeding. It seemed to confirm, in that distinctive decisive way of his, that in all the circumstances I was doing the right thing, I was taking the only possible course, the only logical step.

Earlier, he had stayed out of sight as I loaded our belongings into the car, and now he was waiting at the top of the steps. I felt his eyes burning into our backs as we went down.

We settled ourselves in the car. I switched on the engine, then glanced up for a last look at the tall motionless figure of the man who had been my husband for fourteen incredible agonis-ing years, a well-known stranger standing in the doorway of our home. His face revealed very little. The large brown eyes held mine with an unwavering stare; if anything they held a touch of relief tinged with quiet satisfaction, as if something, some well-considered lengthy transaction or other, had been sensibly and logically concluded.

Inclining his head to one side, he touched it briefly with his hand in a conventional parting gesture and let his hand fall to his side again. We were dismissed. Not disowned, for that would have implied some kind of former ownership or kinship, but annulled, consigned to oblivion, cancelled out like an out-of-date passport. I caught myself resisting a powerful urge to rush back like a mother to a distressed child and make a last desperate attempt to rescue the isolated soul from himself.

I engaged first gear, released the hand-brake and let in the clutch. The car moved slowly up the narrow lane.

Gerald, and the white stone of the house, were immediately lost to view.

I fixed my gaze on the road ahead.

Epilogue

Late one evening in August 1979 when I was living in Norfolk and Melanie was in her last year at the UEA, I received a sudden telephone call from Gerald's sister. A voice from the past. I hadn't heard anything of her for more than fifteen years.

Gerald was very ill, she said, in hospital in Plymouth, and she 'couldn't go'. Could I go for her?

'What is it?' I asked. 'What's wrong with him?'

'I don't know, exactly. But he's very ill.' Her voice was quavery, pleading.

Something was seriously wrong.

'All right,' I said, 'leave it to me. I'll ring you when I have some news.'

'Thanks, Elaine.'

I rang the hospital and the ward sister would only say that he was 'very poorly'. I knew from her voice it was bad.

Melanie agreed with me that we must leave for Plymouth right away.

Melanie had been in touch with Gerald since she was eleven, something she'd always wanted since we'd left him, and eventually I'd written to him, care of Mavis and Jack, to say that she'd passed the eleven-plus, and did he want to contact her? To my surprise and relief, and to her great joy, he was very keen, and immediately started writing to her, typing the letters on the old Underwood typewriter I'd left him. Melanie still has them all. Then they both wanted to meet, so I sent her on the train from Norfolk to London and he met her there; they'd looked along the platform and had known each other straight away. He took her on the train to Plymouth and installed her in a very good local hotel, calling for her every day after breakfast. She stayed a week and they got on famously. He kept looking at her with admiration, saying, 'My daughter! My daughter!' It makes me tearful now to think of it.

He wasn't with Mavis and Jack any more. He'd apparently got a job as caretaker in a big rundown bedsit house in the city where he had a grotty room, a set-up which I suppose gave him the privacy he craved. An unsuitable place for Melanie, hence the hotel.

They repeated the visit a number of times, then she went to university and he took a keen interest in that.

It was nearly midnight when Melanie and I set out from Norfolk. We drove all night into heavy rain coming relentlessly from the west, the Devonian gods berating us for our long absence from their kingdom. No motorway in those days. We stopped at the all-night restaurant on the Oxford bypass at four o'clock in the morning and I phoned the hospital.

Gerald was dead.

I don't know how I went on to the hospital, what with my eyes streaming with tears and the windscreen streaming with rain all the way. We saw him when we got there, and I've always wished I hadn't. His face was shrunken and waxen. It was hard to believe he'd died only a few hours ago. The effect of the massive doses of drugs they have to give you at the end, the doctor told us; it was cancer of the stomach.

I couldn't stop crying. It was as though I was doing all the crying I hadn't been able to do when I left him. It was weeks before I'd finally cried myself out. Amid my tears I rang his sister and told her, and she asked me to arrange the funeral, which I did, and she and her husband came down for it a week later.

Melanie and I booked into a quiet little private hotel and went to the place where he'd been living, a comfortable detached bungalow on the outskirts of Plymouth. He's buried there in the local churchyard. Melanie went back later on to arrange for a headstone.

It seemed that in return for board and lodging he lived in the bungalow with Dolly Carter, an elderly partly disabled widow who needed someone to drive her car. She was very upset to hear of his death. 'Such a nice man, such a gentleman!' she said, uncannily echoing the words of the young nurse at the hospital as she turned her head away, unprofessionally near to tears, when we mentioned Gerald's name.

'The only thing was,' Dolly Carter continued, 'I couldn't understand why he spent so much time alone in his room, when he wasn't out with his bird-watching. Never sat with me and watched the telly. I don't know what he did in there.'

I knew only too well what he had done in that bleak space – a single bed, small wardrobe, small chest of drawers. And his old oak bureau-bookcase, filled with books. No notes, no papers. He must have destroyed them all before he went into hospital; he knew he wasn't coming back. It must have been one of the hardest things he ever did.

Gerald's bureau-bookcase, with all his books, to this day stands sentinel in a corner of Melanie's sitting-room.

Author's Note

In *The Oxford Companion to the Mind* (Oxford University Press, 1987), the following passage on page 30 in the article on 'Anxiety' very precisely describes my own observations in 1957 of my newborn baby daughter:

> An anxious person is in suspense, waiting for information to clarify his situation. He is watchful and alert, often excessively alert and over-reacting to noise or other stimuli.

In the same work, on page 106 under 'Brain Development', the following sentence has a direct bearing on my early experiences with my daughter:

> More changes occur in the cellular structure of the cortex in the first six months after birth than at any other time in development.

Acknowledgements

I am grateful to Georgina Capel and everyone at Capel & Land for their enthusiastic support, and to Penny Daniel and everybody at Profile Books for their courtesy and zealous publishing, also to Claire Peligry for her meticulous editing. My special thanks to Fay Weldon for her unfailing encouragement.